Baseball Research Journal

Volume 45, Number 1
Spring 2016

Published by the Society for American Baseball Research

THE BASEBALL RESEARCH JOURNAL, Volume 45, Number 1

Editor: Cecilia M. Tan
Design and Production: Lisa Hochstein
Cover Design: Lisa Hochstein
Fact Checker: Clifford Blau

Front cover photos: National Baseball Hall of Fame Library, Cooperstown, NY

Published by:
Society for American Baseball Research, Inc.
Cronkite School at ASU
555 N. Central Ave. #416
Phoenix, AZ 85004

Phone: (602) 496–1460
Web: www.sabr.org
Twitter: @sabr
Facebook: Society for American Baseball Research

Contents

Letter from the Editor

Are we all on a quest to glean meaning from life around us? Well, maybe not all people are, but I am, and I strongly suspect that many SABR members funnel that urge into their study of baseball. It doesn't matter what creed you ascribe to—you'll find ample parables in baseball. This is because, fractal-like, the game itself is part of the fabric of life, and every part contains microcosms of the whole.

Team versus team—league versus league!—can represent nation striving against nation or faith against faith. The batter versus pitcher brings the conflict down to a personal level. Or does the batter-pitcher matchup represent the battle of wills in a partnership? It could be all that and more. I look at the stories and the analysis presented in this issue of the *Baseball Research Journal* and I see tales of hubris, growth, the overcoming of obstacles, the lessons of failure. There's a lot going on.

You can see the Kansas City Royals' triumph in 2015 as a storybook sequel to their 2014 heartbreak, or you can see it as a not-unlikely outcome of a team that did well doing well again in similar circumstances. Both are "true." It's fairly rare for the *BRJ* to feature such recent history as "last year" but in this issue we have two articles spawned in the wake of the 2014 World Series. Jeffrey Howard takes a deep dive on what may or may not have been happening in the minds of the men on the field during the fateful penultimate play of the Series, and Wade Kapszukiewicz presents a startling way of conceptualizing the kind of climax that Series had. At least, I found it startling that I had never thought of it that way before. Which just goes to show no matter how much life you've lived, epiphanies can still happen.

Sometimes we look back, sometimes we look forward, and—as is very often the case—we look back so that we can look forward with sharper eyes. We're still examining the notorious Black Sox, as Bruce Allardice does in his article on the team's activities in 1920, and we're still examining the way baseball, the press, and society reacted to the Black Sox scandal, as Jacob Pomrenke demonstrates in his piece about a particular myth that persists despite facts to the contrary. Richard Hershberger's and Brian Marshall's inquiries into Paul Hines's 1878 triple play gives us another prime example of people's feelings coloring their perception of an event that was witnessed in broad daylight on a baseball field and yet there's doubt about what happened.

When all avenues of inquiry have been exhausted and a question remains unanswered, what's left? Belief. There are many such debates in baseball: was the triple play unassisted? did Ruth call his shot? And in life: was Oswald working alone? I do not think the urge to pick a side is a flaw in humans, nor is the need to believe. We draw conclusions. That's how our brains work. What would be a flaw is not to be able to change one's belief in the face of new evidence.

History, whether made on the baseball field or not, gives us heroes and goats, parables, fables, and cautionary tales, because of the way we interpret it. The hottest musical on Broadway right now is about Alexander Hamilton. The subject matter in the past is inexhaustible and the lessons we can glean are only made finite by the span of our lives.

— Cecilia Tan
Editor

Golden Pitches

The Ultimate Last-at-Bat, Game Seven Scenario

Wade Kapszukiewicz

In the immediate aftermath of the exciting Game Seven between the Kansas City Royals and San Francisco Giants in 2014, the baseball world fixated on one question: should Alex Gordon have been sent home with two outs in the bottom of the ninth inning as his hit was being botched and booted somewhere near the left-center field wall? Indeed, no less a numbers guru than Nate Silver tweeted that—regardless of the outcome on that potential play-at-the-plate—it would have been one of the five greatest moments in baseball history. However, what happened immediately after that play (with Gordon on third and Madison Bumgarner pitching to Salvador Perez) is far more remarkable, and this paper presents data to support that claim.

The six pitches Bumgarner threw to Perez had the ability to win the World Series for either team. That is, each of those six pitches could have produced a World Series championship for the Royals (had Perez hit a home run) or the Giants (had Perez grounded out to shortstop, flown out to right field, or, as he did, fouled out to the third baseman).

This is an occurrence so incredibly rare that it has only happened seven times since the 1903 World Series: 1912, 1926, 1962, 1972, 1997, 2001, and 2014. Only on these seven occasions have single pitches been thrown that simultaneously held the potential to win a World Series for either team.

THE GOLDEN PITCH: A DEFINITION

For lack of a better phrase, and for ease of conversation, I will refer to these pitches as "Golden Pitches," borrowing perhaps from the concept of a Golden Goal in sudden death overtime of a soccer or hockey game. By definition, under the current best-of-seven World Series format, a Golden Pitch can only be thrown in Game Seven of the World Series and only in the bottom of the ninth inning when the road team has the lead (or in the bottom of an extra inning, if the road team scores in the top, as was the case in Game Seven of the 1912 World Series, the first time a Golden Pitch was thrown[1]). Indeed, in no other situation could either team win the World Series on a given pitch.

Some of the greatest and most dramatic moments in World Series history did not involve Golden Pitches. Carlton Fisk's epic home run came in Game Six of the 1975 World Series; only the Reds could have won the Series that night. For that matter, Fisk's home run came with the score tied in the bottom of the twelfth inning; only the Red Sox could have won the game on that pitch.

A similar point can be made about Joe Carter's Series-winning home run in 1993: it happened in Game Six, so only the Blue Jays—not the Phillies—could have won the title that night. In the 2011 World Series, the Rangers came within one strike of winning the championship on two separate occasions, but both came in Game Six (in the bottom of the ninth and tenth innings). As dramatic as that game was, only the Rangers—not the Cardinals—could have won the World Series that night.

The pitch Ralph Terry threw to Bill Mazeroski in 1960 comes close to meeting the criteria of a Golden Pitch because it was the bottom of the ninth inning of a Game Seven, but the game was tied when the pitch was made. Only the Pirates could have won the World Series on that pitch. The best the Yankees could hope for was that the game would make it to extra innings.

Game Seven of the 1991 World Series is ranked by some historians as the greatest baseball game ever played, and yet no Golden Pitches were thrown. Several pitches were thrown in the bottoms of the ninth and tenth that could have produced a victory for the Twins (including the one thrown to Gene Larkin that eventually did win the World Series for Minnesota), but not a single pitch thrown in that game could have won it for Atlanta. The exact same can be said about the longest World Series Game Seven ever played (in 1924)—since only the home-team Nationals could have won the World Series during at bats in a tied game in the bottoms of the ninth, tenth, eleventh, and twelfth innings. Since the visiting Giants never took the lead in any of those innings, there were no Golden Pitches thrown.

SOME NEAR-MISSES

A handful of the 37 Game Sevens that have been played were so one-sided that there was no possibility of a Golden Pitch being thrown.[2] Other Game Sevens were close, but since the visiting teams lost, the home teams never had to bat in the bottom of the ninth inning, and thus by definition, no Golden Pitches were thrown.[3] However, several other Game Sevens came close to meeting the criteria for a Golden Pitch, but fell just short.

- **1924**: As discussed previously.
- **1952**: The visiting Yankees took a 4–2 lead into the bottom of the ninth inning at Ebbets Field. Had the Dodgers put at least two runners on base (creating the potential of a Series-winning three-run home run), a Golden Pitch could have been thrown. Instead, Bob Kuzava retired the side in order, retiring Pee Wee Reese on a fly ball to left field to end the game.[4]
- **1955**: The visiting Dodgers took a 2–0 lead into the bottom of the ninth inning at Yankee Stadium. Had two runners reached base (creating the potential of a Series-winning three-run home run), a Golden Pitch could have been thrown. But Johnny Podres retired the side in order.
- **1957**: The visiting Milwaukee Braves led 5–0 in the bottom of the ninth inning at Yankee Stadium. The game ended when Lew Burdette got Bill Skowron to ground into a force out at third base with the bases loaded and two outs. Two more batters would have had to reach for a Golden Pitch to be thrown.
- **1958**: The visiting Yankees took a 6–2 lead into the bottom of the ninth inning against the Milwaukee Braves. The game ended when Red Schoendienst lined out to center field with runners on first and second. Two more batters would have had to reach base for a Golden Pitch to be thrown.
- **1960**: As discussed previously.
- **1965**: With the Dodgers leading the Twins 2–0 in the bottom of the ninth inning, Harmon Killebrew singled off Sandy Koufax with one out. Had one more batter reached base, Koufax would have thrown at least one Golden Pitch, since a double play (with two on and one out) could have won the Series for the Dodgers and a three-run home run could have won it for the Twins. Instead, Koufax struck out Earl Battey and Bob Allison to end the game.
- **1968**: The visiting Tigers took a 4–0 lead into the bottom of the ninth inning in St. Louis. With

two outs, Mike Shannon hit a solo home run to cut the Tigers' lead to 4–1. Had the Cardinals then loaded the bases, thus creating the possibility of a Series-winning grand slam, at least one Golden Pitch would have been thrown. As it was, Mickey Lolich retired Tim McCarver on a foul pop to catcher to end the game.
- **1971**: The visiting Pirates took a 2–1 lead into the bottom of the ninth inning in Baltimore, but Steve Blass retired the Orioles in order, and so no Golden Pitches were thrown. Since no one reached base, no pitch Blass threw in the bottom of the ninth could have won the Series for Baltimore.
- **1975**: After Joe Morgan's go-ahead RBI with two outs in the top of the ninth inning, the Reds took a 4–3 lead into the bottom of the inning. The Red Sox were retired in order, and so no Golden Pitches were thrown. Carl Yastrzemski made the final out, but the best he could have done during his at-bat was tie the game (with a solo home run), not win it, for Boston.
- **1979**: The visiting Pirates took a 4–1 lead into the bottom of the ninth inning in Baltimore. Had the Orioles loaded the bases, thus creating the possibility of a Series-winning grand slam, at least one Golden Pitch would have been thrown. As it was, Kent Tekulve retired the side in order.
- **1991**: As discussed previously.

THE SEVEN TIMES GOLDEN PITCHES WERE THROWN

To gain a full appreciation of just how rare a Golden Pitch is, and to put in perspective how incredibly consequential the Bumgarner-to-Perez sequence was in 2014, I investigated how many (how few) Golden Pitches have been thrown in baseball history. Using Baseball-Reference.com, which charts pitch counts for games beginning in 1974, I was able to definitively calculate the number of Golden Pitches thrown in 1997, 2001 and 2014. Various newspaper accounts were helpful in calculating the number of Golden Pitches that were thrown on the first four occasions in 1912, 1926, 1962, and 1972. In fact, using both Baseball-Reference.com and newspaper accounts of the games in question, we know for certain how many Golden Pitches were thrown to 10 of the 12 batters who have faced such pitches. For only two batters—Bob Meusel in 1926 and Chuck Hiller in 1962—is there ambiguity regarding precisely how many Golden Pitches they faced.

A review of the available data as detailed below leads me to estimate 40 Golden Pitches have been thrown since 1903—with a minimum of 36—and we were lucky enough to see six of them in the 2014 World Series. In detail, here are the seven times pitches were thrown that had the unique ability to win a World Series for either team:

1912: Boston Red Sox 3, New York Giants 2 (10 innings)
Fenway Park in Boston

With the game tied 1–1, the visiting Giants scored a run in the top of the tenth inning on an RBI single to center field by Fred Merkle. Working with a 2–1 lead in the bottom of the tenth inning, Christy Mathewson faced Clyde Engle to lead off the inning. Engle reached second base on an error by center fielder Fred Snodgrass, which brought up Harry Hooper. The pitch (or pitches) Mathewson threw to Hooper were not Golden Pitches, since the Giants could not win the World Series during that at-bat. (Only the Red Sox could have won it at that point, had Hooper hit a two-run home run.)

However, when Hooper flew out to Snodgrass (with Engle advancing to third base on the play), for the first time in baseball history the next several pitches all had the ability to win the World Series for either team.

Steve Yerkes was the next batter, and now with a runner at third base and one out, each pitch Mathewson threw to him was a Golden Pitch. Yerkes could have hit a two-run home run (which would have won the World Series for the Red Sox), or he could have hit into an unconventional double play (which would have won the World Series for the Giants).

According to *The New York Times*, Yerkes walked on five pitches, which brought Tris Speaker to the plate with runners on first and third and one out. Once again, every pitch Mathewson threw to Speaker was a Golden Pitch: a triple or two-run double would have won the World Series for the Red Sox, while a double play (including a conventional 6–4–3, 4–6–3, or 5–4–3 double play) would have won the World Series for the Giants.

According to *The Boston Globe*, on the second pitch Speaker singled to right to tie the game, 2–2, and at that point, no other pitch Mathewson threw that inning was a Golden Pitch. From that point on, since the game was tied, every pitch thrown in the bottom of the tenth inning could only win the World Series for the Red Sox. (Indeed, that is what eventually happened, two batters later, when Mathewson gave up a sacrifice fly to Larry Gardner.)

So, the only Golden Pitches thrown by Mathewson were the five he threw to Yerkes and the two he threw to Speaker. Therefore, Mathewson threw a total of seven Golden Pitches.

1926: St. Louis Cardinals 3, New York Yankees 2
Yankee Stadium in New York

The visiting Cardinals took a 3–2 lead into the bottom of the ninth inning. Pete Alexander retired the first two batters before facing Babe Ruth. The pitches Alexander threw to Ruth were not Golden Pitches, since the best Ruth could do in that at-bat was hit a solo home run and tie the game. Instead Ruth walked, which meant that any pitch Alexander threw to Bob Meusel would be a Golden Pitch. Sources differ on whether Alexander threw one or two pitches to Meusel, but Ruth was caught stealing to end the game. Alexander, therefore, threw either one or two Golden Pitches.

1962: New York Yankees 1, San Francisco Giants 0
Candlestick Park in San Francisco

The Yankees' Ralph Terry took a 1–0 lead into the bottom of the ninth inning and gave up a leadoff bunt single to Matty Alou. He faced Felipe Alou next, but since the pitches he threw to Felipe Alou only had the ability to win the World Series for the Giants (had Alou hit a two-run home run) and not the Yankees (since the best Terry could hope for during that at-bat was a double play that would still have left New York one out shy of victory), they were not Golden Pitches.

Terry struck out Felipe Alou, which meant that he did throw Golden Pitches to the next batter, Chuck Hiller, since a double play at that point would have produced a World Series victory for the Yankees.

There are no reliable accounts of Hiller's at bat, but since we know he also struck out, at least three Golden Pitches must have been thrown. Fortunately, newspaper accounts do make clear what happened next. After Hiller struck out, Terry threw three Golden Pitches to the next batter, Willie Mays, who doubled down the right field line on a 2–0 pitch to put runners

Ralph Terry has thrown more Golden Pitches than any other pitcher, all in the 1962 World Series.

and second and third with two outs. Willie McCovey then fouled off the first pitch before lining out to the second baseman on Terry's final Golden Pitch, thereby ending the game.

The pitches Terry threw to Hiller, Mays, and Mc-Covey were all Golden. Since Hiller struck out, we know he faced at least three Golden Pitches, but it is reasonable to assume he may have faced a few more. We know for certain that Mays faced three Golden Pitches and McCovey faced two. Therefore, Terry threw at least eight Golden Pitches, and probably a few more, giving him the distinction of having thrown more Golden Pitches than any other pitcher.

1972: Oakland A's 3, Cincinnati Reds 2
Riverfront Stadium in Cincinnati

Working with a one-run lead entering the bottom of the ninth inning, the A's Rollie Fingers retired the first two batters before hitting Darrel Chaney with a pitch. With a runner at first and two outs, every pitch Fingers threw to the next batter, Pete Rose, was a Golden Pitch. Rose could have hit a two-run home run to win the World Series for the Reds, or he could have made an out (as he did, flying out to left fielder Joe Rudi), thereby giving the championship to the A's. Both *The New York Times* and *The Washington Post* reported that Rose hit the first pitch to Rudi, so we know that Fingers threw one Golden Pitch.

1997: Florida Marlins 3, Cleveland Indians 2 (11 innings)
Pro Player Stadium in Miami

With the Indians holding a 2–1 lead, Jose Mesa gave up a single to Moises Alou to lead off the bottom of the ninth inning. Mesa next faced Bobby Bonilla, but the pitches he threw were not Golden Pitches, since they

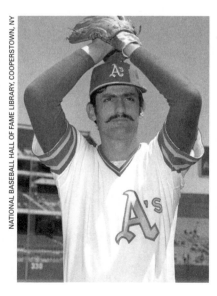

The single pitch Rollie Fingers threw to Pete Rose in the 1972 World Series was Golden and won the series for the Oakland A's.

only had the ability to win the World Series for the Marlins. (A two-run home run by Bonilla would have won the World Series for the Marlins, but the best Mesa could hope for in that at-bat—a double play—would still have left the Indians one out short of victory.)

Bonilla struck out, which brought Charles Johnson to the plate with a runner at first and one out. The four pitches Mesa threw to Johnson were Golden Pitches, since now a potential double play would have won the World Series for the Indians.

Johnson singled to right field on a 1–2 pitch, which put runners at first and third with still only one out. The three pitches Mesa then threw to Craig Counsell were also Golden Pitches, since every pitch could have won the World Series for either the Marlins (had Counsell hit a two-run double or three-run home run) or the Indians (had Counsell, for example, hit into a 6–4–3 double play).

Counsell hit a sacrifice fly to Manny Ramirez in right field on a 1–1 pitch to tie the game 2–2. Mesa would go on to throw 21 more pitches before he was relieved by Charles Nagy with two outs in the tenth inning, but none of those 21 were Golden Pitches. Once the Marlins tied the game, the pitches thrown in the bottom of the ninth, tenth, and eleventh innings only had the ability to win the World Series for the Marlins.

Because Baseball-Reference.com provides pitch counts for this World Series, we know that Mesa threw a total of seven Golden Pitches—four to Johnson and three to Counsell.

2001: Arizona Diamondbacks 3, New York Yankees 2
Bank One Ballpark in Phoenix

The Yankees took a 2–1 lead into the bottom of the ninth inning and had Mariano Rivera on the mound. Mark Grace led off with a single, and Damian Miller reached on a fielder's choice while attempting to bunt pinch runner David Dellucci over to second base. Dellucci reached second on an error, which put runners on first and second with nobody out.

The two pitches Rivera threw to Miller were not Golden Pitches, since only the Diamondbacks could have won the World Series on those pitches (had Miller hit a two-run home run). The best Rivera could hope for in Miller's at bat was a double play, which would have left the Yankees one out short of victory.

However, once two runners reached base with nobody out, the conditions for a Golden Pitch were present, since the next batter (Jay Bell) could have either hit a two-run double or three-run home run (which would have won the World Series for the Diamondbacks), or, at least theoretically, could have hit into a game-ending triple play (which would have won the World Series for the Yankees).

Rivera threw one Golden Pitch to Bell, who bunted into a force out at third base, which put runners at first and second with one out. Tony Womack then faced five Golden Pitches from Rivera—each pitch could have produced a two-run double or three-run home run (which would have won the World Series for the Diamondbacks) or a double play (which would have won the World Series for the Yankees).

On a 2–2 pitch, Womack lined an RBI double down the right field line, which scored pinch runner Midre Cummings (who had run for Miller) to tie the game 2–2. Rivera then hit Craig Counsell with a non-Golden pitch to load the bases before giving up the Series-winning RBI single to Luis Gonzalez. None of the pitches Rivera threw to Counsell or Gonzalez were Golden Pitches. Rivera, then, threw a total of six Golden Pitches: one to Bell and five to Womack.

2014: San Francisco Giants 3, Kansas City Royals 2
Kauffman Stadium in Kansas City

As was discussed briefly above, Bumgarner and the Giants took a 3–2 lead into the bottom of the ninth inning. Had he retired the side in order, Bumgarner would not have thrown any Golden Pitches, since no pitch would have had the ability to win the World Series for the Royals. But once Gordon singled and reached third base on the two-base error, every pitch Bumgarner threw to the next batter, Perez, had the ability to win the World Series for either team.

On Bumgarner's sixth and final Golden Pitch, Perez fouled out to third base to end the game and the Series.

THE STATISTICAL RARITY OF THE GOLDEN PITCH

We know definitively that Mathewson (7), Fingers (1), Mesa (7), Rivera (6) and Bumgarner (6) threw a total of 27 Golden Pitches. We know that Alexander threw one or two Golden Pitches and Terry threw at least eight. Therefore, while we know at least 36 Golden Pitches have been thrown, it is safe to estimate that the number of Golden Pitches thrown since 1903 is roughly 40.[5]

For all the talk following Game Seven of the 2014 World Series about whether Gordon should have tried to score, there does not seem to be much appreciation of how consequential it was to see Bumgarner throw six pitches to Perez, each with the awesome power of being able to deliver a World Series title to either team.

Since we know there have been roughly 40 Golden Pitches thrown since 1903, I thought it might be illustrative to estimate how many pitches have been thrown in World Series history, playoff history, or even in baseball history.

There have been 111 World Series played since the one in 1903 between the Pittsburgh Pirates and Boston Americans for a total of 643 games. Assuming 130 pitches per game per team, that means a total of roughly 260. That would yield 167,180 pitches.

That means that only .02% of all pitches thrown in the World Series have been Golden Pitches.

Beginning with the 1969 season, the playoffs were expanded to include two league championship series. Since then, 230 games have been played in the ALCS and 239 in the NLCS. In 1995, the playoffs were expanded to include two division series for each league. Including the strike-caused division series of 1981, there have been 179 ALDS games and 172 NLDS games. Finally, after another expansion of baseball's playoff format, eight one-game wild card games have been played since 2012.

Years in which Golden Pitches were thrown	1912, 1926, 1962, 1972, 1997, 2001, 2014
Pitchers who have thrown Golden Pitches	Christy Mathewson (1912): 7 pitches Pete Alexander (1926): 1 or 2 pitches Ralph Terry (1962): at least 8 pitches Rollie Fingers (1972): 1 pitch Jose Mesa (1997): 7 pitches Mariano Rivera (2001): 6 pitches Madison Bumgarner (2014): 6 pitches
Batters who have faced Golden Pitches	Steve Yerkes (1912): 5 pitches Tris Speaker (1912): 2 pitches Bob Meusel (1926): 1 or 2 pitches Chuck Hiller (1962): at least 3 pitches Willie Mays (1962): 3 pitches Willie McCovey (1962): 2 pitches Pete Rose (1972): 1 pitch Charles Johnson (1997): 4 pitches Craig Counsell (1997): 3 pitches Jay Bell (2001): 1 pitch Tony Womack (2001): 5 pitches Salvador Perez (2014): 6 pitches
Number of Golden Pitches thrown (since 1903)	At least 36, probably closer to 40
Total number of pitches thrown (since 1903)	48.9 million (estimate)

Including the World Series starting in 1903, then, 1,471 postseason games have been played. Again assuming roughly 260 pitches per game, that yields 382,460 postseason pitches.

That means that only .01% of all pitches thrown in the postseason since 1903 have been Golden Pitches.

Estimating the number of pitches thrown in regular season games since 1903 would have been an extraordinarily difficult endeavor without the assistance of Baseball-Reference.com. Fortunately, that site has calculated that 186,579 regular season games have been played since 1903. Again assuming 260 pitches per game, I estimate that 48.5 million pitches have been thrown in the regular season since 1903. Adding the estimated 382,460 pitches that have been thrown in the playoffs and World Series, that brings the total number of pitches thrown since 1903 to roughly 48.9 million.

That means that only .00008% of all pitches thrown since the beginning of the 1903 season (regular and postseason) have been Golden Pitches.

CONCLUSION

Golden Pitches have only been thrown by seven pitchers, on seven different occasions, to 12 different batters, over the course of the 113 years since our current World Series format came into existence. Roughly 40 Golden Pitches have been thrown out of the roughly 48.9 million total pitches thrown during that time. The throwing of a Golden Pitch is so incredibly rare, and so potentially consequential, that I found it worthy of note.

Consider this final point. The 2015 postseason consisted of 36 games (two wild card games, 19 games in the ALDS and NLDS, 10 games in the ALCS and NLCS, and five games in the World Series). There were exactly 10,538 pitches thrown.[6] None were Golden Pitches. Roughly 631,800 pitches were thrown during the 2015 regular season.[7] This means that, excluding the 2015 exhibition season, roughly 642,000 pitches have been thrown in major league baseball games since Bumgarner ended the 2014 World Series by throwing six Golden Pitches to Perez. None have been Golden Pitches since.

This is precisely the point of highlighting the existence of the Golden Pitch. How many pitches does a baseball fan see during one season, following the game on television or in person? Thousands? Tens of thousands? How many does he or she see over the course of five years? Hundreds of thousands? How many does he or she see over the course of a lifetime? Millions?

The pitch is so elemental to the game of baseball, and it also enjoys a unique place in the fabric of our shared heritage. A parent plays catch with a child in the backyard. The President tosses out the so-called first "pitch" of the season. We've all participated in so many pitches in our lives—one way or another—but how may Golden Pitches have we seen? And when, we may wonder, will we ever see one again? ■

Acknowledgment

The author is deeply indebted to Clifford Blau for his work in getting this essay ready for publication. His knowledge of the game and attention to detail leave little doubt as to why he has been described as "the gold standard" for fact-checkers at the *Baseball Research Journal.*

Notes

1. The final game of the 1912 World Series was actually Game Eight, since Game Two ended in a 6–6 tie after 11 innings due to darkness. For purposes of this discussion, it shall hereafter be referred to as Game Seven, since it was the seventh and final game of that World Series in which a winner was declared.
2. This was the case for Game Seven of the World Series in 1909, 1934, 1945, 1956, 1967 and 1985.
3. This was the case for Game Seven of the World Series in 1925, 1931, 1940, 1946, 1947, 1964, 1973, 1982, 1986, 1987, 2002 and 2011.
4. This sequence was re-recreated from information contained at Baseball-Reference.com, which was also used for game data contained elsewhere in this discussion (unless otherwise noted).
5. Three of the seven pitchers to have thrown a Golden Pitch had their teams eventually lose the World Series—Christy Mathewson (1912), Jose Mesa (1997), and Mariano Rivera (2001)—almost certainly the only time Mesa's name will ever be mentioned in the same breath as the two Hall of Famers.
6. MLB.com.
7. 30 teams playing 162 games means a total of 2,430 games are played during the regular season. The total pitch count for the season assumes 260 pitches, on average, are thrown during a game.

Flashback Gordon

Cryptic Communication within a Base-Running Relay-Throw Event

Jeffrey N. Howard

No sooner had Kansas City Royals catcher Salvador Perez popped up for the last out in the 2014 World Series, the pundits, second-guessers, arm-chair managers, and even scientists embarked on quests to address third base coach Mike Jirschele's decision to hold KC's Alex Gordon at third, instead of sending him home to try to tie the game. In a moment that will haunt KC fans, Gordon stayed at third. We will never know with any reasonable degree of certainty if Gordon could have been safe. Or will we?

Analyses of the play have addressed variables that range from Gordon's speed and the breakdown of the relay throw, to Giants shortstop Brandon Crawford's throwing accuracy and Giants catcher Buster Posey's ability to get back to the plate in time from an off-line throw.[1,2] However, a thorough analysis of the entire scenario and its constituent variables requires one to ask "Was everything done strategically—both on offense and on defense—to extract the maximum amount of advantage from the scenario for its participants?" Such a question goes beyond a well-executed relay-throw chain and a base runner heading toward third base—it extends to the fundamentals of offensive and defensive baseball itself, and whether important strategic elements of the game were in place when Gordon's trek began.

CRYPTIC COMMUNICATION IN BASEBALL

Baseball is a sport of hidden communication; there is always a "game within the game" being played somewhere on the field. Catchers give covert signals to pitchers to establish pitch type and location, when to pitch out, and cuing events such as snap-throws behind a runner on base. Fielders give each other signals regarding who should cover a base or take a relay throw, and managers and base coaches pass signals to players and each other in numerous strategic situations. As many as a thousand of these signals can be exchanged in an average major league game, and coordination of comprehensive offensive strategy among players and coaches can be critical in a close contest.[3] However not all situations where cryptic communication may be of benefit are exploited in baseball. One such situation was indeed the Game Seven bottom-of-the-ninth baserunning situation that Kansas City's Alex Gordon found himself in.

Gordon's situation was not unusual outside of having occurred when and where it did. A team might find itself in this same situation once or twice every five to ten games—perhaps even more frequently. Sending the runner from third is reliant upon the most critical set of signals.[4] Why, then—in a game where cryptic communication is of paramount importance in assuring success—would the offense allow the defense free access to their "stop" and "go" signals as conveyed by their third base coach? To answer such a question, one has to look at what an alternative strategy to allowing such "theft" of signals to occur, might look like.

THE "TROJAN-HORSE"

The cryptic nature of communication among baseball coaches and players generally relies upon a master-signal called an "indicator," whereby the indicator consists of a specific act or behavior on the part of the coach (or player) conveying the signals. The intent of an indicator is to obfuscate the signals to an opponent who may also have visual access to the communication. For example, signals occurring prior to an indicator are false signals that convey no meaning. Only a signal given directly after the indicator—called the "hot sign"[5]—is valid. Thus the indicator serves as a sort of "decryption key" for those privy to it.

Alex Gordon and the Kansas City coaching staff found themselves in a situation that called for an indicator that could cryptically signal Gordon to keep running and simultaneously convey false information to the defense, thus causing a delay/hesitation on the part of the San Francisco Giants' relay-throw chain. In particular, with respect to the play as it unfolded, second baseman Joe Panik would be the target of such a "deke"—a word derived from the word "decoy"—where the intent is to mislead or fool an opposing player in some way.[6] Such dekes have been well-documented with respect to delaying an opposing player's behavioral response using situational cues such as body-language.[7] The "automatic switch" also exists which reverses the meaning of a specific signal until further notice.[8] But in Gordon's situation it was clear that the regular stop/go signal sequence was in place.

The application of a cryptic indicator by Kansas City third base coach Mike Jirschele would in essence have constituted a "Trojan-Horse" of sorts whereby the true intent of the signal given to the base runner is hidden from the defense. A consultation of the video replay provides a clear view of the effect that Jirschele's signal had not only on Gordon, but the effect it had on Panik and Crawford and how it influenced their defensive strategy.[9] The MLB.com video is fairly conclusive as to "where" Panik is gleaning his information from during the relay throw. At the 38-second mark Panik begins looking back over his left shoulder toward Jirschele—and it is fairly clear that Panik is not looking at Gordon. (Gordon is directly behind him at this point in the video.) At the 41-second mark Panik, having seen Jirschle give the "stop" sign, throws up his arms nearly in-concert with Jirschle, while turning toward Crawford who is receiving the relay throw. Jirschle, Gordon, and Panik are all visible in the frame.

As mentioned, Panik would be the main target of the deke, and Panik indeed readily watches for Jirschele's signal so he can turn and verbally relay to Crawford what is transpiring on the basepaths while Crawford concentrates on receiving the relay throw from left fielder Juan Perez. Crawford was likely mentally contemplating his next move based upon some verbal signal by Panik—and the video seems to bear this out. The ball can be seen in the air about 15 to 20 feet in front of Crawford (and Gordon about 12 feet from third base) at 40 to 41 seconds. A verbal warning to a cutoff man could be beneficial in two ways:

1. In the event the runner is going, the cutoff man can mentally prepare to make the relay throw. A fluid throw, utilizing continuity of momentum, will allow for the quickest possible relay.

2. In the event that the runner is not going, the verbal warning avoids an unnecessary relay

Alex Gordon was held at third instead of sent home with the potential tying run in Game Seven of the 2014 World Series.

NATIONAL BASEBALL HALL OF FAME LIBRARY, COOPERSTOWN, NY

throw—a throw that could be errant or get away from a fielder, potentially allowing runners to advance.

Indeed, being deked into making a relay throw could be the intent of some strategy, as a bad throw may create opportunities for the offense. A June 26, 2014, Giants and Reds game demonstrates such a relay (absent any "deke" situation) with two outs in the top of the eighth, with Crawford as the relay man and Brandon Phillips of the Reds as the intended home plate target. Crawford's relay throw was slightly high and to the left of Buster Posey the catcher, and so slow such that despite Posey having moved in front of the plate several feet to meet it, he had to dive and reach back toward the plate to nick Phillips on the arm and secure the out. Had there been a even a minute delay in Crawford's relay throw, Phillips would have clearly been safe.[10]

If a deke-inducing signal strategy had been in indeed in place, Panik would have falsely warned Crawford that Gordon was a "no-go"—but Gordon would have kept running. Most interestingly, even if San Francisco knew ahead of time that the Royals might deke the cutoff man in this type of base-running event, such knowledge would render useless any verbal warning that an infielder might give. The cutoff man would then have to wait on the ball, turn, assess the situation himself, and then make (or hold) the throw—all of which would buy more time for a runner on the move.

Although the previously mentioned "automatic switch" could attain similar results in a "Gordon situation," the Trojan-Horse strategy incorporates three options as opposed to the on/off binary option provided by the automatic switch. The Trojan-Horse indicator strategy can take on one of three forms:

1. The "literal" indicator—where status quo prevails and the stop/go signs are presented as they always have been;

2. The "deke"—an indicator is used (e.g. helmet in hand) that conveys the inverse of the status quo—where stop means "go"… and go means "stop"; or

3. The "ignore" indicator—where an indicator is used, but said indicator is ignored in favor of the status quo. Implementing such a cryptic signal permanently as a part of a team baserunning strategy could increase runs scored within certain types of play-at-the-plate situations.

INSIDE THE BOX

Major League Baseball players invest a great deal of time watching video and studying tendencies of pitchers to maximize the result of each at-bat (and pitchers study batters in the same manner). This intense study places the batter under the cognitive load to simultaneously process what they learned about a pitcher—such as how the current count aligns with known pitcher tendencies—with all the other sensory inputs in the batters box such as coaching signals, changing pitch count, and other situational hitting information.

Alex Gordon was probably not ruminating in-depth about running hard and fast out of the box prior to making contact; it is far more likely he was internally analyzing his own actions, assessing the pitch sequence he had seen up to that point, trying to predict what the next pitch might be in the sequence with respect to the current count, recalling what Bumgarner's tendencies were, and what—if anything—might tip him off to the next pitch. In short, the power of the situation had control of Gordon—and research has shown that even the power of situations which are clearly artificial can have a profound effect on behavior to the point where those in the situation can seemingly lose touch with reality.[11]

Batters can become consumed with critiquing their actions on a pitch-by pitch basis; they meticulously self-monitor their performance. Action-control research supports the view that high self-monitoring individuals are sensitive to external (situational) cues, and exceedingly influenced by unanticipated events.[12] Few would argue against the idea that baseball players

during an at-bat will self-monitor pitch-by-pitch so as to make adjustments. Ultimately, Gordon cannot be faulted if he went into a routine response mode, for according to Singer, Lidor, and Cauraugh, "attaining a state of automaticity in routine acts is the goal in any mastery situation."[13] Such "automaticity" would clearly explain Gordon's reserved start in leaving the batter's box upon making what he deemed to be a "routine" hit.

OUTSIDE THE BOX

A number of sources direct criticism at Gordon's speed to first in that situation.[14] In Gordon's defense, his behavioral response was natural with respect to human nature and the means by which humans interpret "cues" within the immediate environment. This can be particularly true of contextual cues which convey information that is highly relevant to one and one's current situation.[15] Outfielders provide us with a prime example of such cues and their influence. Outfielders use cues from batters to discern their immediate action upon batter contact with the ball.[16] These cues can consist of things such as whether the batter has dropped their shoulder or the bat at a low angle, where the batter's head is facing, or if the batter's body positioning upon contact is an open stance (which can cause a ball to "slice") or remains closed (which can cause a ball to "hook"). These cues allow outfielders to get a more accurate "jump" or first step in pursuit of the ball.[17] A batter is no different after making contact—a batter will immediately receive physical feedback from the contact, as well as visual feedback from the flight path of the ball and will interpret behavioral cues from fielders where the ball is headed. Such cues quickly convey information regarding the fielder's likelihood of making a play on the ball. A hitter who receives fielder cues indicating the fielder is playing a "routine hit" will likely respond with behavior consistent with a routine hit—particularly if the fielder cues coincide with the physical feedback a hitter receives upon making contact.

Gordon could have overridden any influence from fielder cues by making the conscious effort to tell himself at the plate beforehand to run full-bore no matter what type of contact he made. But he responded to the situational cues that were available to him in the manner he always had. Gordon had no way of knowing that center fielder Gregor Blanco's response would be punctuated with a "slip" of Blanco's plant foot, resulting in the ball skipping beneath his glove and headed for the wall in center field. Gordon's mental processes as he moved out of the box would likely have reflected that of the earlier-mentioned concept of automaticity. Before seeing the error by Blanco, Gordon was simply responding (physically and mentally) to what he thought looked like a routine hit.

RUNNING THE NUMBERS

Accounts of Gordon's velocity toward first base indicate that he was traveling at approximately 19.31 feet per second, and arrived at 4.66 seconds—an arrival time that coincides with the lowest possible score of "2" as per the major league scouting system.[18] This is consistent with physical feedback and fielder cues a batter would receive upon contact with a ball that was indicative of a routine single. In comparison, Gordon's triple on April 5, 2013, in Philadelphia had Gordon arriving at third one second faster—with a time of 11.03 seconds—than he arrived in the World Series scenario.[19] The most telling contrast between these two events is the type of hit that was delivered by Gordon. The Philadelphia triple was driven hard to the right-center gap, with immediate response cues of the fielders indicating not a "play" on the ball, but rather a "chase."[20] Gordon reacted to the situational cues the context warranted and ran hard and fast.

Knowing that Gordon's peak velocity and arrival time at third base during the Philadelphia triple was better than in the World Series scenario begs the question: would the base-running parameters of the Philadelphia triple, when coupled with the theorized "Trojan Horse" strategy, have allowed Gordon to score in Game Seven?

Had Gordon's base-running performance been the equivalent of his Philadelphia 2013 triple, and if a Trojan-Horse strategy were in-place—e.g. where Jirschele held his protective helmet in his hand while simultaneously giving the universally accepted baseball "stop" sign to Gordon (both hands held up in the air)—Crawford (the cutoff man) would have received a false verbal base-running status warning from Panik that could have amounted to a delay in Crawford's relay throw. Could such a delay while Gordon was running at full speed (the same velocity as the Philadelphia 2013 triple) account for the distance Gordon needed to be called safe? The sequence of events listed below supports the argument that there was sufficient variability in the system that could have been manipulated by the offense allowing Gordon to arrive safe, but that this variability simply was not addressed by Kansas City physically or strategically during the play.

1. In his April 5, 2013, triple at Philadelphia, Gordon traveled 270 feet over 11.03 seconds—a velocity of 24.47 feet per second. However, this rate includes Gordon's head-first slide into third. With sustained momentum absent any slide, Gordon most likely attains a 26 feet per second rate rounding third base (more conservative than Freed's calculated rate of 30 feet per second[21]) which is the equivalent of a sustained 4.615 40-yard dash time; a reasonable estimate given such a unique adrenaline-charged situation. It's also important to note that Gordon's actual distance travelled would not have been linear as a path, but rather it would have been "parabolic" at times given that base runners do not make exact 90-degree turns at full speed when contacting bases, nor do they run straight toward a base on all occasions. The aforementioned conservative estimate of 26 feet per second rate upon arriving at third base does serve to slow Gordon down to some degree so as to compensate for the fact that Gordon's journey would not have been precisely linear, and would have deviated to some extent from an exact 270 feet.

2. If there was no stop sign, Gordon's momentum around third base at the 26 feet per second rate puts him .97 seconds past third base at the 12-second mark when Crawford receives the ball (11.03 + .97 = 12.0). That .97 seconds beyond third base at 26 feet per second equals 25.22 feet, which places Gordon 295.22 feet into his journey, or 64.78 feet away from home plate.

3. Crawford has the ball at the 12 second mark—but Giant's second baseman Joe Panik has been yelling at him for 1.25 seconds to "hold up! hold up!" In the video Panik sees Jirschele's stop-sign before Crawford receives the relay throw, then turns to Crawford, and puts his arms up in the air, repeating the stop-sign.[22] Crawford would have known to "hold up" prior to catching Perez's relay throw due to the auditory signal from Panik—and Panik's auditory warning means that Crawford may have mentally "relaxed" to a certain extent because he knows before turning around that he does not have to make a throw. However, Crawford is still in a ready-state when he turns around, as evidenced by the video. In addition, at this point, and likely due to the auditory signal from Panik, Crawford no longer has the need to prepare to make a relay throw.

National Baseball Hall of Fame Library, Cooperstown, NY

Could Gordon have broken out of the box more quickly, overcoming the automatic programming of thousands of previous situations, or was his reaction too ingrained?

4. Suppose that the stop-sign Jirschle gave was indeed a "Trojan" stop-sign—where Jirschele passed an indicator to Gordon, such as giving the stop-sign with his helmet in his hand. This Trojan signal would tell Gordon to keep going, but would appear to be the stop sign to the Giants. If the deke caused Crawford to hesitate a mere 1.1 seconds before realizing it, Gordon would have covered 31.2 more feet, putting him 33.58 feet from home plate.

5. According to Freed, "If Crawford reaches 70 miles per hour on his throw, probably the most realistic estimate; he gets it home in 1.36 seconds."[23] Crawford's throw (which due to the deke he now has to launch without optimal momentum and rhythm toward home plate) covers the 140 feet to home plate in 1.36 seconds at 70mph—but Gordon will cover 35.36 feet in this same time frame—which puts Gordon at home plate 1.78 feet ahead of Crawford's throw.

CONCLUSION

The intent of this paper was to demonstrate that maximized offensive manpower resources within the "Gordon situation," when coupled with maximized offensive strategic resources, could have exacted the result of tying the game for Kansas City, and more importantly, that the status quo for communicating base runner advance information under the circumstances that Gordon endured, is a good candidate for offensive strategic change within the game of baseball.

From a psychological perspective, the pundits, journalists, fans, and scientists have not been entirely fair to Gordon, as "the power of the situation" reasonably vindicates Gordon for his late start.[24] Gordon was not only a participant in the situation, he was also a victim of it. Gordon's triple in Philadelphia and his error-stricken single in the 2014 World Series are clearly two different types of hits. It is unreasonable to conclude that Gordon should have exhibited the same behavioral reaction to two very different behavior-eliciting situations.

The same commentary that targets Gordon's late start assumes Crawford would have been accurate on a throw home—leaving Salvador Perez to face Bumgarner as Kansas City's last hope. But accuracy in throwing under pressure is only one aspect of Brandon Crawford's multi-faceted job; for Bumgarner, it's nearly his entire job. When faced with the choice of who will fail to perform under pressure when it comes to throwing accuracy, gambling on one hurried throw from a very good shortstop at 140 feet, over an at-bat against a World Series MVP pitcher like Bumgarner from 60.5 feet, seems like a good choice. ∎

Notes

1. Andrew Joseph, "Alex Gordon's late start costs the Royals in 9th inning," *The Arizona Republic*, October 30, 2014. Accessed October 30, 2014. http://www.azcentral.com/story/sports/heat- index/2014/10/30/alex-gordons-late-start-costs-the-royals-in-9th-inning/18176123.
2. Chris Chase, "Alex Gordon going for inside-the-park HR would've been the greatest end to the World Series." *USA Today*, October 30, 2014. Accessed October 30, 2014. http://ftw.usatoday.com/2014/10/alex-gordon-triple-inside-the-park-home-run-score-could-world-series-game-7
3. Paul Dickson, *The Hidden Language of Baseball*, Walker Books, 2005, 6.
4. Wayne Patterson, "The Cryptology of Baseball," *Cryptologia* 35, no. 2 (2011): 158, 156–163.

5. William R.Cheswick, "Johnny Can Obfuscate: Beyond Mother's Maiden Name." In Proceedings of the 1st USENIX Workshop on Hot Topics in Security. 2006, 33.

6. Jason Turbow and Michael Duca, *The Baseball Codes: Beanballs, Sign Stealing, and Bench-Clearing Brawls: The Unwritten Rules of America's Pastime*, Anchor, 2011, 81.

7. Jason Turbow, "Deking Propriety." *The Baseball Codes*, April 28, 2010. Accessed February 1, 2015. http://thebaseballcodes.com/2010/04/28/deking-propriety.

8. William R. Cheswick, 2006, 33.

9. MLB.com. 2014. "Gordon takes third on error," October 29, 2013. Accessed November 15. http://m.mlb.com/mia/video/topic/63106348/v36878067/ws2014-gm7-gordon-singles-takes-third-on-error

10. MLB.com. 2014. "Relay nabs Phillips," June 26, 2014. Accessed February 4, 2015. http://m.mlb.com/video/v34074955/cinsf-relay-throw-cuts-down-phillips-at-the-plate/?c_id=mlb

11. Craig Haney, Curtis Banks, and Philip Zimbardo, "Interpersonal dynamics in a simulated prison." *International Journal of Criminology & Penology* (1973), 90.

12. Julius Kuhl, and Jürgen Beckmann, eds. "Action control: From cognition to behavior." *Springer Science & Business Media*, 2012, 22.

13. Robert Singer, Ronnie Lidor, and James H. Cauraugh, "To be aware or not aware? What to think about while learning and performing a motor skill." *Sport Psychologist* 7 (1993): 21, 19–309.

14. Rob Neyer, "What if Alex Gordon had hustled?" FOXSports.com, Accessed February 4, 2015. http://www.foxsports.com/mlb/just-a-bit-outside/story/alex-gordon-world-series-game7-mike-jirschele-royals-third-base-coach-103114.

15. Eric Buckolz, Harry Prapavesis, and Jack Fairs, "Advance cues and their use in predicting tennis passing shots." *Canadian Journal of Sport Sciences; Journal Canadien des Sciences Dusport*, 13, no. 1 (1988): 20, 20–30.

16. Mike Evans, "Outfield Fundamentals. Evans Pressure Baseball," n.d. http://www.evanspressurebaseball.com/books-articles/outfield.php

17. David Krival, and Tito Landrum, "Tito Landrum on Outfield Play: Getting a Good Jump on the Ball," *Hardball Magazine*, 1993 (Winter). http://www.msblnational.com/HardBall-Archives/Blog/Tito-Landrum-on-Outfield-Play-39-193.htm.

18. Andrew Joseph, October 30, 2014.

19. Rob Neyer, February 4, 2015.

20. MLB.com. 2014. "Gordon's RBI triple," April 5, 2013. Accessed January 10, 2015. http://m.mlb.com/video/topic/42930092/v26025851/kcphi-gordons-rbi-triple-puts-royals-in-the-lead/?query=alex%2Bgordon%2Btriple.

21. David Freed, "Should Alex Gordon Have Been Sent Home?" *The Harvard Sports Analysis Collective* (HSAC), October 31, 2014. http://harvardsportsanalysis.org/2014/10/should-alex-gordon-have-been-sent-home.

22. MLB.com. 2014. Gordon.

23. David Freed, 2014.

24. Craig Haney, Curtis Banks, and Philip Zimbardo. 1973.

Never Make the First or Last Out at Third Base... Perhaps

Ryan Gantner

Baseball players, even those playing as children, have likely heard the familiar adage *Never make the first or last out at third base*. This advice warns players to exercise extreme caution when deciding to advance to third base when there are presently zero or two outs, imploring them to remain at second unless successful advancement is virtually certain. But are there data to support this wisdom? In this paper, we explore the soundness of the advice in this adage, including various interpretations of it, by looking at Major League Baseball data in various ways.

EXPECTED NUMBER OF RUNS GENERATED PER INNING

One way to determine whether advancing to third base is prudent is to examine the expected number of runs scored in each of three possible scenarios: the runner successfully advances to third base, the runner is out while attempting to advance to third base, and the scenario in which the runner does not attempt to advance and remains safely at second base. One can examine the average number of runs scored per half inning in each of these situations by looking at MLB data from an entire season. These data are readily available. For instance, the Baseball Prospectus website contains the data in Table 1 based on the 2014 MLB season.[1]

Table 1.

Baserunners	Exp. runs, 0 outs	Exp. runs, 1 out	Exp. runs, 2 outs
000	0.4552	0.2394	0.0862
003	1.2866	0.8873	0.3312
020	1.0393	0.6235	0.2901
023	1.8707	1.2714	0.5351
100	0.8182	0.4782	0.1946
103	1.6496	1.1261	0.4396
120	1.4023	0.8623	0.3985
123	2.2337	1.5102	0.6435

The expected number of runs in a half inning from various base runner configurations. Data are from the Baseball Prospectus website. The presence of a runner on a base is indicated by that base number appearing in the configuration code; there is a 0 in that spot if there is no runner at the base.

Using tables like Table 1 we can compute *threshold* values for the probability of successful advancement to third: the probability of successful advancement which would yield identical expected values for runs scored for both situations (the runner attempts to advance and the runner makes no such attempt). Anytime the actual probability of success exceeds the threshold value, the expected number of runs scored will be maximized by having the runner attempt to advance to third base. These probability calculations are done assuming that the future events (such as the number of runs scored in subsequent play) in the inning are independent of past events, given the current baserunner configuration. In reality, future events are dependent on who is batting, who is running, who is pitching, where the game is played, the weather, etc. Modeling probabilities based on these dependencies is not only beyond the scope of this paper but also not in the spirit of a simple adage that advises one to never make an out at third. Furthermore, work done by David W. Smith suggests that considering these dependencies actually does not drastically change the transition probabilities anyway.[2]

There are two situations to examine. One situation is when a runner is attempting to advance to third base and this runner is the only baserunner. This situation could arise when a batter attempts to stretch a double into a triple, when a runner on second tries to steal third base, or when a runner on second attempts to advance to third on a fly ball or when a pitch gets past the catcher. When there is nobody out, the expected number of runs per half inning is 1.2866 when there is a runner on third and nobody out and 0.2394 when there are no baserunners and one out (which would occur if the runner were unsuccessful in advancing to third). Thus, if the probability of successful advance to third base is denoted by p, the expected number of runs by attempting to advance to third base with nobody out is $1.2866p + 0.2394(1-p)$. Setting this equal to 1.0393 (the expected number of runs scored with a runner on second with nobody out, the situation in which no advance is attempted) and solving for **p** gives the threshold value of **p** for this situation; in this case **p = 0.764**. A runner will increase the team's expected number of runs scored in the inning by attempting to advance from second to third if he anticipates a probability of success better than 0.764. Other threshold values appear in Table 2.

Table 2.

2014 thresholds	0 outs	1 out	2 outs
one base runner	0.764	0.671	0.876
also runner on 1st	0.789	0.717	0.907

Threshold values for advancing from second to third base, based on 2014 MLB data.

As we can see by Table 2, the threshold values for going to third base are higher with zero or two outs than with one out. This does give some evidence to support the adage. This is true whether or not we assume that there is a runner behind the one who is attempting to advance to third (which we assume will stay at first base regardless of whether the other runner attempts to advance to third).

To show that these thresholds are not a fluke, a similar analysis can be done using the 2013 MLB season. The threshold values obtained appear in Table 3:

Table 3.

2013 thresholds	0 outs	1 out	2 outs
One base runner	0.774	0.680	0.866
Also runner on 1st	0.800	0.724	0.899

Threshold values for advancing from second to third base, based on 2013 MLB data.

While this does support the adage, it is worth noting that the thresholds with zero or one out are not extremely different.

It is worth mentioning that this particular analysis was done with older MLB data (not immediately clear which year or whether it was an entire season or the whole league, etc.) in a series of two blog posts by Zachary Levine of the *Houston Chronicle* in 2009.[3,4]

In those articles it was mentioned that the thresholds for going to third with zero outs and with one out are fairly close to each other, while the threshold for going to third with two outs is substantially greater. With the 2013 and 2014 data, that effect is not quite as pronounced. Levine even offers a change to the axiom to say:

Don't make the last out at third (The first is forgivable).

It is also interesting to note that numerous analyses involving the expected number of runs after various baserunning transitions are done in the work of David W. Smith. While Smith doesn't specifically address this particular threshold calculation, he does specifically mention it as one that could be performed using this type of analysis.

EXPECTED NUMBER OF RUNS FORFEITED PER INNING

Also mentioned in the *Houston Chronicle* blogs is that rather than examining the expected number of runs generated per inning by each of the three baserunner configurations that could arise, we could look at how many runs per inning we expect to forfeit if the runner attempts to advance to third base but is unsuccessful. For instance, in 2014 the mean number of runs per half inning scored after we reach a situation in which there is a runner on second and nobody out (the runner does not try to advance) is 1.0393 and the mean number for nobody on and one out is 0.2394. Therefore, a runner being thrown out at third for the first out has squandered 0.7999 runs. Table 4 shows the mean number of runs forfeited with each attempt at advancing to third.

Table 4.

	0 outs	1 out	2 outs
Successfully advance to third, lone runner	1.2866	0.8873	0.3312
Unsuccessfully advance to third, lone runner	0.2394	0.0862	0
No attempt to advance to third, lone runner	1.0393	0.6235	0.2901
Runs forfeited by unsuccessful advance	0.7999	0.5373	0.2901
Successfully advance to third, also runner on 1st	1.6496	1.1261	0.4396
Unsuccessfully advance to third, also runner on 1st	0.4782	0.1946	0
No attempt to advance to third, also runner on 1st	1.4023	0.8623	0.3985
Runs forfeited by unsuccessful advance	0.9241	0.6677	0.3985

The expected number of runs in each situation and the number of runs forfeited if the advancing runner is unsuccessful.

In both situations, while the threshold for advancing to third with two outs is quite high (we need to be all-but-certain of a successful advance in order for our average number of runs to increase), the number of runs lost by an unsuccessful advance is actually substantially less with two outs than with one or no outs. This, together with our previous skepticism about the wisdom of not making the last out at third base, might seem to indicate that we should say:

Never make the first out at third base.

MAYBE WE ONLY NEED ONE RUN

The previous two subsections contain arguments based on the increase or decrease in the expected number of runs scored from various situations. However, there are many times in baseball that we don't need to maximize the expected number of runs scored in the inning, rather we would like to maximize the probability of scoring at least one run (or at least 2 runs, etc.). To perform this analysis, the author wrote a computer program to scour through the play-by-play files provided by Retrosheet.org to determine the fraction of the time from each situation when at least one run is scored.[5] The results are presented in Table 5.

Table 5.

Situation	At least 1 run	At least 2 runs	At least 3 runs	At least 4 runs
000, 0 out	0.255	0.114	0.049	0.020
100, 0 out	0.404	0.229	0.108	0.046
020, 0 out	0.609	0.259	0.112	0.050
003, 0 out	0.857	0.283	0.125	0.047
120, 0 out	0.596	0.379	0.222	0.109
023, 0 out	0.849	0.573	0.243	0.129
103, 0 out	0.876	0.426	0.251	0.112
000, 1 out	0.147	0.057	0.022	0.008
100, 1 out	0.258	0.140	0.056	0.020
020, 1 out	0.384	0.150	0.059	0.023
003, 1 out	0.660	0.166	0.071	0.028
120, 1 out	0.398	0.234	0.133	0.049
023, 1 out	0.692	0.390	0.163	0.070
103, 1 out	0.620	0.255	0.139	0.055
000, 2 out	0.061	0.018	0.006	0.002
100, 2 out	0.122	0.040	0.013	0.004
020, 2 out	0.206	0.065	0.025	0.009
003, 2 out	0.255	0.059	0.021	0.006
120, 2 out	0.210	0.106	0.058	0.016
023, 2 out	0.234	0.185	0.062	0.019
103, 2 out	0.249	0.102	0.049	0.014

The fraction of the time each event occurs subsequently in the same inning when the baserunners are in a particular situation. For instance, when a runner is on third base (and only third base) with one out, at least one run is scored 66% of the time.

We can then perform a similar analysis to what we did before. For example, suppose we would like to maximize the probability of scoring at least one run. With one out, a batter gets a good hit and is trying to decide whether he should remain happy with a stand-up double, or try to extend to a triple. If he is successful in his advance to third, the probability of scoring at least one run is 0.660. If he is unsuccessful, the probability drops to 0.061. If he doesn't attempt to advance, the probability is 0.384. Again assuming that what occurs after this batter is independent of how the

batter runs the basepath, the runner should try to advance to third if his probability of success is at least 0.54. We can do a similar analysis of each situation, which yields the probabilities in Table 6:

Table 6.

Situation/Runs needed	1 run	2 runs	3 runs	4 runs
Go to third, 0 outs, lone runner	0.651	0.896	0.874	1.063
Go to third, 1 out, lone runner	0.540	0.893	0.813	0.798
Go to third, 2 outs, lone runner	0.806	1.103	1.216	1.359
Go to third, 0 outs, runner on 1st	0.547	0.834	0.850	0.968
Go to third, 1 out, runner on 1st	0.553	0.901	0.952	0.874
Go to third, 2 outs, runner on 1st	0.843	1.036	1.180	1.128

The critical probabilities for advancing to third if we need a certain number of runs. If the probability the runner will successfully advance to third is greater than these values, advancing to third will improve the probability of achieving the desired result. Values are based on 2014 MLB data.

The most striking feature of the values in Table 6 is that some of the probabilities are more than one. For example, sending a runner to third base with two outs actually decreases the team's probability of acquiring two or more runs in the inning, based on 2014 data. The only logical explanation that the author can think of for this is that with a runner on second, the opposing team may be tempted to walk the next batter to yield a force play, and this strategy may backfire. According to this analysis, runners should stop at second base with two outs in this situation, even if a triple were guaranteed!

In Table 6, we notice that with a lone runner the critical probabilities for advancing to third are lower with one out than with two or zero, regardless of how many runs are needed in the inning. This may speak to the adage in the sense that attempting to advance to third base is less risky with one out than with zero or two. However, in most cases there is not much difference between the critical probabilities for zero outs and for one out. Furthermore, with a runner on first the critical probabilities are actually higher (except if the team needs four runs) with one out than with zero outs. Perhaps most importantly, the only values in the table which are less than 0.8 are when attempting to advance to third with zero or one out and only one run is needed. Perhaps the axiom should say:

When only one run is needed, don't make the last out at third base. When more than one run is needed, don't get out at third base no matter how many outs there are.

IS THIRD BASE UNIQUE?

What's so special about third base? Perhaps the axiom should read *Don't make the first out at second base, or Don't make the third out...anywhere!* In this subsection, we'll examine whether there is anything different about third base that makes it worthy of such advice.

Using a similar analysis, we compute the threshold values for going to second (stretching a single into a double, stealing second, advancing from first to second on a wild pitch, etc.). We also compute the threshold values for attempting to score from third base (sorted according to where any other baserunners are). The results are displayed in Table 7. For example, in order to increase a team's expected number of runs scored in the inning, a runner should only advance to second with one out if the probability of successful advance is greater than 0.7296.

Table 7.

	0 outs	1 out	2 outs
Going to 2nd	0.72347	0.72957	0.6708
Going home (lone runner)	0.86133	0.69468	0.30492
Going home (runner on 1st)	0.87424	0.72569	0.36799
Going home (runner on 2nd)	0.88092	0.73594	0.41477
Going home (runner on 1st & 2nd)	0.89052	0.75946	0.46014

Threshold values for advancing to selected bases. Computed using 2014 MLB data.

What we see is that the threshold values for advancing to second do not exhibit substantial differences with respect to the number of outs, though advancing to second with two outs has a slightly lower threshold than with 0 or 1. However, the threshold

LIBRARY OF CONGRESS: BAIN COLLECTION

Bill Reynolds of the 1914 New York Yankees attempts a play at the plate on second baseman Charles Seitz of the Houston Texas League club.

values for advancing to home do vary dramatically: much more dramatically than the thresholds for advancing to third. Because the threshold for advancing to home plate with 0 outs is so much more than the thresholds with other numbers of outs, perhaps our adage should say:

Never make the first out at home plate.

We can also repeat our analysis of the situation where we need a certain number of runs. We calculate the critical values for situations in which we need only one, two, three, or four runs and present them in Table 8. Threshold values for advancing to home are presented in the case when there is only one baserunner; the other baserunner configurations give similar conclusions.

The critical values for scoring at least n runs in an inning are computed as

$$critical\ value = \frac{p-q}{s-q}$$

where

$p = P$ (scoring n runs if no attempt to advance is made)

$q = P$ (scoring n runs if attempt fails)

$s = P$ (scoring $n-1$ runs if attempt succeeds)

Table 8.

Situation/ Runs needed	1 run	2 runs	3 runs	4 runs
Go to 2nd, 0 outs	0.55759	0.85141	0.95093	0.92033
Go to 2nd, 1 out	0.60957	0.92389	0.95074	0.87034
Go to 2nd, 2 outs	0.59367	0.61714	0.5288	0.48912
Go home, 0 outs (lone runner)	0.83186	1.1398	1.11877	0.94296
Go home, 1 out (lone runner)	0.6383	1.14744	1.28224	1.29507
Go home, 2 outs (lone runner)	0.25537	0.96659	1.15459	1.0564

Critical probabilities for advancing to second base and home plate when a specified number of runs is needed. The data were calculated using 2014 MLB data.

We notice a few things immediately. For example, when only one run is needed the critical value of the probability of successful advance to second base is essentially the same regardless of the number of outs. However, when more than one run is needed, the critical probability for going to second is very high with zero or one outs and much lower with two outs, suggesting that it is rarely worth it to advance to second base in zero or one out situations when more than one run is needed. Also, the critical probability for attempting to score is only reasonably small when one run is needed, and even then it is still high when there is nobody out.

Indeed, many of the critical probabilities in Table 8 are greater than one, indicating that a team is actually more likely to score, say, at least three runs in an inning when the baserunner is kept at third instead of scoring, even if successful advance is certain. The author acknowledges that this advice seems a bit suspicious and offers some interpretation. First, the independence assumption (that the events of the game following a baserunner advance are independent of the past events) is not entirely sound. The presence of a runner on third base may indicate something about the pitcher's current state, for instance, and may improve the probability of scoring more subsequent runs in an inning, thus driving the threshold probabilities below one. Second, the numbers came from MLB data, so they are based on what MLB teams actually did, not based on the results of some unbiased experiment (there were no "clinical trials" in the way that a medical treatment would get approved). Finally, as the events in question get more specific (e.g., a team scores four or more runs in an inning with a runner on third and two outs), the number of occurrences begins to lessen somewhat, so a smaller sample size may begin to distort the results. In any event, the upshot is that the critical values for advancing to home when more than one run is needed in an inning are extremely high.

We could pen a more elaborate adage:

If more than one run is needed in an inning, never get out at home and never make the first or second out at second base. If only one run is needed, never make the first out at home plate, but making the third out at home is entirely forgivable.

However, the first sentence of our new adage has forgotten the critical values for third base. In fact, if more than one run is needed, the only situation in which it makes sense to advance a baserunner is when attempting to advance to second with two outs. Putting this together, we could say the following.

If more than one run is needed in an inning, the only time a runner should be advanced when success is not completely certain is when going to second base with two outs.

RESULTS BASED ON A MARKOV MODEL

Another way to analyze the situation is to build a model to examine baserunning situations. As is mentioned by Smith in his paper, one way this has been done is to model the game of baseball as a Markov chain.[6] We use for states of the Markov chain the combination of which bases contain runners and the number of outs. For example, one state is "nobody on base with one out" and another is "runners on first and third with two outs." Modeling the game as a Markov chain is natural for our purpose for two reasons. First, as mentioned earlier, the calculation of threshold values presumes the independence of future events from past events, given the present situation. Therefore, we are in effect employing a Markov assumption even in that case. Furthermore, by using a Markov model we are extending the foundation of empirical probabilities to a more generalized context, while still keeping the foundation in realized data.

To determine transitions between these states, we examined play-by-play data from the 2013 and 2014 Major League Baseball seasons. Every single play was examined and tallied in order to assess the probabilities of these transitions during these seasons. For example, in 2014 there were 257 instances of a transition from a runner on first base with nobody out to a state with nobody on base with nobody out. Likely, the vast majority of these transitions were due to a two-run home run, but perhaps a stolen base or pick-off attempt together with a grossly errant throw which allowed the baserunner to score could have happened a few times. Since there were 10,951 instances of a runner on first base with nobody out, the transition probability from (runner on first with nobody out) to (nobody on with nobody out) we model as 257/10,951 in the 2014 season.

We add an extra state to the Markov chain called the "end of inning" state, which acts as an absorbing state. In such, there are 25 states in this Markov chain. Let P denote the 25 × 25 transition matrix generated using MLB data. If P_T represents the 24 × 24 transition matrix which is the same as P but with the row and column representing the end of inning state (the absorbing state) removed, then it is a standard result (see, for instance, Sheldon Ross's book[7]) that S_{ij}, the expected number of visits to state j starting from state i, is given in matrix form by:

$$S = (I - P^T)^{-1}$$

We can also define an expected number of runs produced for each transition by looking at MLB data.

The number of runs produced for each transition were recorded, then divided by the total number of transitions to get an expected number of runs generated per transition. For instance, in 2014 there were 133 runs generated by transitions from (runner on first with nobody out) to (runner on second with nobody out). There were 823 such transitions in that season, so the expected number of runs per transition is 0.1616. (Here, most of the time the transition was made by the runner on first stealing second, but occasionally the transition was made by the batter hitting a double in which the runner scored from first.) Let R denote the matrix whose entries r_{ij} are the expected number of runs per transition from state i to state j. Then the vector r, with $r_i = \Sigma_j R_{ij}$, will give us the expected number of runs scored by transitioning out of state i. The product Sr will then give us the expected number of further runs scored in a half inning from each base running situation under this model. We can use this to evaluate the wisdom of making the first or last out at third base using some of the metrics introduced in the last section.

We can analyze the threshold values for sending a runner from second to third base in the same way as we did before. A summary of the data for the 2014 season appears in Table 9. We notice that the threshold values for sending a runner to third base in the absence of a runner on first are higher than the threshold for sending a runner to second when there are zero or two outs, but lower when there is one out. Also, the Markov model has threshold values in line with those generated using the Baseball Prospectus data.

Table 9.

Advance to	0 outs	1 out	2 outs
2nd base	0.704	0.717	0.689
3rd base (lone runner)	0.791	0.663	0.839
3rd base (also runner on 1st)	0.715	0.738	0.902
Home (lone runner)	0.888	0.730	0.320
Home (runner on 1st)	0.950	0.706	0.364
Home (runner on 2nd)	0.891	0.794	0.387
Home (runner on 1st and 2nd)	0.904	0.777	0.478

Threshold Values for sending a runner in various situations under the Markov chain model, using 2014 MLB data.

Upon closer inspection we see that it would actually be more damaging to make the first out at home plate. The threshold value here of 0.888 (as a lone runner) indicates that we really don't want to make the first out at home plate. Also, the fact that the threshold value for sending a runner to third in the presence of a runner at first with one out (0.738) is greater than the threshold for sending a runner to second with one out (0.717) is not consistent that there is anything "special" about third base with zero or two outs which would allow us to be less careful about making the second out at third base.

In order to verify the consistency of this model, we did the procedure indicated above for the 2013 MLB season. That is, we examined all of the play-by-play data to build a transition matrix for that season, examined the runs scored for each transition in that season, and calculated the threshold values based on those. The results are shown in Table 10. In 2013, we do see that sending a runner to third base with one out seems less risky than sending a runner to second with one out, while this is not the case with zero or two outs. However, we also note that the situation which requires the highest threshold is still sending a runner home with zero outs.

Table 10.

Advance to	0 outs	1 out	2 outs
2nd base	0.686	0.730	0.712
3rd base (lone runner)	0.780	0.653	0.859
3rd base (also runner on 1st)	0.748	0.715	0.843
Home (lone runner)	0.886	0.726	0.321
Home (runner on 1st)	0.919	0.730	0.406
Home (runner on 2nd)	0.916	0.788	0.419
Home (runner on 1st and 2nd)	0.853	0.777	0.515

Threshold Values for sending a runner in various situations under the Markov chain model, using 2013 MLB data.

Again using the Markov chain model as a guide, we formulate separate Markov transition matrices for each MLB team based on 2014 play-by-play data. The number of runs scored per transition were also sorted per team in order to calculate all of the values above for each team in 2014. The data here do not always support the adage nearly as well.

As we did in the first section, we can examine the threshold for advancing to third base. We first look to see whether the threshold for advancing to third base is lower with one out than with zero or two outs. For two of 30 teams (Baltimore and Boston), the thresholds for going to third with one out was higher than that with zero outs with no other runners on base. For four teams (Oakland, San Diego, Cleveland, and Chicago White Sox), the threshold for going to third with one out was higher than that with two outs with no other runners on base. When there is an additional runner on first base, the situation is even less consistent. For seven of the 30 teams the threshold for advancing to third with one out eclipses that with two outs and for 17 of 30 teams the threshold for advancement with one out exceeds that with zero outs when there is another runner on first base. Only 10 of the 30 teams had all four of these inequalities in a direction consistent with the adage.

We can also calculate thresholds which examine why advancing to third, rather than a different base, is worthy of such an adage. Only 22 of the 30 teams had thresholds for going to third base with zero outs that were higher than the thresholds for going to second with zero outs. The situation isn't too much different with two outs: 23 of the 30 teams had higher thresholds for going to third with two outs than for going to second with two outs. And with one out, nine of the 30 teams have a higher threshold for going to third than for going to second. In order to have a threshold analysis support the familiar *never make the first or last out at third base* adage, one might expect that the thresholds for going to third base are higher than those going to second base for zero and two outs, but not for one out. This was indeed the case for the MLB as a whole using the Markov model generated by 2013 and 2014 data (though this is not the case in 2014 in the case that there is a runner behind the runner attempting to advance to third who will remain on first base; with one out the threshold for advancing to third in this instance is actually higher than the threshold for a single runner to advance to second). However, this threshold analysis breaks down when viewed on a team-by-team basis. Only 13 of the 30 teams had all three inequalities consistent with the adage using the 2014 model. And using 2013 data to build a model, only nine of 30 teams show all three inequalities consistent with the adage.

Finally, we calculate all of the thresholds for each team to see which are the highest. Of the 30 teams in 2014, 27 had their highest thresholds for either sending a runner home with zero outs (with various configurations of baserunners on the other bases) or sending a runner to third base with two outs in the presence of a runner on first base. One team for which these advances did not have the highest threshold using the Markov model is the Kansas City Royals. Their highest thresholds were sending a runner to third with nobody else on base with zero outs and with two outs. In fact, both of these thresholds are greater than one, indicating that the 2014 Royals should never have a runner try to stretch a double into a triple with zero or two outs, even if success is certain. The other two teams are the Cincinnati Reds and the Baltimore Orioles, which had the highest threshold in sending a runner home with one out in the presence of two other baserunners. Putting this together, we can say the following:

Never make the first out at home. Don't make the last out at third base if there is another runner behind you.

CONCLUSIONS AND DISCUSSION

We have examined a few ways of using data to support or refute a popular adage.

Through the computation of threshold values for advancing to each base given the current configuration of runners, we initially find that, in general, advancing to third base with one out has a lower threshold than doing so with zero or two outs (though this is not true of all data sets with all runner configurations). This seems to suggest that making the second out at third base is less damaging than the first or last. However, the threshold for advancing to third with one out is usually close to that with zero outs, so it is not immediately clear that there is really anything special about making the first out at third base.

We also examined the expected number of runs forfeited by unsuccessful advance. With this, we saw that we are poised to do the most damage by unsuccessfully advancing a runner from second to third with 0 outs. By analyzing this, it seems odd to recommend that we *never* make the last out at third base; doing so simply doesn't squander as many expected runs as we would by making the first or second out there.

If all we need is one run in an inning, the threshold for advancing to third base is much higher with two outs than with zero or one. If more than one run is needed, then the thresholds for advancing to third base are all pretty high.

We also looked at other bases to see if third base is special enough to warrant such an adage. We find the highest thresholds to occur when advancing to third with two outs, advancing to home with zero outs, and advancing to home anytime more than one run is needed in an inning.

By generalizing this analysis to a Markov chain model, we reach similar conclusions. However, when using team-by-team data rather than MLB data as a whole, we find large variation among the threshold values. Even so, the vast majority of the teams seem to be best served with the updated adage:

Never make the last out at third base. Never make the first out at home plate. And never make any out at home plate if more than one run is needed in the inning.

The evidence that making the first out at third base is substantially worse than other situations is just not that strong. We've presented a few arguments for it, but all seem like cherry-picking the data that support the argument. Because there is no "right" or "wrong" way to analyze data which are relevant to the adage, the best we can do is to use data to help make our point. Doesn't this seem to be the case with any baseball argument that one thing/player/strategy is better than another?

Finally, it should be noted that all of these analyses were done using Major League Baseball data. Whether the adage provides wisdom backed with data for Little Leaguers or recreational baseball leagues remains to be seen. ∎

Notes

1. "Baseball Prospectus/Statistics/Custom Statistics Reports: Run Expectations," accessed November 20, 2015, http://www.baseballprospectus.com/sortable/index.php?cid=1657937.
2. David W. Smith, "Are outs on the bases more harmful than other types of outs?" accessed December 30, 2015, http://www.retrosheet.org/Research/SmithD/OutsOnBases.pdf.
3. Zachary Levine, "Don't make the last out at third (The first is forgivable)," *Houston Chronicle*, February 14, 2009, http://blog.chron.com/unofficialscorer/2009/02/dont-make-the-last-out-at-third-the-first-is-forgivable.
4. Zachary Levine, "More on the last out at third base; goodbye to a friend," *Houston Chronicle*, February 16, 2009, http://blog.chron.com/unofficialscorer/2009/02/more-on-the-last-out-at-third-base-goodbye-to-a-friend.
5. "Retrosheet Event Files," accessed October 21, 2015, http://www.retrosheet.org/game.htm.
6. Mark D. Pankin, "Baseball as a Markov Chain," in *The Great American Baseball Stat Book*, ed. Bill James (New York: Ballantine Books, 1987), 520–24.
7. Sheldon M. Ross, *Introduction to Probability Models, Tenth Edition*, (Burlington, MA: Academic Press, 2009).

Player Win Averages (1946–2015)

Pete Palmer

After the 1970 season, two brothers, Eldon and Harlan Mills, unveiled a new approach to baseball statistics: Player Win Averages. Eldon was a retired Air Force colonel and an expert in computer programming and data processing, while Harlan was a professor and mathematics consultant to IBM. What they did was develop a model for calculating win probability as a function of inning, score, and base-out situation and then measure the change for each at-bat during the 1969 season for every batter and pitcher. They paid Elias Sports Bureau to enter the data on punch cards and then tallied the results. The model started with 0 points for each team and at the end one team had 1000 and the other minus 1000, so 1000 points equaled one win. For each player they added up all the plus points and minus points, with the player win average being plus points over the sum of both, so .500 was average. Willie McCovey (.677) and Mike Epstein (.641) led their respective leagues. They did not publish a copy of the win probability, but did show a play-by-play for the 1969 World Series, which contained many values.

Unfortunately, the idea did not catch on. They calculated data for 1970, but did not publish, although they did send me a copy of the results. I shared the data with Dick Cramer, who joined with me to produce an article in the 1974 *Baseball Research Journal* on Batter Run Average, which was basically on-base average times slugging average. Since those data were independent of game situation, you could compare them to player win averages. Players with higher win averages than expected therefore might be considered clutch hitters. However, in his famous article in the 1977 *Baseball Research Journal* ("Do Clutch Hitters Exist?"), Cramer showed there was no correlation from one year to the next. Dick and I gave a presentation at the 2008 SABR national convention, which was also published in the *BRJ* that year, which supported this conclusion over a much larger sample—about 1000 players from 1957 through 2007.

Earnshaw Cook introduced me to Dick Trueman, a professor at Cal State Northridge in the 1960s. Dick had gotten copies of the raw figures from Mills and done quite a bit of work on them. He discovered that a key relief pitcher can actually have about double the effect of a starter on game outcomes because of the situations he faces. Trueman also presented a paper on clutch hitting at the ORSA/TIMS Meeting in 1977. His conclusion was that it might exist, but more data were needed. Trueman gave me a tape of the raw data, which I sent to Dave Smith of Retrosheet who converted them to floppies. I recently turned a copy over to Sean Lahman to have it made available to SABR members. (I also believe Retrosheet used it to reconstruct play-by-play data missing from games 1969–70.)

In order to compare normal stats to player win averages, I punched up all the batting and pitching data for 1969. This turned out to be fairly easy, which started me on creating my baseball database. I kept up with each year and worked backwards, so by 1984 when *The Hidden Game of Baseball* (co-authored by me and John Thorn) came out, I had done to 1925. By then I also had a full basic register based on my work on the old A.S. Barnes baseball encyclopedia, to which I had added at-bats, hits, walks, total bases, innings pitched, and earned run average for all players. Later I added all the other categories back to 1871, which was used for *Total Baseball* with Thorn and the *ESPN Baseball Encyclopedia* with Gary Gillette.

I created a win probability program in the 1970s. It actually wasn't that hard. All you do is start with two outs in the last of the ninth and play the game backwards. I had earlier created a table of runs scoring distribution from 0 to 12 versus the 24 base-out situations. So, in the last of the ninth, one run behind, with two outs and a runner on third, the win probability is simply half the probability of scoring one run from that situation plus the probability of scoring more than one. When you get back to the bases empty, none out situation, you now have ending points for each score difference for the top of the ninth. The run distribution table was created from a game simulation I wrote, using probabilities of each event, plus various transitional frequencies from going from first to third on

NATIONAL BASEBALL HALL OF FAME LIBRARY, COOPERSTOWN, NY

Barry Bonds tops the list of player wins among hitters since 1946.

single, advance on an out, being picked off or getting thrown out stretching, etc. There were very little play-by-play data in those days. Most of my calculations for these figures came from play-by-play of 34 World Series games shown in the baseball guide from 1956 through 1960. Of course now, thanks to Bill James, Gary Gillette, Dave Smith, and others, we have play-by-play of games back to 1946, a full 70 years, plus a great many before that date.

So now I can create the run distribution table from real data, but the win probability table still needs to be done by a program because many of the cells simply don't come up often enough in a season to produce reliable results. I made up a run distribution table and the derived win probability table for each league each year for 1946 through 2015.

The original win probability tables developed by the Mills brothers came from thousands of computer simulated games starting at the 24 different base-out situations (empty, none out through full, two outs). In my model, I used plus-or-minus 8 runs, which would be 24 x 18 x 15 or 6480 different calculations. Using the run-distribution data, I was able to calculate the win probability for all 6480 cases in one short computer run. The problem with using simulations is even after a thousand runs, the margin of error is still three percent. This is calculated by finding the square root of one half times one half times a thousand, or 16, which is the standard deviation (sigma). The margin of error is plus or minus 2 times sigma. The true answer should be in that range 95 percent of the time, assuming that you have a perfectly random sample. If you have a sample of 1000 games and get 530 wins,

that means the true value should be between 500 and 560, which is a pretty big range. Using ten thousand simulations reduces the margin by the square root of ten, which would mean the true answer should be between fifty-one and fifty-three percent. Very few people understand what the margin of error means. When you see a poll of a thousand people and the answer comes out fifty-three percent, the usual interpretation is that since fifty percent is within the margin of error, the result is too close to call. Actually, since the true answer would be between fifty and fifty-six percent, 95 percent of the time, the probability that true answer is in the majority is actually 97.5 percent.

The win probability table is useful in calculation of leverage, a concept that Tom Tango (www.tangotiger.net) and I invented independently. What you do for each cell in the table, you calculate the average change for the various items—single, double, triple, home run, walk, or out—each weighted by the appropriate frequency. Then add up the absolute value of each for the total. I called mine "stress," but Tom's name (leverage) was much better. There are usually about 700 cases a year (about one every three or four games) where the leverage is 200 points or more (one-fifth of a win). Almost all are in the ninth inning or later with the team one run behind or tied. The highest level is around 400 points, depending on the league and year. It is two out, last of the ninth, one run behind. The win probability is around 28 percent. If a batter makes out, you lose 280 points. If driving in a run, you gain 360 points, and if you drive in two, you gain 720 points. Starting pitchers average around thirty five leverage points per plate appearance, but key relievers can get up to seventy. Mop-up men can go as low as twenty. This shows one of the drawbacks of player win averages. A few key appearances can swamp out hundreds of ordinary ones. For example, in 2015, Mike Trout's top ten leverage situations average 162 points, which was about equal to the sum of his lowest two hundred appearances.

My method of calculating player win averages was slightly different from the Mills method. I started with each team at 500 points or fifty percent win probability, and added or subtracted the change after each at bat to the batter and pitcher. Thus at the end of the game, one team gains 500 points and other team loses 500. The Mills brothers used 1000 points for each win, which did not affect the value of their average, since both numerator and denominator were doubled. But I used the sum of points, not the ratio, so a player with 5000 points over the season would have contributed five wins more than average. The split between batting and pitching for the winning team in a particular game could vary, but the difference would always be plus 500 and the losing team would be minus 500. In a poorly pitched game, the winning team might have 900 batting points and the losing team 400 batting points. Successful defense points, which are equal to other teams' offense points, are negative. A balanced game would be 250 batting points and 250 pitching points (or minus 250 batting points for the other team).

There are a few more adjustments to be made. Even though the win tables were calculated from the league batting stats, the sum of all points for the year might not be quite zero. The league total usually comes out off by about 0.1 points per appearance (one ten-thousandth of a win). A much bigger correction has to do with the designated hitter rule. The league average for the AL from 1973 to 1996 contained very little pitcher hitting (slightly more since interleague play started). Thus the AL players were being compared to a higher standard than the NL. In order to handle this, I took an average of batting by pitchers and non-pitchers. Pitchers were about 9 points lower than average per at-bat through 1960 and have crept up to 12 point lower today. Since so few AL pitchers have batted since 1972, I used the NL value for the AL in the DH era. This resulted in a correction of about .7 points per appearance for NL batters and AL batters before 1973. Thus I subtracted a bit less than half a win from each batter who played a full season. The correction was zero for the AL until 1997, when it became around .05.

For the ballpark correction, I took the sum of all batters, visitor and home, for each park and compared it to the same players on the road (pitchers excluded). About half the teams were within plus or minus one point per appearance. However, no surprise, Colorado dominated the largest corrections, with 11 of the top 13 spots. The largest was 6.36 points per appearance in 1995. This would mean a regular player would have two wins subtracted from his season record for approximately 300 appearances at home. It is strange that from 2003 through 2009 the adjustment was only about two points, but in recent years it has gone up again and 2012, 2014, and 2015 are in the top ten. There is no such domination on the low end, although Houston does have three of the ten bottom teams. The lowest was the Mets in 1988 with minus 4.29. I took appearances in each park for each player and applied the corrections for that team and year. Thus the fact that the NL West plays a lot more games in Colorado than other divisions is properly taken care of. The park correction is not entirely fair because players are affected differently. Power hitters can take advantage of a short fence better than singles hitters. Asymmetrical parks can benefit batters based on handedness, although not consistently. Lefties Carl Yastrzemski and Wade Boggs were able to take advantage of Fenway Park, while Ted Williams had just a normal home advantage. Joe DiMaggio was hurt by Yankee Stadium, but so was Lou Gehrig.

The batters shown in Table 1 are rated by player wins over average. I included all players with 2800 or more at-bats. Barry Bonds wins by three touchdowns.

Table 1. BATTERS

Name	G	PW	RW
Barry Bonds	2986	120.3	123.2
Henry Aaron	3298	97.2	94.6
Willie Mays	2992	95.7	87.5
Mickey Mantle	2401	92.4	92.3
Ted Williams	1706	75.0	85.2
Stan Musial	2571	71.5	77.4
Rickey Henderson	3081	71.3	67.9
Albert Pujols	2274	69.3	68.0
Willie McCovey	2588	66.6	56.2
Frank Robinson	2808	64.3	69.5
Frank Thomas	2322	62.5	74.3
Alex Rodriguez	2719	60.8	71.1
Manny Ramirez	2302	57.2	68.6
Eddie Mathews	2391	57.1	60.2
Joe Morgan	2649	57.1	59.1
Miguel Cabrera	1938	56.3	55.9
Gary Sheffield	2576	56.2	55.7
Mark McGwire	1874	54.4	56.6
Reggie Jackson	2820	53.4	57.4
Jeff Bagwell	2150	53.2	59.3
George Brett	2707	52.8	52.5
Harmon Killebrew	2435	52.7	48.8
Billy Williams	2488	52.4	46.9
Chipper Jones	2499	52.3	57.9
Al Kaline	2834	52.3	50.0
Jim Thome	2543	51.7	63.1
Jason Giambi	2260	51.1	57.2
Eddie Murray	3026	50.7	50.5

The 120.3 represents 120,300 player win points. Rw is the increase in wins based on runs above average, independent of game score or inning, which was 1232 runs. For example, a single with one out sending the runner to third will always be worth about six tenths of a run (or .06 wins), regardless of the game situation. But if it occurs in the last of the ninth with the score tied, it could be worth about 200 win points, or .20 wins. The difference between the two for 1156

players since 1946 with 2800 or more at-bats was random, supporting the theory that clutch hitting doesn't exist. I ran a simulation of 18 identical batters with their performance dictated by a random number generator through 750 games (about 3000 at-bats), for 200 times and came up with a difference between the wins above average calculated by player win average and by runs from average. The standard deviation (sigma) was 2.2 wins, meaning 95 percent of the time the difference would be between plus and minus two sigma or 4.4 wins. Since this number is proportional to the square root of the number of at-bats, a player with 12,000 at-bats would be within plus or minus 8.8 wins. Five percent of the sample (or 58 players) should be beyond the two-sigma limit. There were actually 47. There should have been three beyond the three sigma limit, and there were actually five.

Ted Williams and Stan Musial show figures only since 1946. Musial probably would have about 15 more wins, plus another five for missing 1945 in the military. Ted would have about 30 more wins from his actual play, plus another 35 for the almost five seasons missed in the air force, which would have moved him to the top. Joe DiMaggio had only 20 wins from 1946, but had 34 before and could have had another 13 during the war, which would have put him on the list below, which shows everyone with 50 or more. Willie Mays missed two years in military service, but it was at the start of his career, so it is difficult to give it a number, perhaps six to twelve wins.

Player win average is a batting statistic, so there is no accounting of fielding. The original Mills method charged an error to the fielder, not the pitcher, and gave the batter and pitcher an out on the play. This does not allow credit for fielding range. Infielders make more errors, but also have more difficult plays. I gave the batter credit for reaching on an error and charged the pitcher. A shortstop who hits like a typical first baseman can be worth a couple of wins a year more than an average first sacker. This is because his team will have a first baseman in the lineup, where the other team will need a shortstop. Shortstops and catchers average about minus ten runs batting per season compared to average non-pitchers, second basemen around minus five, third basemen and center fielders zero, corner outfielders five and designated hitters and first basemen ten. In addition, a fielder can get a swing of another win or two based on his fielding being better or worse than average.

Pitchers were done in the same manner. As shown in Table 2 Roger Clemens and Greg Maddux came out on top. I listed the leverage to show that most starting pitchers have a value of about 35. This means the average change in win probability is only 35 points or 3.5 percent. The difference between win calculated by ordinary run difference and actual win probability is small, as was the case with the batters. There was one notable exception, Mariano Rivera, who had a leverage figure about double that of the starters. He was the only reliever to have 36 or more career wins. This was because relievers can be used in more crucial game situations, so their effect is stronger. By runs alone, he had only 35 wins, but taking the game situation into account, he produced 54 wins. Bob Feller had 20 wins from 1946, but had 21 before and could have had another 19 in the four years his missed in the military which would put him at 60.

Table 2. PITCHERS

Name	IP	PW	RW	LEV
Roger Clemens	4916.2	79.6	81.8	36.5
Greg Maddux	5008.1	73.3	74.9	36.2
Tom Seaver	4783.0	69.2	64.9	36.7
Warren Spahn	5228.0	64.1	60.1	38.1
Randy Johnson	4135.1	59.1	63.3	36.5
Pedro Martinez	2827.1	59.1	60.1	35.8
Bob Gibson	3884.1	56.8	55.6	38.2
Mariano Rivera	1283.2	54.8	35.5	67.8
Tom Glavine	4413.1	49.0	53.4	36.7
John Smoltz	3473.0	48.9	49.8	39.3
Jim Palmer	3948.0	48.3	43.6	35.4
Steve Carlton	5217.2	46.7	48.2	37.2
Robin Roberts	4688.2	46.6	47.3	36.9
Gaylord Perry	5350.0	45.8	44.4	38.0
Juan Marichal	3507.0	43.8	37.4	35.3
Curt Schilling	3261.0	42.5	51.6	35.2
Don Sutton	5282.1	40.9	37.2	36.1
Sandy Koufax	2324.1	40.8	34.1	37.7
Fergie Jenkins	4500.2	40.6	41.3	35.9
Bert Blyleven	4970.0	39.3	45.8	36.3
Roy Halladay	2749.1	39.1	37.2	35.5
Whitey Ford	3170.1	38.3	44.7	36.9
Billy Pierce	3296.2	38.0	39.1	38.2
Mike Mussina	3562.2	37.3	40.7	34.3
Jim Bunning	3760.1	36.2	38.0	37.0

I charted relievers only, 3000 or more batters faced, discounting any season where they started at least 10 games, or started more than they relieved. The leverage values are typically 50 to 70 as shown in Table 3. Rivera is really in a class by himself. And this doesn't even include his playoff games. He pitched 141 innings and had an earned run average of 0.70 there and then added nine s innings with no earned runs in All-Star

Roger Clemens tops the list of players wins among pitchers with almost 80 (79.6). His next nearest contender is Greg Maddux at 73.3.

Table 3. RELIEVERS

Name	IP	PW	RW	LEV
Mariano Rivera	1216.2	55.6	36.0	69.8
Trevor Hoffman	1089.1	36.0	20.4	69.0
Rich Gossage	1585.1	33.1	19.3	59.9
Billy Wagner	903.0	30.5	23.2	65.3
Tug McGraw	1435.0	28.4	17.9	49.5
Hoyt Wilhelm	1881.1	27.6	25.7	49.0
Francisco Rodriguez	892.1	26.7	17.4	64.7
Lee Smith	1289.1	24.4	20.7	67.3
John Franco	1245.2	21.7	14.5	67.8
Bruce Sutter	1042.0	21.5	15.4	71.7
Stu Miller	1055.0	21.3	11.7	50.8
Randy Myers	752.2	21.2	12.0	70.9
Tom Henke	789.2	20.5	14.8	62.1
Dan Quisenberry	1043.1	20.0	12.3	55.5

Mariano Rivera is the only reliever to make the top 25 in player wins among all pitchers, and is far and away the number one reliever with 55.6 player wins. Trevor Hoffman comes in a distant second at 36.0.

Table 4. PITCHERS HITTING

Name	AB	PW	RW
Bob Lemon	1174	10.3	10.0
Don Newcombe	878	9.1	12.0
Earl Wilson	740	9.0	8.3
Early Wynn	1424	8.2	7.7
Mike Hampton	725	7.2	7.8
Tom Glavine	1323	7.0	8.4
Steve Carlton	1719	6.4	7.7
Bob Gibson	1328	6.0	9.5
Warren Spahn	1866	5.9	8.6
Vern Law	883	5.3	5.5
Johnny Sain	747	5.3	6.4
Carlos Zambrano	693	5.2	6.0
Fred Hutchinson	584	5.1	4.9
Bob Forsch	893	5.0	4.8
Gary Peters	807	4.6	6.4
Rick Rhoden	761	4.4	5.2
Don Robinson	631	4.4	5.6
Tommy Byrne	590	4.3	6.1
Jason Marquis	663	4.2	5.1
Jim Kaat	1251	4.0	5.5

Bob Lemon tops the player win rankings for pitchers hitting.

games for good measure. In his final all-star appearance in 2013, he went out to pitch the eighth inning. When he got to the mound, he found himself alone on the field, as all the other players stayed in the dugout. He received a well-deserved two minute standing ovation in honor of his remarkable career.

One of Bob Davids' favorite subjects was pitcher hitting. He wrote a book about it, *Great Hitting Pitchers*, originally published by SABR in 1979. I rated pitchers against the average of all pitchers, which meant adding about ten points per appearance to their total. ∎

Appendix (For the complete listing of Player Win Averages: Batters and Pitchers, see http://sabr.org/node/40520)

BATTERS Name	AB	PW	RW	BATTERS Name	AB	PW	RW	BATTERS Name	AB	PW	RW
Barry Bonds	2986	120.3	123.2	Pete Rose	3562	40.3	41.1	Ryan Howard	1460	27.4	24.5
Henry Aaron	3298	97.2	94.6	Fred McGriff	2460	39.5	43.8	Scott Rolen	2038	27.2	26.0
Willie Mays	2992	95.7	87.5	Paul Molitor	2683	39.4	41.6	Bob Watson	1832	27.2	28.0
Mickey Mantle	2401	92.4	92.3	Yogi Berra	2120	39.0	36.5	Bernie Williams	2076	27.0	28.5
Ted Williams	1706	75.0	85.2	Frank Howard	1895	38.5	33.7	Kirby Puckett	1783	26.8	26.0
Stan Musial	2571	71.5	77.4	Todd Helton	2247	37.1	40.9	Eric Davis	1626	26.7	24.0
Rickey Henderson	3081	71.3	67.9	Minnie Minoso	1835	36.4	34.2	Roberto Alomar	2379	26.6	29.2
Albert Pujols	2274	69.3	68.0	Wade Boggs	2440	36.3	44.5	Jackie Robinson	1382	26.3	25.8
Willie McCovey	2588	66.6	56.2	Boog Powell	2042	36.2	36.7	Jose Cruz	2353	26.2	25.5
Frank Robinson	2808	64.3	69.5	Brian Giles	1847	36.1	38.8	Ken Griffey	2097	25.9	21.3
Frank Thomas	2322	62.5	74.3	Joey Votto	1110	35.7	33.4	Craig Biggio	2850	25.5	27.2
Alex Rodriguez	2719	60.8	71.1	Mike Piazza	1912	35.4	41.3	Greg Luzinski	1821	25.5	25.2
Manny Ramirez	2302	57.2	68.6	Rusty Staub	2951	35.2	35.3	Roy White	1881	25.5	21.2
Eddie Mathews	2391	57.1	60.2	Tony Perez	2777	35.1	31.6	Brian Downing	2344	25.3	29.4
Joe Morgan	2649	57.1	59.1	Darrell Evans	2687	34.9	32.5	Johnny Bench	2158	25.1	28.0
Miguel Cabrera	1938	56.3	55.9	Reggie Smith	1987	34.9	32.1	Pedro Guerrero	1536	25.1	27.2
Gary Sheffield	2576	56.2	55.7	Harold Baines	2830	34.8	35.4	Ryan Braun	1219	24.6	27.4
Mark McGwire	1874	54.4	56.6	Jack Clark	1994	34.7	36.8	Ted Simmons	2456	24.3	26.2
Reggie Jackson	2820	53.4	57.4	Ralph Kiner	1472	34.5	34.5	Ron Fairly	2442	24.1	23.3
Jeff Bagwell	2150	53.2	59.3	John Olerud	2234	34.4	38.9	Don Mattingly	1785	24.0	24.1
George Brett	2707	52.8	52.5	Jimmy Wynn	1920	33.2	29.6	Toby Harrah	2155	23.7	19.8
Harmon Killebrew	2435	52.7	48.8	Norm Cash	2089	32.9	36.9	Ernie Banks	2528	23.6	26.9
Billy Williams	2488	52.4	46.9	Mark Grace	2245	32.8	26.9	Andre Dawson	2627	23.5	19.1
Chipper Jones	2499	52.3	57.9	Prince Fielder	1522	32.2	30.8	Joe Mauer	1456	23.5	28.8
Al Kaline	2834	52.3	50.0	Orlando Cepeda	2124	32.1	33.1	Ron Santo	2243	23.5	21.1
Jim Thome	2543	51.7	63.1	Derek Jeter	2747	32.1	37.7	Fred Lynn	1969	23.3	27.2
Jason Giambi	2260	51.1	57.2	Carlos Beltran	2306	32.0	34.3	Andrew McCutchen	1037	23.2	22.4
Eddie Murray	3026	50.7	50.5	Bobby Bonds	1849	32.0	32.4	Moises Alou	1942	23.1	30.3
Willie Stargell	2360	49.7	52.2	Joe Torre	2209	32.0	30.1	Rico Carty	1651	23.0	24.4
Tony Gwynn	2440	48.7	43.9	Adrian Gonzalez	1648	31.9	32.5	Tony Oliva	1676	23.0	25.7
Carl Yastrzemski	3308	48.7	50.5	Matt Holliday	1663	31.9	34.4	Gene Woodling	1788	23.0	25.1
Edgar Martinez	2055	47.8	53.4	Dwight Evans	2606	31.6	33.1	David Justice	1610	22.9	26.1
Mike Schmidt	2404	47.6	51.1	Keith Hernandez	2088	31.6	33.1	Sal Bando	2019	22.8	21.8
Lance Berkman	1879	46.3	48.2	Dave Parker	2466	31.2	32.1	Rocky Colavito	1841	22.7	25.2
David Ortiz	2257	45.8	46.9	Ken Singleton	2082	30.3	30.0	Barry Larkin	2180	22.7	21.9
Will Clark	1976	45.1	41.7	Jose Canseco	1887	29.9	31.7	Jim Rice	2089	22.5	23.3
Bobby Abreu	2425	44.6	49.4	Larry Doby	1533	29.9	32.4	Kirk Gibson	1635	22.4	22.9
Dick Allen	1749	44.2	40.8	Kent Hrbek	1747	29.9	27.2	Ted Kluszewski	1718	22.3	21.5
Ken Griffey	2671	44.2	48.9	Jim Edmonds	2011	29.7	31.2	Roger Maris	1463	22.2	22.4
Rafael Palmeiro	2831	43.2	49.5	Vic Wertz	1862	29.6	27.5	Aramis Ramirez	2194	22.2	17.1
Rod Carew	2469	43.1	48.0	Lou Whitaker	2390	29.1	28.9	Juan Gonzalez	1689	22.1	26.4
Duke Snider	2143	42.9	45.7	Darryl Strawberry	1583	28.7	32.0	Gene Tenace	1555	22.1	26.4
Dave Winfield	2973	42.4	43.4	Enos Slaughter	1714	28.3	27.4	Robin Yount	2856	22.1	28.8
Carlos Delgado	2035	42.3	44.5	Bobby Murcer	1908	28.2	22.8	Luis Gonzalez	2591	22.0	25.6
Roberto Clemente	2433	42.2	36.7	David Wright	1546	28.1	27.6	Amos Otis	1998	22.0	18.5
Tim Raines	2502	41.8	40.6	Albert Belle	1539	27.6	33.5	Steve Garvey	2332	21.8	21.9
Larry Walker	1988	41.6	40.0	Cesar Cedeno	2006	27.6	23.2	Wally Joyner	2033	21.6	25.1
Vladimir Guerrero	2147	41.3	38.7	Mark Teixeira	1746	27.5	36.1	Sammy Sosa	2354	21.6	30.6

Working Overtime

*Wilbur Wood, Johnny Sain and the White Sox
Two-Days' Rest Experiment of the 1970s*

Don Zminda

In Game Seven of the 2014 World Series, Madison Bumgarner of the San Francisco Giants entered the contest in the fifth inning with his team leading the Kansas City Royals, 3–2. Bumgarner, working on two days' rest after a complete-game shutout victory over the Royals in game five, proceeded to pitch five scoreless innings to secure the championship and electrify the baseball world.[1] "Now he belongs to history," wrote Tyler Kepner in the next morning's *New York Times*. Kepner went on to praise Bumgarner for "his excellence in shouldering a workload that brings to mind the durable and dominant aces of old."[2]

Wilbur Wood never performed any postseason heroics during a 17-year career that produced 164 major league victories. In fact, none of the three MLB teams he pitched for even reached the postseason during his career. But any discussion of "the durable and dominant aces of old" should rightly include the lefty knuckleballer. From 1971 through 1975, Wood won 106 games for the Chicago White Sox, working an average of $336\frac{1}{3}$ innings a year. Nearly 30 percent of Wood's starts during that five-year period—66 of 224—came while working on two days' rest or fewer since his previous start (what we'll call "short rest" for the duration of this article[3]). In the 102-season span from 1914 through 2015, only one major league pitcher topped Wood's 70 career starts on short rest: a durable and dominant ace named Grover Cleveland Alexander, who logged 72 short-rest starts between 1914 and 1928.[4]

How did Wilbur Wood, a pitcher who had worked primarily in relief prior to the 1971 season, become an iron-man starter with a workload out of the deadball era? And why did he pretty much stop pitching on short rest after 1975? The answers lie in the confluence of Wood's career with that of Johnny Sain, a successful pitcher who became an even more successful pitching coach. It was Sain, along with White Sox manager Chuck Tanner, who turned Wood into a starting pitcher in spring 1971. Johnny Sain believed that nothing was wrong with working a pitcher hard— one of his quotations about a pitcher's arm was, "It'll rust out before it wears out."[5] And in the soft-tossing knuckleballer Wood, he found the ideal candidate for pushing his pitching theories to the limit.

JOHNNY SAIN

Like Wilbur Wood, John Franklin Sain achieved success as a major-league pitcher without benefit of a blazing fastball. As Jan Finkel wrote of the right-hander, "Sain came to realize and accept that although he was large for his era at 6-feet-2 and 180–200 pounds, he didn't have high-octane velocity. Accordingly, he'd have to rely on mechanics, finesse and guile…."[6] Beginning in 1946, Sain won 20 or more games four times in five years for the Boston Braves. In his best season, 1948, he helped the Braves reach their first World Series in 34 years, while leading the National League in wins (24), games started (39), innings pitched ($314\frac{2}{3}$) and complete games (28). Notably, Sain's 1948 season included eight starts on two days' rest. Six of those eight starts came in a 25-day stretch from August 24 through September 17. Over that period, Sain threw eight straight complete games while going 6–2 with a 1.57 ERA as the Braves neared the pennant.[7]

Sain's major-league career ended in 1955, and four years later he returned to the majors as pitching coach of the Kansas City Athletics. He didn't earn much notoriety with an A's team that went 66–88, but after a year out of baseball, Sain returned to the game in 1961 as pitching coach of the New York Yankees. Jan Finkel wrote that with the powerful Yankees "Sain showed what he could do with good material."[8] Under Sain's tutelage, Whitey Ford—who had never won more than 19 games in any of his previous nine major league seasons—went 25–4 in 1961 and won the Cy Young Award for the World Series champion Yankees. In 1962 Ralph Terry had his only 20-win season as the Yankees repeated as champions. Then in 1963, both Ford and Jim Bouton won 20-plus games for the Yanks, who captured another American League pennant before being swept in the World Series by the Los Angeles Dodgers. Bouton would later refer to Sain as "the greatest pitching coach who ever lived."[9]

Sain left the Yankees after the 1963 season—amid

conflicting stories about whether he resigned or was fired—but returned to the majors in 1965 as pitching coach of the Minnesota Twins. Sain's 1965 Twins included a first-time 20-game winner (Jim "Mudcat" Grant), and again his team won the AL pennant. The Twins finished second in 1966, but Sain had another first-time 20-game winner in Jim Kaat, who won a career-high 25 games. Kaat, who led the American League in games started in both 1965 and 1966, started five games on short rest in each season. Like Jim Bouton, Kaat was full of praise for his pitching coach. "If I'd had Johnny Sain as my pitching coach for 10 years during my career," he said in a 2015 interview, "I'd have had some of the best years in the history of the game."[10]

Despite his success with the Twins, Sain was fired after the 1966 season, and moved on to Mayo Smith's Detroit Tigers.[11] In 1967 Sain had yet another first-time 20-game winner, Earl Wilson, for a team that finished one game behind the pennant-winning Boston Red Sox. In 1968 the Tigers won their first pennant and World Series championship since 1945; this time Johnny Sain's mound staff included the major leagues' first 30-game winner since 1934, Denny McLain (who went 3–0 in three starts on two days' rest in 1968). Despite that success, Sain's career as a pitching coach took a familiar turn when the Tigers fired him in August 1969.[12]

In 1970, Sain spent most of the season as a roving minor-league instructor in the California Angels' farm system. He became friends with Chuck Tanner, the manager of the Angels' Pacific Coast League farm team in Hawaii, and when Tanner was named manager of the

Johnny Sain was a "finesse and guile" pitcher in the major leagues who went on to serve as pitching coach for multiple big league teams.

NATIONAL BASEBALL HALL OF FAME LIBRARY, COOPERSTOWN, NY

White Sox that September, he brought Sain along as his pitching coach.[13] Sain and Tanner had their work cut out for them: the last-place Sox were on their way to a franchise-record 106 losses, ranking last in the majors with a 4.54 team ERA. The team obviously needed rebuilding, and one player who Tanner and Sain saw as part of the rebuilding effort was the staff leader in saves (with 21): Wilbur Wood. With the Sox starting rotation needing a major upgrade—in 1970, veteran Tommy John was the only Sox starter with 10-plus games started who posted an ERA under 4.75—they decided to shift Wood from reliever to starter.[14]

WILBUR WOOD

Wilbur Forrester Wood, a native of the Boston area (Cambridge), led Belmont High to the state championship in 1959, his junior year, as a "self-described fastball-curveball pitcher."[15] Wood threw four no-hitters and posted a 24–2 record in high school, drawing interest from a number of major league teams before signing with the Boston Red Sox for "a bonus variously reported from $25,000 to $50,000."[16] But after making his major league debut with Boston at age 19 in 1961, Wood went 0–5 for the Sox in several trials over the next four seasons before the team released him to Seattle of the Pacific Coast League in May of 1964. "The little sonofagun just couldn't throw hard enough," said Red Sox manager Johnny Pesky.[17]

THE WHITE SOX

After Wood posted a 15–8 record for the Seattle Rainiers in 1964, the Pittsburgh Pirates purchased his contract in September. Pittsburgh used Wood mostly in relief in 1965 before sending him back to the minor leagues. The White Sox acquired Wood in a trade with Pittsburgh for left-hander Juan Pizarro following the 1966 season, and in 1967 Wood made the Sox roster as a relief pitcher and occasional starter. In the Sox bullpen, Wood—only a part-time knuckleballer when he joined the team—began working with one of the all-time masters of the pitch, Sox reliever Hoyt Wilhelm. The future Hall of Famer told Wood, "You either throw the knuckleball all the time or not at all. It's not a part-time pitch."[18] Utilizing tips from Wilhelm, Wood blossomed into one of the most effective, and durable, relievers in baseball. From 1968 to 1970 Wood led the American League in games pitched each year, setting a single-season major league record (later broken) with 88 appearances in 1968. His 386⅔ relief innings over that three-year span were the most in baseball.

Entering the 1971 season, Wood had started 21 games in nine major league seasons, going 5–10 with a 3.99 ERA as a starter; he had appeared in 344 games as a reliever, posting a 32–36 record with a 2.67 ERA. Put into the number-four spot in the rotation after Joel Horlen suffered a knee injury, Wood commented that "I never got any work because of all the off days early in the season."[19] Wood didn't win his first game as a starter until May 2, but by the All-Star break he had a 9–5 record and ranked second in the American League with a 1.69 ERA. Along with advocating Wood's move from reliever to starter, according to Pat Jordan, Sain "made one other suggestion to Wood, and that was he pitch often with only two days' rest. Sain felt that as a knuckleballer, Wood put less strain on his arm than did other pitchers with more orthodox stuff, and therefore he could absorb the extra work with ease."[20]

Wood made his first start on two days' rest on June 30, 1971, in an 8–3 complete-game victory over the Milwaukee Brewers. From then until the end of the season, he started 14 times on two days' rest, going 8–4 with a 1.86 ERA in those games. The Sox won 10 of the 14 starts. "The more he pitches, the more it helps the club," Sain said about Wood in August of 1971. "He loves the work and it doesn't bother him."[21] Wood himself was so comfortable with his heavy workload that in a *Sporting News* story the same month, he told Jerome Holtzman that "he'd love to try" starting both games of a doubleheader. "If you have a nice and easy delivery [in the first game] and don't have to throw too many pitches," Wood said, "I don't think it would be too hard to pitch the second game, too."[22]

By season's end, Wood had started 42 games (he also worked twice in relief) and pitched 334 innings while going 22–13 with a 1.91 ERA. He finished second in the league in ERA behind Vida Blue (1.82) of the Oakland Athletics. In the Cy Young Award balloting, Wood finished third behind Blue and 25-game winner Mickey Lolich of the Detroit Tigers, a former Johnny Sain protégé who worked a staggering 376 innings in 1971. The short-rest experiment with Wood was considered a success, and the White Sox plan for 1972 was for more of the same. "Wood is proof that pitchers can work more often," Sain told David Condon of the *Chicago Tribune* in spring training in 1972. "I've known many who could do the job with only two days' rest.... But Wood has to be tops."[23]

With Wood leading the mound staff, the White Sox had improved by 23 wins from 1970 to 1971, finishing third in the American League West with a 79–83 record. Hoping to contend for a division title in 1972, the club made several trades over the 1971–72 off-season. The moves included trading the team's third-leading winner in 1971, Tommy John, to the Los

Angeles Dodgers in a deal that netted slugger Dick Allen, and replacing John in the rotation with right-hander Stan Bahnsen, acquired from the Yankees for infielder Rich McKinney. But perhaps the club's boldest move for 1972 was a commitment to using Wood on two days' rest throughout the season, while also giving Bahnsen, Tom Bradley, and number-four starter Dave Lemonds occasional short-rest starts.

Wood started 25 times on two days' rest during the 1972 season, the most short-rest starts for any major league pitcher since at least 1914 (This article utilized the Retrosheet and STATS LLC databases, which included day-by-day player and team data back to 1914).[24] Bahnsen and Bradley each started eight games on two days' rest, and Lemonds made three short-rest starts. Like Wood, who posted a 2.62 ERA in his 25 starts on two days' rest in 1972, neither Bahnsen nor Bradley had any issues with pitching on short rest.[25] "I actually feel stronger in the games with only two days' rest," Bradley told the *Chicago Tribune*. Bahnsen agreed. "I've felt strong," he told the *Tribune* about starting games on short rest. "I think they have shown that a lot of the theory of rest is a mental thing."[26] The results seemed to back what Bahnsen and Bradley were saying. As a group, White Sox starting pitchers posted a 3.04 ERA in their 44 starts on two days' rest in 1972, a figure actually a shade lower than the club's 3.12 ERA in their 110 starts with three or more days' rest. Overall, the team's 44 starts with two days' rest or fewer between starts was the most by a major league team since the 1918 Philadelphia Athletics. (See Table 1)

The demands on Wood's durable left arm in 1972 were often staggering. A frequent pattern for Wood that year was to alternate a start on three days' rest with one on two days' rest—in essence, starting two games a week. But at times Sain and Tanner asked him to do even more. During one 16-day period from June 20 to July 5, Wood started six straight times on two days' rest.

Table 1. Most Pitcher Starts with 2 or Fewer Days' Rest Since Last Start, 1914–2015

Year	Team	Starts	Team W–L	ERA
1918	Philadelphia Athletics	47	18–28	3.19
1972	Chicago White Sox	44	23–21	3.04
1973	Chicago White Sox	41	23–18	3.62
1916	Philadelphia Phillies	39	25–13	2.02
1918	Cincinnati Reds	39	23–16	2.78
1914	Washington Senators	38	22–15	2.37
1917	Cincinnati Reds	36	20–14	2.14
1922	Detroit Tigers	35	22–13	3.66
1916	Boston Braves	33	18–12	1.66

(Source: Sam Hovland, STATS LLC)

Thanks to the knuckleball and Sain's belief that it put less strain on his arm, Wilbur Wood found himself pitching quite a bit more often than usual for a starting pitcher with the Chicago White Sox.

(The Sox lost five of the six games, though Wood posted a 3.43 ERA during the period.) During another 14-day span from July 30 to August 12, Wood started five games, including four on two days' rest, and threw four complete games; the last start was an 11-inning, two-hit victory over the Oakland Athletics that put the Sox in first place in the AL West race by one percentage point over the A's. This time Wood and the Sox won four of the five games, with Wood posting a 1.00 ERA.

With the numerous short-rest starts made by Wood, Bahnsen, and Bradley playing a big role, Chicago's top three starters found themselves taking on a heavy workload. Between Wood (49 games started), Bahnsen (41), and Bradley (40), the trio started 84.4 percent of the club's 154 games in the strike-shortened 1972 season, the highest percentage of starts by a team's three most-frequently used starters since Joe McGinnity, Christy Mathewson, and Luther "Dummy" Taylor of the 1903 New York Giants started 85.2 percent of the Giants' 142 games.[27] As for Wood, his 49 games started in 1972 were the most for any MLB pitcher since Ed Walsh of the White Sox recorded the same number of starts in 1908, and his 376.2 innings the most since Pete Alexander worked 388 innings for the 1917 Phillies.

Tanner, Sain, and company weren't performing a lab experiment in 1972, of course; they were trying to win a division title. With Wood, Bahnsen, and Bradley leading the mound staff and first baseman Dick Allen on his way to the AL Most Valuable Player award, the team made a strong challenge to the defending Western Division champion Athletics. The Sox led the division as late as the morning of August 29, but the team went 16–17 the rest of the way, finishing in second place, five and a half games behind Oakland. Despite the disappointing finish, the season was widely seen as a triumph for the South Siders, only two years removed from their 106-loss 1970 campaign. Along with Allen's MVP Award, *The Sporting News* gave Tanner its 1972 Manager of the Year award and named White Sox Director of Player Personnel Roland Hemond Major League Executive of the Year. Wood, who finished the year 24–17 with a 2.51 ERA, ran just behind Gaylord Perry of the Indians in the AL Cy Young Award voting.

In truth, the White Sox were probably a little lucky to go 87–67 in 1972. The club won an MLB-high 38 one-run games in '72, and their .655 (38–20) win average in one-run contests was best in the American League. According to Bill James' "Pythagorean" formula, which projects a club's won-lost record based on its runs scored and allowed, the 1972 White Sox won six more games than expected. Additionally, despite (or perhaps, in part, because of) all the games started by the trio of Wood, Bahnsen, and Bradley, the White Sox ranked eighth in the 12-team American League in ERA (3.12). The starting rotation also showed signs of fatigue over the last six weeks of the season. From opening day through August 19, Sox starting pitchers had an overall record of 53–37 (.589) with a 2.92 ERA; over the remainder of the season, the starters went 10–18 (.357) with a 3.61 ERA.

Nonetheless, the White Sox continued to use Wood regularly on short rest in 1973, along with occasional starts on two days' rest for Bahnsen and newly-acquired Steve Stone, obtained (with outfielder Ken Henderson) from the San Francisco Giants for Tom Bradley. The new number-four starter, 36-year-old knuckleballer Eddie Fisher, was also a candidate for occasional short-rest starts. The Sox started the season strongly, and by the end of May led the American League West by three games at 27–15. Thirteen of those 27 wins belonged to Wood, who had started 15 of the team's 42 games, plus a five-inning relief stint. The relief appearance came on May 26, two days after Wood had worked eight and two-thirds innings in a victory over the California Angels. Two days later, on May 28, Wood threw a four-hit complete-game shutout at the Cleveland Indians. At that point Wood had a 13–3 record and a 1.71 ERA in 131⅓ innings—33 more innings than he had logged by the end of May in 1972. His early-season success was one of the biggest stories in baseball, engendering a cover story ("Wizard with a Knuckler") in the June 4 edition of *Sports Illustrated*.

But the rest of 1973 proved to be a struggle for Wood and the White Sox. Wood lost his first two starts in June, allowing 12 runs and 19 hits in 12⅔ innings. From June 1 to the end of the season, he posted an 11–17 mark with a 4.47 ERA in 33 starts. Over that same time span, the White Sox were 20 games under .500 (50–70) and ultimately finished fifth in the six-team AL West with a 77–85 record. Projected as a possible 30-game winner early in the year, Wood finished 24–20, becoming the first major league pitcher since Walter Johnson in 1916 to both win and lose 20-plus games in the same season. Stan Bahnsen (18–21) also slumped after a strong start; Bahnsen, 15–11 with a 2.76 ERA after a victory over the Texas Rangers on August 5, went 3–10 with a 5.86 ERA the rest of the way.

The nadir for Wood in 1973 most likely came on July 20, when the White Sox took on the Yankees in a twi-night doubleheader at Yankee Stadium. Wood failed to retire a batter in game one (one Yankee reached first after a dropped third strike) as the Yanks scored eight runs in the first inning (six charged to Wood) en route to a 12–2 victory. In game two, Wood finally got his wish to start both games of a twin bill. This time he lasted 4⅓ innings but gave up seven runs as the Sox lost again, 7–0. In doing so, Wood became the first pitcher since Jack Russell of the 1929 Red Sox to start, and lose, both games of a doubleheader.[28]

There were reasons for Chicago's slump beyond Wood's (and Bahnsen's) poor finishes, most notably a broken leg suffered by Dick Allen on June 28. (Allen had only five more at-bats the remainder of the season.) It was a team-wide collapse, as both the team's offense and pitching staff suffered sharp declines in production after the hot start. But the club's starting pitchers, who had posted a 2.89 team ERA through the end of May, recorded a 4.35 mark the rest of the way, and Tanner and Sain's frequent use of their starting pitchers on short rest began to come under increased scrutiny. For the 1973 season, Sox pitchers made 41 starts on two days' rest or fewer, 19 by Wood. (Bahnsen made eight starts on short rest, Steve Stone seven, and Eddie Fisher four, with two going to Bart Johnson and one to Jim Kaat.) While the team posted a winning record (23–18) in those games and the starters' ERA (3.62) in short-rest starts was again better than the club's 4.04 mark in its other 121 starts, the slumps by Wood and Bahnsen, in particular, caused some observers to blame fatigue.

"Wilbur is not tired,"[29] Tanner asserted after Wood defeated the Brewers 6–1 on August 27, for his first victory since July 29. Wood, however, made only one more start on short rest over the remainder of the year, that one on September 3, and did not pitch at all during the final week of the regular season. Asked prior to the start of the 1974 season if his eight starts on two days' rest in 1973 had contributed to his late-season slump, Stan Bahnsen replied, "I don't know. I think I

Ultimately it wasn't the wear on his arm but a kneecap fractured by a ball off the bat of the Tigers' Ron LeFlore that curtailed Wood's career.

could start on two days' rest maybe every fourth start and it wouldn't hurt me. But once last year I made three of those in a row. We were in a pennant race.... I figured: What have I got to lose? But maybe I lost more than I thought."[30]

As the White Sox prepared for the 1974 season, Johnny Sain was no longer talking about using Wood and other Sox starters on short rest. "Our goal from the beginning has been a four-man starting rotation," he told George Langford of the *Chicago Tribune*. "We wouldn't use the two days' rest thing if we had four solid starters. Actually, we've been B.S.'ing our way thru the last few years and we might have gotten away with it last year if it hadn't been for all the injuries."[31] Over the next two seasons, Chicago's use of its starting pitchers on short rest was greatly reduced. After making 44 starts on short rest in 1972 and 41 more in 1973, Sox starting pitchers made only six short-rest starts in 1974 and 13 in 1975. Only eight of those 19 starts were made by Wood.

Wood didn't exactly get a light workload in 1974 or 1975, as he led the American League in games started both years. But his won-lost records were around .500 or worse (20–19 in 1974, 16–20 in 1975), and his ERA had risen every year since his 1.91 mark in 1971 (2.51,

3.46, 3.60, 4.11). Wood, though, refused to blame his decline on the frequent short-rest starts in 1971–73. "The only way that could have had a bad effect was if my arm were sore or I felt physically tired," he told Robert Markus of the *Tribune* in June of 1975. "I never did."[32]

Following middling seasons in 1974 (80–80) and 1975 (75–86), with attendance falling to 750,802 in 1975, White Sox team president John Allyn put the cash-strapped club on the market.[33] The club was nearly sold to a Seattle-based syndicate before former Sox owner Bill Veeck stepped in with a new ownership group and purchased the club for a second time.[34] Veeck replaced Chuck Tanner as Sox manager with Paul Richards, and Johnny Sain moved on as well, becoming pitching coach of the Atlanta Braves. With rare exceptions, the short-rest experiment was over for good on the South Side.

Wilbur Wood pitched for three more seasons after Tanner and Sain left the White Sox. Richards and new Sox pitching coach Ken Silvestri used Wood very conservatively early in 1976; after Wood shut out the Kansas City Royals on opening day, all but one of his next six starts were made with four or more days' rest (the exception was a start on three days' rest at Boston on April 18). But on May 9 at Detroit, Wood, working on a shutout in the sixth inning, took a line drive off the bat of the Tigers' Ron LeFlore that fractured his left kneecap.[35] Wood, who had posted a 2.24 ERA in 1976 up to that point, missed the remainder of the season. He returned the next year but was neither durable nor effective in 1977–78, posting a 17–18 record with a 5.11 ERA in 52 appearances (45 starts) in the two years combined.

Wood made his final career start on short rest on July 6, 1977, three days after pitching a complete-game shutout of the Minnesota Twins, and he brought back his early short-rest magic one last time with a complete-game 4–2 seven-hitter against the Seattle Mariners. But the White Sox never again started him on fewer than three days' rest since his last start, and 26 of his 45 starts in 1977–78 were made with four or more days' rest since his last start. Wood became a free agent after the 1978 season, but was unable to land a job with another major league team and opted to retire. "I just couldn't do what I did before I got hurt. That took the fun out of it," he later told the *Boston Globe*. [36]

END OF AN ERA

Johnny Sain spent the 1977 season with the Atlanta Braves, a team whose top starter was Phil Niekro—a knuckleballer like Wilbur Wood. The Braves used Niekro on short rest only once in 1977, and Braves' starting pitchers made only two short-rest starts all season; Niekro, however, led the National League in games started, innings pitched and complete games, fashioning a 16–20 mark for a 101-loss team. Sain then became a coach in Atlanta's minor league system before returning to the Braves in 1985.[37] His last job as a major league pitching coach was with the 1986 Braves, when he was reunited with new Atlanta skipper Chuck Tanner. Neither the 1985 nor 1986 Braves had any pitcher starts on short rest, though Rick Mahler did lead the NL in starts both years.

Four-plus decades after his heyday as a major league pitching coach, Sain's philosophies about starting-pitcher workloads have essentially been abandoned. According to Sam Hovland of STATS, there were only 40 short-rest starts in all of major league baseball in the 16 seasons from 2000 through 2015; Sain's White Sox teams had more short-rest starts than that in both 1972 and 1973. Hovland's data also show that during the 1960s and seventies, between 25 and 30 percent of all MLB starts were made with three days' since the pitcher's last start; from 2010 through 2015, the starts on three days' rest fell to a minuscule 0.527 percent. Even the term "short rest" is now defined differently; in this millennium, a short-rest start is usually defined as any start with fewer than four days' rest.

The main rationale for lightening pitchers' workloads has been that it helps reduce the chance for injuries. That is hardly a new idea. "At the beginning of major league time, teams used their starting pitchers all game every game, without concern for long-term consequences," Bill James wrote in 2001. "Since then, managers have tried to reduce the workloads of their top pitchers, so that they might last longer. This process began in 1876, and continues to this moment."[38] In the free-agency era, with salaries increasing and clubs often signing pitchers to long-term, multi-million dollar contracts, teams have grown increasingly conservative about how much rest to give their pitchers between starts. Table 2 tracks the percentage of major league

Table 2. Percentage of MLB Starts by Days' Rest Since Last Start, 1960–2015

Days' Rest	1960–69	1970–79	1980–89	1990–99	2000–09	2010–15
0–2 Days	1.80	1.10	0.23	0.15	0.06	0.03
3 Days	29.40	26.40	9.40	2.50	0.70	0.27
4 Days	31.10	38.00	51.00	55.20	512.00	47.80
5+ Days	37.70	34.60	39.40	42.10	480.00	51.90

(Source: Sam Hovland, STATS LLC)

starts since 1960 by the number of days' rest since a pitcher's last start. The trend is obvious: with each successive decade, pitchers have been given more rest between starts on average.

In that context, the philosophies of Johnny Sain, who had no qualms about giving pitchers very heavy workloads, seem increasingly out of step. Even pitchers who worked under Sain have been critical of him. Steve Stone, who started seven games on two days' rest for Sain's 1973 White Sox, commented in 2015: "I thought at the time it could have been the dumbest idea I'd ever heard and since then it becomes even dumber, because you deteriorate pitchers. If a guy isn't a knuckleballer then you have a big problem. I didn't think it was revolutionary. It was very nice for Wilbur. He was very happy about it because the innings piled up and so did the wins—and the losses, by the way."

Tommy John, who pitched for Sain's White Sox in 1970 and 1971 and was a teammate of Tom Bradley, told SB Nation in 2011: "[Chuck Tanner] and Johnny Sain were big on pitching on two days' rest, three days' rest, and he had Tom Bradley—Bradley could pitch. God, that son-of-a-gun could throw the ball … they rode him right into the river, man. And Bradley, I thought, was never the same pitcher after that first year…."[39] Bradley's post-White Sox pitching record seems to support John's criticism. The White Sox traded Bradley to the San Francisco Giants for Ken Henderson and Steve Stone after the 1972 season, in which Bradley had started 40 games (including eight starts on two days' rest), posting a 15–14 record with a 2.98 ERA. Over the remainder of his career, Bradley started only 61 more games, going 23–26 with a 4.56 ERA. Bradley ultimately suffered a torn rotator cuff and threw his last major-league pitch at age 28.[40]

But while Sain undoubtedly pushed the envelope in working Wood and other pitchers with great frequency, he was hardly alone during that era. To cite one example, there were 22 instances of a pitcher working 325 or more innings during the 12-season period from 1968 through 1979. In all the other years of the expansion era (since 1961) before and since that 12-year period, only one other pitcher had a 325-inning season: Sandy Koufax in 1965.

The 1960s and 1970s—Johnny Sain's primary years as a major-league pitching coach—also featured:

- Mickey Lolich, who was anything but a knuckleballer, starting 45 games, throwing 29 complete games and pitching 376 innings in 1971.

- Seasons featuring 30 complete games from Juan Marichal (1968), Fergie Jenkins (1971), Steve Carlton (1972), and Catfish Hunter (1975).

- Nolan Ryan's 1974 season, in which he recorded 367 strikeouts, 202 walks, 26 complete games, and 332⅔ innings pitched.

- Mike Marshall's 106 games pitched and 208⅓ relief innings in 1974.

It was a different game, without a doubt. In that context, Johnny Sain wasn't that much of an outlier in preaching that a pitcher could stand a heavy workload.

Wilbur Wood was definitely an outlier, and Table 3 puts his short-rest workload into context. Did all that

Table 3. Most Career Starts with 2 or Fewer Days' Rest Since Last Start, 1914–2015

Pitcher	Years	Starts	W–L	Team W–L	ERA
Pete Alexander	1914–28	72	43–22	47–24	2.25
Wilbur Wood	1971–77	70	36–27	42–28	2.71
Eppa Rixey	1914–29	57	27–21	32–24	3.30
Bobo Newsom	1934–46	56	20–29	22–34	4.42
Burleigh Grimes	1916–32	54	29–22	30–23	2.93
Red Faber	1914–31	53	30–16	35–17	2.98
Lee Meadows	1915–27	52	17–26	24–28	3.39
Urban Shocker	1918–27	52	27–16	33–18	3.40
Hippo Vaughn	1914–21	51	34–12	36–14	1.93
Dick Rudolph	1914–23	48	28–12	30–15	2.04

(Source: Sam Hovland, STATS LLC. Tie Games not counted in Team W–L)

work eventually reduce his effectiveness, and perhaps shorten his career? That is certainly an arguable point, but Wood never complained and never questioned what Chuck Tanner and Johnny Sain were asking him to do. "You know, it's comical," he told Robert Markus when the losses were starting to pile up late in 1973. "Guys come here and ask the exact opposite of what they asked in May. Then they wanted to know if I could win 40. Now they ask me if I'm going to lose 20. And I say the same thing to them that I said then."

And what was that? "I hope I can win the next one."[41] ∎

Notes

1. To clarify our terms, "days' rest" in this article refers to the number of days off between appearances. A pitcher who pitches a game on Sunday and another on Wednesday is working on two days' rest; if his next appearance is on Friday, he would be pitching on four days' rest.
2. Tyler Kepner, "Madison Bumgarner Rises to the Moment, and Jaws Drop," *The New York Times*, October 30, 2014.

3. Another point of clarification: when the article refers to days' rest between starts, any intervening relief appearances are not considered. So if a pitcher starts a game on Sunday, makes a relief appearance on Wednesday and then starts again on Friday, the study considers him to be working on four days' rest between starts the same as a pitcher who made no intervening relief appearances.

4. Alexander's major-league career began in 1911, but this article utilized the Retrosheet and STATS LLC MLB database, which includes player and team day-by-day data since 1914. All data for this article on MLB pitchers working on two days' rest or fewer since their last start were provided by STATS LLC programmers Sam Hovland and Jacob Jaffe.

5. E-mail from Jim Kaat, May 4, 2015.

6. Jan Finkel, SABR BioProject biography of Johnny Sain.

7. Retrosheet.org data and daily logs.

8. Finkel.

9. Ibid.

10. Telephone interview with Jim Kaat, May 8. 2015.

11. Finkel.

12. Ibid.

13. Ibid.

14. Gregory H. Wolf, SABR BioProject biography of Wilbur Wood.

15. Ibid.

16. Ibid.

17. Ibid.

18. Rich Thompson, "Time Was Right for Wood," *Boston Herald*, May 28, 1989.

19. George Langford, "Still More Work for Wilbur," *Chicago Tribune*, August 31, 1971.

20. Pat Jordan, The Suitors of Spring (New York: Dodd, Mead & Company, 1973), 209.

21. Langford, "Still More Work for Wilbur."

22. Jerome Holtzman, "Iron-Man Wood Has Goal—Wants to Pitch a Twin Bill," *The Sporting News*, August 7, 1971.

23. David Condon, "In the Wake of the News," *Chicago Tribune*, March 12, 1972.

24. STATS LLC data, programming by Sam Hovland.

25. Ibid.

26. George Langford, "More Work? Really It Works!" *Chicago Tribune*, June 2, 1972.

27. E-mail from Jacob Jaffe of STATS LLC, May 7, 2015.

28. Historical data on pitchers' starting doubleheaders courtesy of STATS LLC.

29. George Langford, "Wood posts 21st, 6–1," *Chicago Tribune*, August 28, 1973.

30. George Langford, "Bahnsen is not unhappy over losing arbitration," *Chicago Tribune*, March 1, 1974.

31. George Langford, "Gopher balls bugged Fergie," *Chicago Tribune*, March 24, 1974.

32. Robert Markus, "Sox' Wood not worried about mound problems," *Chicago Tribune*, June 11, 1975.

33. Richard C. Lindberg, *Total White Sox* (Chicago: Triumph Books, 2006), 86.

34. John Snyder, *White Sox Journal* (New York: Clerisy Press, 2009), 438–39.

35. Wolf.

36. Elizabeth Karagianis, *Boston Globe*, April 27, 1985.

37. Finkel.

38. Bill James, *The New Bill James Historical Abstract* (New York: The Free Press, 2001), 866.

39. Jim Margalus, "Talking White Sox history with Tommy John," SB Nation South Side Sox, June 24, 2011 (http://www.southsidesox.com/2011/6/24/2241067/talking-white-sox-history-with-tommy-john)

40. John Gabcik, SABR BioProject biography of Tom Bradley.

41. Robert Markus, "Wilbur drinks his beer and thinks," *Chicago Tribune*, August 29, 1973.

The Planting of Le Grand Orange

The Strange Circumstances Surrounding Rusty Staub's Trade from the Astros to the Expos

Norm King

No one knew it at the time, but the January 22, 1969, trade that sent Rusty Staub from the Houston Astros to the Montreal Expos was arguably the most significant player transaction in baseball since Harry Frazee sold Babe Ruth to the New York Yankees in 1920. The actions of the players involved showed that baseball management was beginning to lose its hold on the absolute power it enjoyed over players for nearly a century. The trade brought a new franchise its first iconic player and gave a new, fill-in Commissioner a chance to flex his muscle and become a fixture as head of Major League Baseball. The trade also eventually led to a miracle.

The Astros sent Staub to Montreal in return for first baseman Donn Clendenon and outfielder Jesus Alou, but the mechanics of the deal go back to October 14, 1968, when Montreal drafted Clendenon and Alou in the expansion draft. Clendenon's 1968 numbers with Pittsburgh were solid: He had a .257 batting average with 17 home runs and 87 RBIs. But he was turning 33 and was on the downside of his career. The method to the Expos' madness in drafting Clendenon and Alou was to choose players who could serve as potential trade material. "We went for players, who number one had a name, who could still play, and who had trading value, or value period to someone else," explained former Expos general manager Jim Fanning.[1]

Houston expressed interest in Alou as early as the 1968 winter meetings, offering pitcher Mike Cuellar in exchange for the former Giants outfielder. Montreal turned that down. The Expos also initially nixed the Staub for Clendenon and Alou deal because Expos management thought they'd be giving up too much to get Staub. (Montreal also had a chance to swap Clendenon for pitchers Jim McAndrew and Nolan Ryan, but Mets manager Gil Hodges vetoed the trade). Some back-and-forth talks took place over the next several weeks until the transaction was concluded.

On the surface, it seemed like an odd deal from Houston's standpoint. The Astros (then known as the Colt .45s) signed Staub as a much-ballyhooed bonus baby out of Louisiana in 1961 at age 17, and brought him up to the big club after one year in the minors. He struggled his first two years before finding his stride and stroke in 1967 when he batted .333—fifth in the National League—with 10 home runs, 74 RBIs, and a league-leading 44 doubles. In 1968, Staub hit .291 (good enough for ninth place in the batting race), with six home runs and 72 RBIs—good numbers in "The Year of the Pitcher." Also, he would be only 25 years old on April 1, approaching the prime of his career. In return, the Astros were getting players that had been left off their original team's protected list.

The fact was that Houston wanted to get rid of Staub. He had held out for the first eight days of spring training in 1968 before signing for a reported $45,000. That didn't endear him to Astros general manager "Spec" Richardson; all general managers in that era deemed any player demanding a larger salary or thinking independently to have an attitude problem. Staub's decision to sit out the game against the Pirates on June 9, 1968—in commemoration of the assassination of Robert Kennedy—didn't win him any brownie points with Astros brass, either. President Lyndon Johnson had designated that date as a day of national mourning. The Astros chose to go on with the game as scheduled, but

Rusty Staub was signed at age 17 by the Houston Colt .45s.

Staub and teammate Bob Aspromonte chose not to play. The two players were each fined a day's pay, which in Staub's case amounted to $300.

"There was mutual disenchantment between Staub and the Astros management, which had been compared—with reason—to a Boy Scout operation," wrote Mark Mulvoy in *Sports Illustrated*. "At spring training the players are locked into barracks every night. Almost every night during the season there's a bed check. 'The entire operation is gripped by fear,' Staub says. 'Everything is an ultimatum.'"[2]

Staub was having contract issues with Houston again at the time of the trade, and was blunt in telling the media he was glad to leave the Astros. "I like this town, yes, but the organization—no," he said. "The contract they sent me was almost laughable. It was an insult to my intelligence. They did not ask me to take a minute cut, they asked me to take a nice cut."[3]

The Expos, for their part, were thrilled to get Staub. Expos manager Gene Mauch was delighted to have him. "I always knew Rusty had beaucoup power even before I knew what beaucoup meant," Mauch said.[4]

The Houston-area media were confounded by the deal. "With .300 hitters in short supply everywhere, a team with no one else remotely in that class certainly wouldn't deal one away," wrote columnist Emil Tagliabue in a piece aptly titled "Staub Mystery." "But Richardson would, and has, sending the smooth-stroking redhead to the new Montreal franchise in exchange for a couple of journeymen with credentials something less than eyebrow-raising."[5]

Journeymen would be an apt description for Alou and Clendenon. Alou was only 26, but he had had a mediocre year with the Giants in 1968, batting .263 with no home runs and only 39 RBIs. He would have trouble improving his productivity playing his home games in the pitcher-friendly Astrodome. (He did hit five home runs in 1969, but four of those were on the road; he also batted only .248 and drove home 34 runs).

The deal was also unusual in that Houston had already acquired Curt Blefary from Baltimore to play first base in a trade which sent Mike Cuellar to Baltimore. (Cuellar went on to share the 1969 Cy Young Award with Denny McLain.) Clendenon was also primarily a first baseman, and while he had power, his numbers were declining. After hitting for a .299 batting average with 28 home runs and 98 RBIs in 1966, his batting average fell to .249 with 13 home runs and 56 RBIs in 1967.

At first it seemed as if the trade would proceed routinely. Clendenon even attended a press conference at the Astrodome Club in Houston in February. While there, he and Richardson talked contract, at which point Richardson told him to expect a pay cut. Clendenon returned to Atlanta without signing.

Richardson didn't know what he was getting into dealing with Clendenon, who was an anomaly among ballplayers at the time; he was well educated, and had used the offseason to pursue other career interests. In 1961, for example, he worked as a management trainee with the Mellon Bank in Pittsburgh. In 1967, he became the assistant personnel director at the Scripto Pen Company.

Clendenon's position with Scripto gave him something few players had—leverage. After his discussion with Richardson, Clendenon returned to Atlanta and met with Scripto CEO Arthur Harris who offered to double his salary if he would work for the company full time. On February 28, Clendenon stunned the Astros by abruptly announcing his retirement in order to work at Scripto. He even sent a telegram to the Astros informing them of his decision and asking them to place him on the voluntarily retired list.

While the evidence seems to indicate that Clendenon's retirement announcement was a tactic to get a higher salary, some people thought his motives went deeper than that. In his autobiography, Jimmy Wynn—who was Staub's teammate in Houston and a friend of Clendenon's—wrote that Clendenon did not want to play for Astros manager Harry "The Hat" Walker.[6] Walker was from Birmingham, Alabama, and the brother of Fred "Dixie" Walker, who was infamous for requesting a trade from the Brooklyn Dodgers rather than play with Jackie Robinson. Harry's racial attitudes weren't any more enlightened, a fact that Clendenon knew from having Walker as his manager with the Pirates.

"Clendenon had played for Walker at Pittsburgh and he wanted no further part of him," wrote Wynn. "Donn even explained to several of us [Houston players] by phone that he would love to play with us in Houston, but not if it meant again enduring the racist stupidity of another spin with Harry Walker."[7]

Clendenon's tactic of using retirement as a bargaining chip was not unprecedented; it was about the only ammunition players had in the days of the reserve clause. In 1966, Los Angeles Dodgers pitchers Sandy Koufax and Don Drysdale staged a joint holdout during spring training in an effort to get new contracts of $1 million each over three years. At one point during the standoff, Koufax intimated that the two might retire, telling reporters that "he and Drysdale needed time to 'reflect on what we want to do with ourselves if we don't play this season or ever again.'"[8] The two eventually ended their holdout, with Koufax signing for $125,000 and Drysdale settling for $110,000 for the 1966 season.

Clendenon's announcement sent shockwaves through the Astros and Expos organizations. Houston wanted the deal voided, while Montreal wondered whether Pittsburgh owed them a player as compensation for losing Clendenon. There was also the question of whether Clendenon was serious in his intention to retire, and what impact that would have on the Expos' bargaining position. This was, indeed, a situation that called for the wisdom of Solomon. Instead, National League President Warren Giles and new Commissioner Bowie Kuhn entered the fray.

Kuhn hadn't even unpacked the boxes in his office when the matter was dropped in his lap. He became Commissioner on February 4, two months after the owners fired his predecessor, William D. Eckert. His first decision in the matter was to ask the teams to keep Staub and Alou out of uniform. What followed, from Houston's perspective at least, was a farcical succession of events worthy of the Keystone Kops.

Clendenon was suddenly a very popular individual with all kinds of suitors wanting to talk to him. Fanning and Expos President John McHale called him on March 2, a move that Richardson perceived to be tampering. Giles and Kuhn then called Clendenon to tell him—perhaps in an effort to pressure him to comply—that they didn't accept his retirement claim. Giles and Kuhn then held a meeting on March 6 with Expos and Astros senior management in West Palm Beach to hammer out a solution, or at least to allow Kuhn to make a decision. At the same time, McHale and Richardson visited Clendenon in Atlanta to determine if he was going to stay retired. According to Richardson, he walked away convinced that he was still retired. Kuhn and Giles, though, weren't accepting Clendenon's retirement, despite his insistence to the contrary.

It's not as if the Expos weren't above a little subterfuge themselves in the effort to keep Staub. One day when Kuhn was about to arrive at Expos spring training camp for a visit, McHale persuaded team owner Charles Bronfman and Staub to put on uniforms. When Kuhn arrived, Fanning got an Associated Press photographer he knew to shoot a photo of the assembled group.

"So this time he [the photographer] comes out and takes this picture of Bowie, John, Charles, Rusty, and me," said Fanning. "The photographer sent that all over the world. We publicized this picture and it was tantamount to Rusty being a Montreal Expo."[9]

Let's not forget that Alou was also in a predicament because he wasn't sure where he'd be playing. He

At age 19, Staub was signed to a $100,000 contract and played with the major league Colt .45s. After All-Star years for the then-renamed Houston Astros in 1967 and 1968 he was traded to the Expos in 1969 and became the team's first star. He became the first player to win the Expos Player of the Year award and was the team's career leader in OBP before the franchise moved to Washington (.402, minimum 2,000 plate appearances). His stay in Montreal was ultimately short-lived. After three years the New York Mets traded Mike Jorgensen, Tim Foli, and Ken Singleton to get Staub, ending his tenure in Montreal. He would ultimately play 23 years in the major leagues for five teams, including a second stint with the Mets from 1981 through 1985.

went to spring training with Houston and despite his anxieties over the uncertainty of his situation, he acted in a professional manner and worked to get into shape. His behaviour impressed his new teammates.

"[Alou] conducted himself like a big leaguer," said pitcher Don Wilson. "He never said anything but that he was going to get in shape to play baseball and he was going to play the best he could wherever he played."[10]

But trying to go about business as usual was difficult for the players involved. At one point at the end of March Staub said he'd be willing to leave baseball. "I gotta admit it's starting to wear on me now," Staub said. "Not only that, but it's also disturbing my mother and father."[11]

On March 8, Kuhn ruled that the deal would stand and that the Expos would have to give Houston another player to replace Clendenon. Kuhn used his authority as Commissioner to override Baseball Rule 12-F, which said that, "a trade is nullified when one player retires within 31 days after the start of a season without having reported to the assigned club."[12]

"From the moment the Staub trade was announced, and before it hit the skids by Clendenon's refusal to report, the Expos had embarked on an immediate marketing plan of selling Rusty Staub to the fans of Montreal as the new face of Expos Baseball," wrote Wynn. "It was a trade that hit the point of no return from the moment it was announced and Commissioner Kuhn agreed with that kind of thinking."[13]

Kuhn's decision sparked outrage in Houston. Astros president Judge Roy Hofheinz was furious and went so far as to file a petition in a Houston District Court hoping to get a declaratory judgment against the Expos and "at least" $10,000 in damages.

Hofheinz also had some pretty strong words about Kuhn. "This johnny-come-lately [Kuhn] has done more to destroy baseball in the last six weeks than all of its enemies have done in the last 100 years. There is no way we can have 11 clubs protected by the rules and the Houston club unprotected."[14]

Kuhn was in a tough spot. Being new in the position, he could either hold firm or give in to Hofheinz, which would signal to the other owners that they could run roughshod over him as well. Kuhn was an interim commissioner at that point and didn't get a contract for a full seven-year term until 1970. He stood his ground, though, sticking to his decision that Clendenon belonged to the Expos. Finally, on April 3, Clendenon unretired and signed with Montreal after agreeing to a $14,000 raise over his 1968 salary of $35,000. They then offered him to the Astros, but to Houston he was now damaged goods. Instead, Montreal sent Jack Billingham and Skip Guinn, plus $100,000 U.S. Hofheinz dropped his suit after Clendenon signed. (Kuhn also later asked for—and received—an apology from Hofheinz for his remarks.)

The trade was one of the best deals the Expos ever made. Staub had three All-Star seasons for Montreal,

and the player and the city had a mutual love affair that lasted until he was traded to the Mets prior to the 1972 season for Ken Singleton, Tim Foli, and Mike Jorgensen. Clendenon didn't stick around very long; Montreal traded him to the Mets on June 15, 1969, for Kevin Collins, Steve Renko, and three career minor leaguers. At the time of the trade, New York had a 30–26 record, 9 games behind the division-leading Chicago Cubs. They went 70–36 the rest of the way, swooping past the Cubs to win the very first National League East title. After sweeping Atlanta in three games in the NLCS, they upset the Baltimore Orioles in five games, to forever be known as the Miracle Mets. Clendenon hit three home runs in the Series and was named Series MVP.

The Astros? Well, they had their first .500 season in 1969, finishing 81-81, which wasn't much comfort considering that the Mets—who had joined the National League the same year as Houston—went all the way. The Staub and Cuellar deals that Richardson made after the 1968 season not only deprived the Astros of star players, they did not receive adequate compensation in return.

Clendenon's action caused a domino effect. In April 1969 the Boston Red Sox traded Ken "The Hawk" Harrelson to the Cleveland Indians. Harrelson opted to retire instead of reporting to the Indians, citing his Boston business interests. A new contract calling for a $75,000 salary, plus an additional $25,000 for doing promotional work, changed Harrelson's mind.

That June, Expos shortstop Maury Wills pulled the retirement trick in reverse, using the retirement gambit to force a trade. He chose to call it a career rather than continue playing in Montreal because he had a dry cleaning business on the West Coast. On June 11, Montreal traded Wills and Manny Mota to the Dodgers for Ron Fairly and Paul Popovich.

The actions of Clendenon, Staub, Harrelson, and Wills all took place as the Major League Baseball Players Association was beginning to assert itself under its executive director, Marvin Miller. The Staub-Clendenon controversy happened amidst the threat of a player strike during spring training; the walkout was averted when the owners agreed to changes to the players' pension plan. Players could now qualify for the pension after four years of service instead of five, and could begin collecting benefits at age 45 instead of 50.

Oddly enough, the retirement strategy that worked for Clendenon became an impediment for Curt Flood, a center fielder for the St. Louis Cardinals who chose to fight the reserve clause in court rather than report to the Phillies upon being traded to Philadelphia after the 1969 season. Flood received no support from his fellow players, who thought he was just trying to get a raise. When Flood testified at his hearing, no other current major league player attended the proceedings.

As much impact as the Staub-Clendenon trade had, perhaps the folksy wisdom of Luman Harris—manager of the Atlanta Braves in 1969 and a former Astros manager—summed up the Staub deal best. "Houston should lose Staub for even thinking about trading him," Harris said. "Maybe that's what Kuhn was thinking, too."[15] ∎

Notes

1. Video: "Les Expos, Nos Amours," Volume 1, Labatt Productions, 1969.
2. Mark Mulvoy, "In Montreal they love Le Grand Orange," *Sports Illustrated*, July 6, 1970
3. "Staub Says Astro Club Asked Him To Take Big Cut," *El Paso Herald-Post*, January 24, 1969.
4. Mulvoy.
5. Emil Tagliabue, "Staub Mystery," *Corpus Christie Caller Times*, January 26, 1969.
6. He was known as "The Hat" because he continually played around with his baseball cap when he was in the batter's box.
7. Jimmy Wynn with Bill McCurdy, *Toy Cannon: The Autobiography of Baseball's Jimmy Wynn* (Jefferson, North Carolina: McFarland & Company, 2010), 106.
8. Michael Beschloss, "How Sandy Koufax's Motel Helped Lead to Baseball's Big-Money Era," *The New York Times*, May 30, 2014.
9. Jonah Keri, *Up, Up, & Away: The Kid, The Hawk, Rock, Vladi, Pedro, Le Grand Orange, Youppi, The Crazy Business of Baseball, & the Ill-fated but Unforgettable Montreal Expos* (Toronto: Random House Canada, 2014).
10. John Wilson, "Jesus Alou Already Astro Gem," *The Sporting News*, April 19, 1969.
11. "Angry Staub Threatens To Quit If Deal's Voided," *The Sporting News*, March 29, 1969.
12. Wilson, "Hofheinz Blasts Kuhn, Sues Over Staub Deal," *The Sporting News*, April 5, 1969.
13. Wynn, McCurdy.
14. Wilson.
15. Mulvoy.

Additional Sources

The Atlantic
Gordon, Robert. *Then Bowa Said to Schmidt*. Chicago: Triumph Books, 2013
Florence Times-Tri-Cities Daily (Florence, Alabama)
Hardball Times
Indiana Gazette (Indiana, Pennsylvania)
Montreal Gazette
SABR biography of Donn Clendenon by Ed Hoyt
Vernon Daily Record (Vernon, Texas)

The Browns' Spring Training 1946

St. Louis's American Leaguers Hopes Rested on Revived Pitching, Junior, Dick Siebert, and Ducky

Roger A. Godin

The St. Louis Browns' American League (AL) Championship in 1944 was followed by a 1945 campaign best remembered for one-armed Pete Gray and a late season pennant rush which seemed unlikely as late as August. The surprise Cinderella pennant winners of the last full year of WW II stumbled badly the following spring, showing very little of the verve that had surprised the baseball world a year earlier.

Though they were in the first division from May 12 through June 14, early August found the Browns in seventh place when their fortunes changed. Starting with a home stand beginning on August 3, the Browns split a six game set with Cleveland, took three of four from Philadelphia, three of five from Washington, swept four from New York, four of seven from Boston, and five in a row from Chicago. During the home stand in which they played at a .697 clip, the previously erratic pitching staff of Al Hollingsworth, Sig Jakucki, Bob Muncrief, and Nelson Potter caught fire. Particularly noteworthy was Hollingsworth who won six decisions, including a shutout.[1]

Supporting the pitching surge was the superb fielding of second baseman Don Gutterridge and third baseman Mark Christman as well as the hot bats of shortstop Vern "Junior" Stephens, first baseman George McQuinn, and outfielder Chet Laabs. From a position of nine and a half games out of first place on August 3 they found themselves in third place by August 24 and by September 2 were only three and a half games behind frontrunner Detroit.

Though they would eventually falter, the Browns continued to play well enough to finish third, at 81–70, lending optimism to baseball's first post-war season in 1946.[2] The pitching staff that had propelled them to the AL flag in 1944 had come alive in late 1945 and was expected to carry that momentum into the following spring. It was hoped that Denny Galehouse, a stalwart who had spent 1945 in the Navy, could return to his 1944 form. The same could be said of Jack Kramer, while hopes were high for rookie hurlers Cliff Fannin and Ellis Kinder. At third base, much was expected of pre-war second baseman Johnny Berardino and rookie

Bob Dillinger, while newly acquired Dick Siebert would be at first and Stephens was the incumbent star shortstop. In the outfield Laabs, Al Zarilla, and Walt Judnich were projected to return to 1944 form.

The Browns announced their 1946 spring training schedule on December 2, 1945. It consisted of 33 games, 29 against major league opposition. Nineteen would be against the defending National League Champion Chicago Cubs. The remaining major league matchups would include six games against the Pittsburgh Pirates, two versus the White Sox, and the traditional two-game City Series with the Cardinals. Three contests were scheduled against the Hollywood Stars of the Pacific Coast League and one with the Los Angeles Angels. Of the 19 games with the Cubs, six would be played in the Los Angeles area. The two teams would then travel together and play the remaining 13 in Phoenix, Tucson, El Paso, San Antonio, Houston, Dallas, Tulsa, Oklahoma City, Wichita, and Kansas City, Missouri. Players were to report to manager Luke Sewell in Anaheim on February 20.

On February 10 the *St. Louis Post-Dispatch* reported that star shortstop Stephens had returned his contract unsigned.

> …and while he is not complaining about salary terms (he) is objecting to certain clauses in his contract. These are designed, no doubt, to have the club control his conduct during the season.

> …it can be said on positive authority that his chief trouble is a too friendly disposition. He makes many friends and sometimes they cause him to do things which the club thinks is not to the best interests of the Browns or himself. That, the Browns' office is apparently trying to control.

One suspects "too friendly" is a veiled reference to Stephens' well known active libido.[3] However, as events would play out, money was in fact the real issue to the perennially cash-strapped Browns. When the team took the field against the Pirates in Los Angeles in the

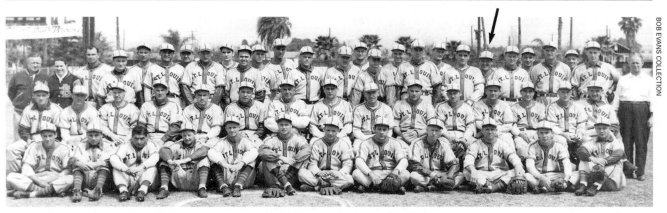

BOB EVANS COLLECTION

In the only known image of Joe Medwick as a member of the Browns, the former Cardinals great appears in the top row, seventh from the right of this spring training team photo.

exhibition opener on March 2, Mark Christman was in his place at shortstop. Junior was now in fact a hold-out. The Browns scored all their runs in the first three innings, including a three-run home run by Judnich, and went on to a 10–5 win. They would lose 7–6 the following day back in Anaheim, but the big news was the signing of former Cardinals star Joe "Ducky" Medwick. Medwick had won the National League triple crown in 1937 en route to being named league MVP, but by 1946 was attempting to extend his major league career. While the ten-time All-Star's best days were well behind him, General Manager Bill DeWitt felt he was worth a look.

> So the story seems to be that if Medwick can approach the hitting form that was his when he got as high as .378 [.374] in the NL, he will have a chance to win a job with the Browns …

> The Browns have outfield strength: they have heavy hitters. A Medwick in form, however, would help to give balance between right and left hand swinging in the outfield department.[4]

Meanwhile Stephens made known his unhappiness with the team and certainly made it clear that the salary he received in 1945, reported in the *St. Louis Post-Dispatch* on March 17 as $12,000, was not what he had in mind for the new season. He told the newspaper:

> They tell me I had a bad year in 1945. I led the league in fielding, led the league in hitting home runs and batted .290 [.289]. And who on the club drove in 89 runs? All that doesn't add up to a bad year for anybody with me.

> I don't know just what I'll do. I'll write DeWitt a letter and tell him I think the club is not being

fair…in a day or two I'll be over in Anaheim and if I see DeWitt, I'll tell him, too, how I feel.[5]

The series with Pittsburgh continued in Anaheim on March 6 with a 13–2 pasting of the Pirates as Bob Dillinger knocked in six runs on three hits, including an inside-the-park home run. Later in the day, Stephens met with DeWitt, but nothing came of it. Christman continued to fill in for him at shortstop and at least defensively seemed his equal as he made two outstanding plays in another rout over Pittsburgh at San Bernardino. After dividing the team into A and B squads and adding two additional games with PCL Seattle, the Browns proceeded to lose those two as well as the two previously scheduled games against Hollywood. The March 13 game against the Chicago White Sox in Pasadena's Rose Bowl was rained out.

Major league play resumed on March 14 when the first of the nineteen games against the Cubs was played in Los Angeles. Despite Walt Judnich's two home runs, the Browns bowed, 8–7, as Bob Muncrief gave up four runs. However, the good news was the arrival in camp of first baseman Dick Siebert, who had been acquired from the Philadelphia Athletics in the offseason in exchange for incumbent George McQuinn. Like Stephens, Minnesotan Siebert was also a holdout for that elusive $12,000 salary that Junior coveted. The next day St. Louis got a good four innings from Fred Sanford, who was viewed as a rotation hopeful, and with a four-run eighth evened the series with a 7–2 win. On the same date the team got strong pitching from Sam Zoldak and Nelson Potter as the B team beat their White Sox counterparts, 11–3.

The team then split a two-game series with the Pirates in Hollywood as Joe Medwick made his A team debut in the first game, an 8–7 loss, when he went 1-for-2 after relieving Glenn McQuillen in left field. In the 4–1 victory the next day, he played the entire game and collected two hits as Tex Shirley pitched four shutout innings.

Major league minded California fans cheered Joe Medwick, National League star, more on his appearance at bat in the first inning than any other member of the A. L. Browns. Joe flied out, but paid off for a second cheer in the third with a line single to left.[6]

On the holdout front, Vern Stephens attended the team's B game at Anaheim against the Pirate B's as his father Vern Sr. umpired on the bases. It's hard to imagine that happening today. There were other developments off the field. Ellis Kinder—who had gone 19–6 with Memphis of the Southern Association in 1944—had received his discharge from the Army and was told to report to Anaheim immediately. As to the other holdout:

First baseman Dick Siebert, in conference this afternoon with Vice President Bill DeWitt…said he was considering going into radio work in St. Paul and declined to sign the contract proffered by the club official. Dick, who arrived yesterday, said the radio station with which he was dickering had just had its channel cleared for broadcasting of ball games, and had he known before coming west of the situation in St. Paul, he would not have made the trip.[7]

Torrential rains then hit Southern California, washing out games against Pittsburgh and the White Sox, but having no effect on the Stephens and Siebert matters. Stephens had another fruitless session with DeWitt on March 19 after having now returned two contracts. As to Siebert, DeWitt offered: "I don't know…If he has decided to quit baseball, I am glad he made up his mind before the season opened, and before we made any moves to work him into our organization. The trade for McQuinn was even up. Connie Mack has McQuinn. If Siebert is through, any move about the trade is up to us. There has been no decision yet."[8]

Siebert recalled his session with DeWitt:

When I walked into the room, there he was, thumbs stuck in his vest and leaning back in his big leather chair. I talked to him for a while. He stayed at the same number. The thumbs in the vest. I finally told him what he could do with his job. What major league baseball could do. Luke Sewell…called me later. So did the Browns owner

(Dick Muckerman). They were willing to pay me the same salary I made with the A's, but I told them no matter what they offered now there was no way I was playing any more…[9]

Rain continued to play havoc with the exhibition schedule at both the A and B squad levels with further cancellations. Luke Sewell: "…We did not make much progress in the last week. It's been too cool. We lost three days in eight when we had games scheduled. We couldn't play the White Sox either of the two games we had scheduled…and it rained when we were to have our final game with Pittsburgh."[10]

After bemoaning the negative effects of California weather, cool with winds and rain, the manager was nonetheless optimistic about where the club stood after almost a month of spring training. He was even willing to make some early projections on who might play and where:

Judnich will be in center. Mancuso is still our No. 1 catcher…It could be that we'll open the season with Mark Christman at shortstop (because of the Stephens holdout). He's been playing a fine game there, looking good on double plays and…getting his hits.

Bob Dillinger likely will start at third. He looks like the player we all heard so much about.

…John Berardino has been…Playing nine innings every time out." Would he be the regular second baseman?

I can't say he has the job cinched. He certainly has improved. He's been playing steady ball.

It may be either Chuck Stevens or George Archie at first base.

Some of the added pitchers look good. Fred Sanford and John Pavlick both are showing plenty. On the left handed side Stan Ferens and Sam Zoldak look good and Clarence Iott has a lot of stuff.

The older fellows have been working slowly and they have not been helped by the weather conditions.[11]

The team finally got back to game action on March 22 with a ten-inning, 5–4 win over the Cubs in

Los Angeles. In the game Zarilla homered, doubled, and tripled (totaling three RBIs). Neither Sanford nor Zoldak lived up to their manager's projections the next day as they combined to give up 19 hits in a 12–9 loss to Chicago. However, on the same day back in Anaheim Joe Medwick kept his hopes alive for a spot with the Browns when he collected two hits in a 6–2 B-team loss to the Hollywood Stars. On March 24, Muncrief became the first St. Louis pitcher to go six innings when he scattered seven hits and the team parlayed a big second inning into a 5–2 victory. The pitching looked good again the next day when the scene shifted to Anaheim with Kramer and Shirley limiting the Cubs to six hits. Meanwhile the Browns pounded out 11 to produce a like number of runs in the shutout win.

On March 25 team President Dick Muckerman and DeWitt met with Vern Stephens, but Junior was still a holdout when the conversations ended. St. Louis would soon break camp, but there remained two exhibition games against PCL teams before the barnstorming with the Cubs would begin. Hollywood bowed, 5–2, before the solid pitching of Hollingsworth and Galehouse on March 26, as did Los Angeles a day later. Both Judnich and Zarilla had home runs in the 8–3 victory over the Angels.

March 28 found the squad in Arizona after dispatching six hopefuls to the minors, including Clarence Iott, whose stuff apparently had deteriorated since Sewell's earlier evaluation. That date also found Vern Stephens in San Antonio, site of the Browns' minor league camp for the home town Missions and Toledo Mud Hens. Between flights to Mexico to meet with Mexican League President Jorge Pasquel, now in the hunt for his services, the holdout shortstop volunteered that he had been offered $13,000, but $17,500 was what he had in mind as a workable number. March 30 found Stephens in Nuevo Laredo, Mexico, where he announced that he would play the coming season for Veracruz's Azules, members of Jorge's loop.[12]

The Mexican League mogul had more than $17,500 in mind. Pasquel's goal in this post-war period was to elevate the status of his league, established in 1925, by attracting big league stars. While previously relative fringe players such as Danny Gardella and Luis Olmo had been lured to Mexico, Stephens was quite another matter. Here was a star player who had led his league in home runs in 1945 and had been a key member of the 1944 pennant winners. What was he willing to pay? Ten times what the Browns were unwilling to provide.

Junior demanded $175,000 over five years. Under the contract's terms the shortstop could break it at any time, but Pasquel could not. The money would be earmarked for salary on a sliding scale from year to year. If the player broke the agreement before a given date in a specific year, he would have to return the balance. These stipulations had been agreed to telephonically before Stephens arrived in Mexico. Once there, the contract had been written accordingly in the simplest terms.

"How do you want your money?" Pasquel had asked his prospective franchise player.

"Make out a check for $5,000 to my wife and send it to her," Stephens replied. "Bank the other $170, 000 in my name."[13]

A few minutes later, talking on the phone to his wife Bernice, Junior told her to deposit the check, but not to spend any of it until she heard from him. Bernice suspected this might be a clue that her husband's stay south of the border might be brief, but for the moment there were games to be played for Veracruz. In his debut on March 31, his clutch ninth-inning hit helped his team defeat Nuevo Laredo. The game had been played in Mexico City and there would not be another until April 4 in Monterrey. The intervening three days of local exploration was enough to convince Stephens that this was not where he wanted to play. He was not fond of the local diet but, more importantly, was unable to locate suitable housing for Bernice and their young son, also named Vern.

"By the time we were ready to leave for Monterrey for our next game, I was thoroughly ready to get out of there. By then, I think I would have signed with the Browns for what they offered me, although I did have my mind pretty well made up that I wanted that extra $4,500. Time was getting shorter…and I didn't want to get myself suspended by [Commissioner] Chandler," he recalled.[14]

Back in Long Beach, Vern Sr., a former amateur player and umpire, had developed serious reservations, as had Bernice, about his son's decision to play in Mexico. After a family discussion, the elder Stephens headed for San Antonio, arriving on April 4, the same day the Browns were scheduled to play the Cubs there. In the lobby of the Plaza Hotel, the senior Stephens ran into Jack Fournier, the Brown' chief scout.

"We've got to do something about getting Junior out of Mexico, in four days, he won't be able to play anywhere else," said Vern Sr. (Chandler had decreed that players returning within ten days of defection would not be suspended from Organized Baseball.)

"It's all settled, " Fournier told him. "The Browns don't want him to stay there anymore than you do. I'm getting ready to drive to Mexico with a contract for $17,500 for him. Come on along."[15]

Stephens had not played well in the April 4 contest and had spent his postgame time anguishing over how to part ways with Pasquel. Breakfasting by himself the next morning, he spotted his father in the hotel dining room and followed him out. About a block away, he caught up to his father who told him, "Fournier's here with his car. We drove all night. You want to come back with us?"

"Do I want to go back with you? I was just trying to figure out a way of getting back to the States." responded Junior.

Two blocks further down the street, Fournier was waiting in his car. "Everything's OK, Junior. The Browns are going to give you what you want."[16]

Back in San Antonio, the three linked up with the team before they left for Houston. Sewell welcomed him back and by April 6 he was back in the lineup against the Cubs as a pinch hitter. The next day in Dallas, playing out of position in right field, he hit a three-run homer. "Naturally, we're tickled to have him back," was Sewell's initial reaction and the manager would make no further reference to Christman taking his place at shortstop.[17]

Stephens had his wife return the $5,000 check to Pasquel and called him from Houston. The owner was understandably upset with the turn of events and offered to up the ante to $250,000, but to no avail. While other "name" players subsequently went to Mexico, notably catcher Mickey Owen and pitcher Sal Maglie (both of whom would return), Pasquel had failed to hold on to the big prize.

While this was playing out, it was reported on March 30 that the Browns were seeking to receive the return of George McQuinn or the equivalent—presumably cash or another player—from the Philadelphia Athletics, in lieu of Dick Siebert's retirement. A formal request for a ruling was being made to Commissioner Chandler. If McQuinn didn't return, it appeared that Chuck Stevens would be his most likely successor over challenger George Archie.[18]

On the diamond, the Browns dropped two of three to the Cubs in Phoenix despite getting solid pitching performances from John Miller in a 5–4 loss on March 29 and Tex Shirley in a 6–4 defeat the next day. The month closed with a 12–9 win which featured a 16-hit attack, including four home runs from Berardino, Laabs (2), and Zarilla.

St. Louis started April in a whirlwind fashion, winning four of their first five games. The fun began with

Vern Stephens was recruited to play in Mexico instead of for the Browns in 1946, but quickly returned to the team after seeing the conditions south of the border.

a 5–4 April Fools Day win in Tucson. Losing 7–4 the next day in El Paso, they got shutout pitching in 1–0 victories on April 3 in Del Rio (from Nelson Potter and Fred Sanford) and April 5 in San Antonio (from Sam Zoldak and Dennis Galehouse). Sandwiched between was a 10–7 triumph in the Alamo city which marked the end of the Joe Medwick experiment. While he went 1-for-2 in left field after relieving Laabs, the team parted ways with the veteran the following day. Playing primarily B team games, the former superstar produced only singles where extra base hits had been the norm. "He had no chance to beat out any of the more youthful...outfielders. His career probably came to an end here today," reported the *St. Louis Post-Dispatch*.[19]

April 6 found the tour in Houston. In Stephens's pinch-hit return he went down on strikes as the Browns bowed 7–1, as they would the next day in Dallas. Despite Junior's fifth-inning blast temporarily tying the game—which drew 7,288, the best of the tour—they fell 10–7. While the home run was no doubt a welcome reminder of Stephens's prowess at the plate, an earlier incident in the game would prove foreboding for the season ahead. Facing only the second batter of the game, starter Bob Muncrief took a smash off the bat of Al Glossop to his right foot and suffered a broken metatarsal.

"Examination immediately after the accident brought the prediction that Bob would not pitch again for a month or a month and a half. Loss of his services is a hard blow to Luke Sewell with the opening of the American League season only a week and a day away. Winner 13 times and loser only four last season, he was high man for the club. He probably would have been the opening day starter for the club..."[20]

Stephens returned to shortstop on April 8 in Tulsa and won the game for the Browns when his sixth-inning single scored Zarilla for the game's only run, while Nelson Potter scattered four hits over seven innings. The next day in Oklahoma City the teams played 13 innings before Joe Grace's solo homer won it for St. Louis, 3–2. April 10 in Wichita proved to be the last game in the series as cold weather and wet grounds forced the cancellation of the Kansas City contest scheduled for the next day. The Browns settled things early in the Wichita game by taking a 4–0 lead in an eventual 7–1 win. Once again, one of the 1944 pitching aces, Denny Galehouse, looked good, giving up just three hits in five innings. Al LaMacchia finished off the game.

The Browns went 12–7 in the spring training series against the NL champs and perhaps that created a false sense of optimism. Four of the victories had been shutouts. Were the glory days of 1944 once again in the offing?

New batting power and good reserves combine to give the Browns a bright outlook for the 1946 American League championship race...Manager Luke Sewell believes.

...Sewell talks of greater power and a higher run-producing potentiality in his club...

...Brownie players are full of confidence. Since the return of Stephens...they believe they have a real chance to land in the first division, and well up. They are confident their pitching will hold up, despite the loss for the first part of the season of Bob Muncrief, ace righthander...

...The hitting power that the club now boasts will have a good representation in Grace, Zarilla, and Judnich, in the outfield. Grace made five hits, including a triple and home run, in the last two games with the Cubs. Judnich...was smashing the ball to the fences all spring, and Zarilla has shown more power than ever before.[21]

Grace would reinforce this positive projection when his eighth-inning home run on top of Sportsmans' Park's right field pavilion proved the margin of victory in a 3–2 triumph on Saturday April 13 in the first City Series game against the Cardinals. Potter started and gave up a run and two hits in three innings while Tex Shirley got the victory with four hitless innings. While the Cardinals would take the Sunday game, 4–3, Galehouse had a strong three innings as the starter. The two games would draw 40,541—as opposed to the estimated 15,000 for the six played a year earlier—reflecting the thirst for postwar major league baseball in St. Louis.

The Browns would finish first in spring training games against major league "A" teams with a 17–10 record; small consolation in a season that would prove agonizingly disappointing.[22] The return of the wartime absentees on the other teams combined with reality proving greater than optimism resulted in a seventh-place finish, though the team drew 526,435, fourth highest in franchise history. The high water mark would be on May 1 when the club stood in fourth place at 8–8.[23] The pitching would prove to be the biggest disappointment as only Jack Kramer finished above .500 at 13–11 and once Muncrief returned from his injury he could do no better than 3–12. No other pitcher won more than nine games.

Among the position players, while Stephens raised his average to .307, his home run output dropped to 14 and his RBIs fell to 64. Most of the position players performed capably, but Zarilla, whose .299 average had been second on the 1944 pennant winners, saw it drop to .259 with only four home runs. Rookie Bob Dillinger was a disappointment at third base, while Chuck Stevens—George McQuinn's successor at first base—actually posted a better batting average than his predecessor did at Philadelphia. The question that remains forever unanswered is how would Dick Siebert have performed? Commissioner Chandler ruled on April 19 that, presumably because they wouldn't meet Siebert's salary demands, the Browns were not entitled to any compensation from the Athletics.[24] Grace was dealt to Washington during the season, but his Senators replacement, Jeff Heath, finished the season with a combined 16 home runs and 84 RBIs, 57 tallied with the Browns. Sewell was replaced by Zack Taylor on August 31.

There would be glimpses of hope for the team between 1947 and 1953, but one can make the case that things might never have looked as bright as they did on Opening Day, April 16, 1946. ∎

References

Books

Carmichael, John; *Who's Who in the Major Leagues*, 15th Edition 1947 (Chicago: B. E. Callahan)

Kashatus, William C.; *One Armed Wonder: Pete Gray, Wartime Baseball, and the American Dream* (Jefferson, NC: McFarland, 1995)

Rippel, Joel; *Dick Siebert: A Life in Baseball* (St. Cloud, MN: North Star Press, 2012)

Newspaper/Magazine Articles

L.A. McMaster, "Joe Agrees to Terms; Pirates Win Game," *St. Louis Post-Dispatch*, March 4, 1946.

L.A. McMaster, "'My Record Doesn't Call For a Cut,' says Vern,'" *St. Louis Post-Dispatch*, March 6, 1946.

L.A. McMaster, "Browns Find New Hurling Prospect in John Pavlick," *St. Louis Post-Dispatch*, March 18, 1946.

L.A. McMaster, "Dewitt and Siebert in Salary Talk," *St. Louis Post-Dispatch*, March 16, 1946.

L.A. McMaster, "Siebert Quits Camp: Plans to Broadcast," *St. Louis Post-Dispatch*, March 20, 1946.

L.A. McMaster, "Sewell Says Team is Ready," *St. Louis Post-Dispatch*, March 22, 1946.

"Stephens Quits Browns: Joins Mexican Nine," *Chicago Tribune*, March 30, 1946 (No author cited).

L.A. McMaster, "Return of McQuinn or Equivalent Sought by Browns From Athletics," *St. Louis Post-Dispatch*, March 30, 1946.

"Browns Release Joe Medwick," *St. Louis Post-Dispatch*, April 8, 1946 (No author cited).

L.A. McMaster, "Batting Power, Better Reserves for the Browns," *St. Louis Post-Dispatch*, April 13, 1946.

"Browns 'A' Champs," *The Sporting News*, April 18, 1946 (No author cited).

"Athletics Keep McQuinn," *The New York Times*, April 20, 1946 (No author cited).

Notes

1. William C. Kashatus, *One Armed Wonder: Pete Gray, Wartime Baseball, and the American Dream* (Jefferson, NC: McFarland, 1995) 116.
2. Kashatus; op.cit. 116.
3. Author's conversation with Don Gutteridge, May 26, 1994.
4. *St. Louis Post-Dispatch*, March 5, 1946.
5. *St. Louis Post-Dispatch*, March 7, 1946.
6. *St. Louis Post-Dispatch*, March 19, 1946.
7. *St. Louis Post-Dispatch*, March 17, 1946.
8. *St. Louis Post-Dispatch*, March 21, 1946.
9. Rippel, Joel; *Dick Siebert: A Life in Baseball* (St. Cloud, MN: North Star Press, 2012) 110.
10. *St. Louis Post-Dispatch*, March 23, 1946.
11. Ibid.
12. *Chicago Tribune*, March 30, 1946.
13. Al Hirshberg "Vern Stephens-Junior Red Socker" *Sport Magazine*, August 1949.
41. Ibid.
15. Ibid.
16. Ibid.
17. Ibid.
18. *St. Louis Post-Dispatch*, March 31, 1946.
19. *St. Louis Post-Dispatch*, April 9, 1946.
20. Ibid.
21. *St. Louis Post-Dispatch*, April 14, 1946.
22. *The Sporting News*, April 18, 1946.
23. *The New York Times*, May 1, 1946.
24. *The New York Times*, April 20, 1946.

No "Solid Front of Silence"

The Forgotten Black Sox Scandal Interviews

Jacob Pomrenke

When legendary sportswriter Furman Bisher died in 2012, his obituary in the *Atlanta Journal-Constitution* repeated a claim that had been casually tossed around for many years—including by Bisher himself:

> One of the biggest "scoops" of his career occurred in 1949, when "Shoeless" Joe Jackson gave Bisher and *Sport Magazine* **his only interview** since 1919, the year Jackson was ousted from baseball in the "Black Sox" scandal.[1]

The interview between Bisher and Jackson, conducted at the latter's home in Greenville, South Carolina, appeared in *Sport*'s October 1949 edition with the headline "This is the Truth!" Jackson's first-person account of the 1919 World Series fix and his subsequent banishment from baseball is, in the words of author Gene Carney, "one of the documents that nobody curious about Jackson can pass up."[2] Thankfully, BlackBetsy.com now makes a copy of the article available online.[3] But even the Internet's most comprehensive Joe Jackson website has erroneously claimed that it is "the only interview Joe Jackson ever gave concerning the infamous World Series."[4]

That couldn't be further from the truth. In the three decades between Jackson's final major-league game in 1920 and his death in 1951, nearly a dozen interviews with Shoeless Joe appeared in such widely read publications as *The Sporting News*, *Washington Post*, and syndicated wire-service articles that ran in newspapers all over the country. Closer to home, Jackson maintained a friendly rapport with veteran South Carolina sports writers Jim Anderson and Carter "Scoop" Latimer, who kept readers updated on Jackson in numerous columns for the *Greenville News* during the 1930s and 1940s.[5]

Jackson wasn't the only Black Sox player to talk to the press in the years following the scandal. In the fall of 1956, Chick Gandil sat down with Los Angeles-based sportswriter Melvin Durslag for a tell-all exposé about the 1919 World Series fix that appeared in *Sports Illustrated*.[6] Gandil's rambling, self-serving interview made national headlines and shined a new spotlight on the old scandal. After the *SI* article was published, the *Chicago Tribune* called Eddie Cicotte and Happy Felsch for their reactions. Hearing of Gandil's assertions, Felsch said, "They're all wrong." Cicotte added, "I took my medicine and I've forgotten about it."[7]

Cicotte and Felsch had more to say about the scandal—and so did many other players involved in the 1919 World Series.

"A SOLID FRONT OF SILENCE"

It's easy to believe the Black Sox had no interest in "talking about the past," as another embattled ballplayer (Mark McGwire) famously told Congress during an investigation into baseball's recent performance-enhancing drug scandal. Ever since the Black Sox were banned in 1921, finger-wagging sportswriters have perpetuated the idea that the Chicago players disappeared from the public eye and lived out the rest of their lives with their heads hung in shame.[8]

When *Eight Men Out* author Eliot Asinof went looking for the surviving Black Sox in the early 1960s, he encountered resistance from almost every ballplayer he found. Happy Felsch was a notable exception, and the old ballplayer finally loosened his lips after Asinof showed up at his door with a bottle of Scotch.[9] Felsch became one of Asinof's primary sources for the book—the author was so appreciative that he dedicated another book, *Bleeding Between the Lines*, to the former star outfielder. But Asinof's attempts to interview Chick Gandil, Swede Risberg, and Eddie Cicotte didn't go so well. Even the "Clean Sox" like Red Faber, Ray Schalk, and Dickey Kerr didn't have much to say to Asinof.

Asinof attributed their reluctance to talk to the stigma that everyone involved—even the innocent players—supposedly felt about the 1919 World Series. As he wrote in *Eight Men Out*:

> Though [the Black Sox] had almost no contact with each other over the decades that followed,

they maintained a solid front of silence to the world. It was as if a pact existed between them and the forces that had brought them to it. It was a silence of shame and sorrow and futility. It was also a silence of fear, for the threats hanging over them made talking a doubly difficult adventure. But mostly, it was a story rooted in the bitterness and frustration of their lives. There seemed to be no way to talk of it that made sense to them, no way that would give some measure of understanding and, perhaps, vindication to their actions.[10]

Asinof's own experiences talking to the ballplayers seemed to back up that claim: The scandal was a subject best left alone. Hall of Fame pitcher Red Faber expressed a similar sentiment when Asinof met with him in Chicago in the early 1960s:

> "It's tough to talk about it. I see some of the boys—like Schalk, for instance—and though he was as straight as an arrow, he won't even mention the Series. They were scared, I guess. Scared of the gamblers.[11]

If a prepared and skilled interviewer like Asinof could not get these players to talk, after doing more homework on the scandal than anyone before him, what chance did any other writer have? Based on his own dealings with the players, Asinof may have gotten the impression that the "solid front of silence" was more widespread than it was. Decades later, Asinof repeated the idea that had become ingrained as part of the mythology of the scandal: "There's a lingering impact on all of baseball. You don't talk about this thing," he told *Sports Collectors Digest* in 1988. "Even sympathetic ballplayers who did not involve themselves in the fix refused to talk."[12]

As Asinof was writing *Eight Men Out*, he was well aware of Joe Jackson's *Sport* interview and Chick Gandil's *Sports Illustrated* account. He also knew that Westbrook Pegler, the Pulitzer Prize-winning political columnist, followed up on the *SI* article in 1956 by visiting Cicotte in Detroit, and Felsch in Milwaukee, and talking on the phone with Risberg.[13,14,15] In Pegler's five-part series on the Black Sox Scandal, which was distributed to hundreds of newspapers by the King Features Syndicate, Cicotte and Felsch expressed some regret for their roles while Risberg remained publicly defiant, as he would for the rest of his life.

These were by far the most prominent Black Sox interviews discovered by Asinof in the course of his

Sports Illustrated *readers saw this image of Black Sox ringleader Chick Gandil in the September 17, 1956, issue, which included Gandil's explosive interview with Melvin Durslag in which he admitted his involvement in the 1919 World Series conspiracy but denied taking any money from gamblers.*

research.[16] But in an era long before text-searchable online archives, many other interviews were lost to obscurity, including those buried in small local newspapers near-impossible to discover prior to digitization. Other writers had been successful in getting not only the White Sox, but also the victorious Cincinnati Reds to talk about the tainted 1919 World Series.

More than 20 White Sox and Reds players spoke on the record about the scandal afterward, in at least 85 separate interviews. The players weren't all forthcoming and their memories weren't always accurate. Their words were sometimes embellished by reporters and, invariably, the players contradicted themselves or each other. There are no "smoking guns," no special insights that help to clear up any of the longstanding mysteries surrounding the scandal. More often, there are claims of innocence or ignorance that don't ring true given what is known now about the 1919 World Series. But like many common myths about the scandal, the idea that the Big Fix was too shameful or too dangerous for anyone to talk about doesn't seem to hold up to scrutiny.

BLACK SOX INTERVIEWS

The Black Sox players were not that difficult to find in their years of exile. While it was sometimes reported they had "dropped out of sight" or "quietly vanished," some writers did their due diligence to look them up.[17,18]

After he was banned by baseball commissioner Kenesaw Mountain Landis in 1921, Joe Jackson settled first in Savannah, Georgia, then moved back home to South Carolina. He played some semipro ball and was a successful businessman in both states, operating a liquor store, a barbeque restaurant, and a dry-cleaners, where he was occasionally visited by curious reporters. In 1927, Harry Grayson of the Newspaper Enterprise Association (NEA) wire service spoke with

Jackson about his punishment: "I don't like being called an outlawed player because I fail to see where I am one," Jackson said. "I was never convicted of any charge in any court."[19] It was a refrain he repeated to anyone who asked.

He also told Grayson he didn't "care a whoop" about having his name cleared, but a few years later, a reinstatement effort was led on his behalf by Greenville mayor John Mauldin in 1933. By then, Jackson's stance had softened. "About all I want now is a minor-league connection," he told the Associated Press. "That'll make me happy."[20]

Judge Landis, predictably, ignored the appeal and Jackson soon stopped asking. But he never failed to take a shot at the baseball commissioner whenever the subject came up. "Sure, I'd love to be in the game," he told the NEA's Richard McCann in 1937. "But I'd rather be out than to be in and bossed by a czar."[21] In 1941, Shirley Povich of the *Washington Post* spent an afternoon with Jackson when the Washington Nationals played a spring training exhibition game in Greenville. Jackson said he was "not bitter toward baseball … [but] I don't care for Judge Landis."[22]

Other than proclaiming his innocence, Jackson rarely offered details in interviews about the 1919 World Series, preferring to let his .375 batting average and Series-high 12 hits stand as his primary defense. One notable exception was in 1932 when he opened up to the NEA's William Braucher about a key detail that he had never revealed publicly: "[I] asked to be suspended before the World Series," Jackson said. "I didn't want to play hard after I heard what was going on. But I had to play and I did play."[23]

Near the end of his life, Jackson repeated this story in 1949 to Furman Bisher and in 1951 to John Carmichael, both writing for *Sport* magazine.[24] But his claim went virtually unnoticed at the time, despite the serious implication that Jackson had tried to inform White Sox officials of the fix before the Series began and they had ignored him. In his groundbreaking book, *Burying the Black Sox*, author Gene Carney devoted most of a chapter to Jackson's request, suggesting that this incident, if verified, would have been the start of a cover-up engineered by White Sox owner Charles Comiskey to sweep the scandal under the rug.[25]

But did it ever happen? The reliability of Jackson's claim is still heavily disputed. He had two chances to tell this story under oath—during his grand jury testimony in 1920 and his civil-trial deposition in 1923—but never said a word about asking to be taken out of the lineup. He also didn't mention it in a long feature profile that appeared in *The Sporting News* in

1942, written by his old friend Scoop Latimer of Greenville.[26] The Furman Bisher interview from 1949 contains a number of details that are inaccurate, such as Jackson misremembering how many outfield assists he had during the World Series, or other anecdotes that cannot be corroborated. In the end, only these vague quotations from Jackson's interviews remain—a tantalizing piece to the puzzle that may never be connected for sure.

Buck Weaver was even more vocal about the 1919 World Series than Jackson. He continued to play semi-pro and outlaw baseball for more than a decade after his banishment in 1921, and then made his home in Chicago, where he regularly could be found at old-timers' banquets with baseball friends like former teammates Red Faber and Ray Schalk. Weaver was outspoken about the injustice of his lifetime ban and often lobbied to have his name cleared.

In January 1922—five months after he was banned—Weaver made his first public plea for reinstatement, telling reporters that he had recently met with Judge Landis to make his case in person. He acknowledged that he was aware of the fix rumors during the World Series: "The only doubt in my mind

LANDIS WRECKS WEAVER'S HOPE OF PLAYING BALL

BARRED FOR LIFE

Denies Buck's Plea for Reinstatement.

Buck Weaver's hope that some day he would return to White Sox ball park and again reign as idol of the south side is shattered. Last night the former star third baseman unfolded a letter from Baseball Commissioner K. M. Landis that ended with these words: "I regret that it was not possible for me to arrive at any other conclusion than that set forth in the decision of Dec. 11, 1922, that your own admissions and actions in the circumstances forbid your reinstatement . . ."

Weaver, appearing as lithe and dynamic as when he raked in line drives on the "hot corner" with the Sox

BUCK WEAVER.

Buck Weaver's fans were disappointed to read the news in the Chicago Tribune *on March 13, 1927, that Judge Kenesaw Mountain Landis had denied the ex–White Sox star's latest effort to clear his name. Later that day, Weaver signed with a local semipro team and resumed playing ball on the South Side to great fanfare that summer.*

was whether I should keep quiet about it or tell Mr. Comiskey. I was not certain just what men, if any, had accepted propositions, or whether they accepted. I couldn't bring myself to tell on them, even had I known for certain. I decided to keep quiet and play my best."[27] After the season, Landis denied Weaver's request on the grounds that he had never adequately explained why he had attended the pre-Series fix meetings with the other players. Landis ominously declared, "Birds of a feather flock together."[28]

Weaver continued to appeal to the judge over the years and used every opportunity to plead for reinstatement. After Landis's death in 1944, Weaver stepped up his efforts, thinking a new commissioner might be more sympathetic to his cause. He appeared on WGN Radio and was interviewed by broadcaster Jack Brickhouse in 1947.[29] He also wrote a letter to commissioner Ford Frick in 1953. In the fall of 1954, Weaver was visited by author James T. Farrell at the Morrison Hotel in Chicago. Buck was still unclear about what he had done to deserve such a harsh punishment: "A murderer even serves his sentence and is let out. I got life. ... Landis wanted me to tell him something that I didn't know. I can't accuse you and it comes back on you and I am... a goof. That makes no sense. I had no evidence."[30]

Weaver's death in 1956, followed shortly thereafter by Chick Gandil's sensational exposé in *Sports Illustrated*, launched another round of attention on the Black Sox Scandal. The syndicated political columnist Westbrook Pegler, who had covered the 1919 World Series early in his career, spoke to Eddie Cicotte, Happy Felsch, and Swede Risberg that summer to ask them more about the tainted Series. Cicotte and Felsch looked back with regrets. "We done wrong and we deserved to get punished," the 72-year-old Cicotte said from Detroit. "But not a life sentence. That was too rough. I could have earned a living coaching later but they wouldn't let me."[31] Felsch, then 65, said he had to give up his tavern in Milwaukee because he "had so much trouble with argumentative drinkers about the 1919 Series."[32] Risberg, at age 61, continued to insist he had done nothing wrong to earn his punishment; instead, he steered the conversation with Pegler more toward his observations on the modern game and about his son Gerald, who was then playing ball at Chico State College in California.[33]

No interviews have turned up yet for the remaining two Black Sox players, pitcher Lefty Williams and infielder Fred McMullin, who both lived quiet lives in California for decades after the scandal. After Gandil's *Sports Illustrated* article appeared in 1956, Williams's wife Lyria wrote a letter to her good friend Katie Jackson, Shoeless Joe's widow, in which she expressed displeasure at the old scandal being brought up: "You sure have trouble with the newspaper men in the South. ... I am glad they do not know where we are. We would send them chasing if they came here."[34] McMullin may not have talked to any reporters, but according to family lore, he once wrote up his version of the scandal in a file that was to be revealed after all the Black Sox players had died—and his wife Delia destroyed the letter.[35] McMullin might have played a much larger role in the scandal than is commonly believed, but without his own words, that may never be known for sure.[36]

The last surviving Black Sox, Swede Risberg, remained defiant over the years and he occasionally took to the press to proclaim his innocence. In 1931, while playing semipro ball in South Dakota, he complained to a reporter for the Sioux Falls *Argus-Leader* about how much money he had lost because of the lifetime ban, which he estimated to be about $150,000 or $200,000. "That's a terrible penalty for a man who believes himself the victim of circumstantial evidence. ... [Risberg] still swears he was innocent of any conniving with gamblers or that he was promised or received any of the money which was accepted by other members of the team."[37]

A few years later, as the Great Depression wiped out his savings and times were tough for an outlaw ballplayer, Risberg moved back home to San Francisco and made a public plea to be reinstated. "If I had held up a bank, I would have paid the penalty by this time and would be out of jail and able to earn a living," he said in 1934.[38] There is no record that Judge Landis ever responded to the Swede, who went on to rebound from his struggles and open a successful nightclub near the California-Oregon border by the time Pegler visited him two decades later.

Risberg spent his final years living with his son Robert in Red Bluff, California. In 1970 he was asked to preview the upcoming World Series as a guest columnist for the local newspaper. Swede's columns were short and amiable, and no mention was made of his sordid past. But anyone who knew his history might have raised an eyebrow at the irony of his prediction: he picked the Cincinnati Reds to win.[39]

Chick Gandil opened up one more time after the *SI* article, in a two-part interview with Dwight Chapin of the *Los Angeles Times* in 1969, for the 50th anniversary of the tainted World Series. He was 82 years old and in poor health, but instantly regained his old fire at the mention of baseball's first commissioner. "We were exonerated," he said. "But that damned Judge Landis took more power than the courts and we were blacklisted for all time. ... I just get tired of being made the goat in all this. I have taken an awful beating in this thing."[40] As he had done in 1956, Gandil again insisted that the World Series was never thrown, citing his own crucial RBI singles in Games Three and Six, and that he hadn't received any money from gamblers. As Chapin wrapped up the interview, Gandil looked squarely at him and said, "I'm going to my grave with a clear conscience, you understand?"[41]

Eddie Cicotte offered a more penitent tone in his final interview, when Joe Falls of the *Detroit Free Press* came to visit his 5½-acre strawberry farm in 1965. "I admit I did wrong," Cicotte said, "but I've paid for it the last 45 years. ... I don't know of anyone who ever went through life without making a mistake. I've tried to make up for it by living as clean a life as I could."[42] He offered no excuses for his involvement in the Black Sox Scandal and seemed genuinely at peace with his life. When Falls shook hands with the old pitcher and waved goodbye, he sized up Eddie's plaid shirt, blue denim pants, and tan shoes. "But what I noticed for the first time were his socks," Falls wrote. "They were white."[43]

CLEAN SOX INTERVIEWS

When Hall of Fame catcher Ray Schalk learned of Eddie Cicotte's death in 1969, he felt a pang of affection for his old, disgraced batterymate. "He made my work easy behind the plate," Schalk told the *Chicago Tribune*. He also said the pitcher had "a great sense of humor and was a great storyteller."[44] But a few months later, when the Associated Press contacted him for a story on the fiftieth anniversary of the tainted series, Schalk clammed up. "You can ask me anything in the world except [that]," he said. "I have my personal feelings about it all. It's one of the saddest things that ever happened."[45]

Over the years, Schalk wavered back and forth on his willingness to talk publicly about the 1919 World Series. At times, he was candid and offered unique insight about the Series that only a participant could provide. On other occasions, he claimed to know nothing about the fix and "had no reason to suspect anything."[46] Eliot Asinof's attempt to interview him at Purdue University, where Schalk was an assistant baseball coach, ended before it even started. Schalk threw the writer out of his office.[47] Asinof later wrote of Schalk's silence, "He could not bear the shame of the fix, for this was his team, these were the men he lived with, this was the game he played and loved."[48]

But Schalk had been more open in the past. In fact, he had been the very first of the "Clean Sox" to open his mouth about the World Series fix rumors back in 1919—and it got him in big trouble. Two months after the Series ended, Schalk spoke to an investigative reporter, Frank O. Klein, for a small Chicago-based gambling trade publication called *Collyer's Eye*. He said seven of his teammates wouldn't return to the White Sox roster in 1920 ... and he even named them: Cicotte, Felsch, Gandil, Jackson, McMullin, Risberg, and Williams.[49] (Everyone but Buck Weaver, whose name wasn't being tossed around in the fix rumors then.) When *The Sporting News* picked up the story, Schalk was chastised by White Sox owner Charles Comiskey and he immediately retracted his comments.[50]

Schalk must have learned his lesson from this incident, because it took him more than twenty years before he spoke openly about the scandal again. In a 1940 profile for *The Sporting News* by veteran Chicago writer Ed Burns, Schalk said he had turned down "considerable sums" to tell the "inside story" of the 1919 Series and still had "confused emotions" about it all.[51] He also denied reports that the Black Sox were disgruntled: "Whatever happened was not traceable to any general discontent."

Eddie Collins was also quick to go on the record soon after the scandal was exposed. In an interview with *Collyer's Eye* on October 30, 1920, he said "there wasn't a single doubt in my mind" as early as the first inning of Game One that the games were being thrown. He added, "If the gamblers didn't have Weaver and Cicotte in their pocket, then I don't know a thing about baseball."[52]

Collins's accusation against Weaver was not the last time he pointed a finger in Buck's direction. In 1943, the Hall of Fame infielder told Joe Williams of the *New York World-Telegram* that he "should have recognized the tip-off in the very first game" when Weaver missed a hit-and-run sign and Collins "was out by a yard at second." Collins asked Buck if he "was asleep," and Weaver snapped, "Quit trying to alibi and play ball."[53]

Weaver's reply could be damning evidence that he was more involved with the fix than is commonly believed, but it also could be just a reflection of his cool relationship with Collins, who wasn't well liked in the White Sox's dissension-riddled clubhouse. But Collins's tone changed over the years and he began to back off from his comments that he had known much about the scandal. "I was to be a witness to the greatest tragedy in baseball's history—and I didn't know it at the time," he told *The Sporting News* in 1950. "I didn't for an instant believe at that time they would engage in anything as dastardly as a conspiracy to throw a ball game or a Series and let the rest of their teammates down."[54]

Join Swede Risberg For 1970 World Series

(Editor's note: Charles August "Swede" Risberg, who will celebrate his 76th birthday on Tuesday, has agreed to analyze the 1970 World Series between the Baltimore Orioles and the Cincinnati Reds for the Daily News. The father of Bob Risberg of Red Bluff, Swede has lived with his son and daughter-in-law and two grandchildren for eight years. He played major league baseball between 1917 and 1920 and participated in two World Series.)

"It looks like the National League will win," says Swede Risberg, who sees the Cincinnati Reds taking it in five or six games.

'They're a good-hitting ball club all right. They have seven right-handed hitters in the lineup and two of the three Baltimore pitchers are left-handers," added Risberg.

Although he's been out of baseball for nearly 50 years, Risberg has always maintained his interest.

Born in the North Beach section of San Francisco and a survivor of the big earthquake and fire in 1906, he avidly watches both Bay area clubs on television and occasionally sees one in person.

"Want to know what's wrong with those Giants? Too many —— stars, too many prima donnas, that's what."

"And the way baseball clubs handle pitching nowadays, wearing a path between the mound and the bullpen."

"I believe in the saying 'You haven't got anything in the bullpen as good as what you start with, so why call in relievers so often?"

"It's a different ball game these days. We used to win by playing percentage ball," added Risberg.

Swede first began pro ball in 1911 in Visalia.

"Didn't play ball in school. Why, they threw me out of the third grade because I wouldn't shave."

In 1912, he moved to Spokane, advancing to Ogden, Utah the following year and then to the Vernon Club in Los Angeles in the Coast League.

In 1917 he was called up to Chicago, where he played all infield positions, mostly at shortstop.

"Knew Babe Ruth well," said Risberg, "He was one of the best left-handers I ever saw. I thought he was making a mistake when they made an outfielder out of him, but it looks like I was wrong."

Swede calls Ty Cobb the best ball player he ever saw, however.

"He could hit, run, throw and think. He also thought he could fight, although he couldn't. His only drawback was his temper. . . he expected everyone to play as good as him."

"That's why good ballplayers don't make good managers," he added.

"I was 6-foot-1 when I played," said Risberg, and then added that age and stooping over to wait for that fast grounder just might "have shrunk me a little."

But when you consider that baseball has doubled its age in the time since Swede Risberg hung up his spikes, what does a little shrinking mean, anyway?

FORMER MAJOR LEAGUER SWEDE RISBERG AND FRIEND AWAIT SERIES

Swede Risberg, banned from baseball for his role in the Black Sox Scandal, later settled in Red Bluff, California, where in 1970 the local newspaper asked the 75-year-old ex-ballplayer to write a daily column with his observations of the World Series between the Baltimore Orioles and Cincinnati Reds. He picked the Reds to win.

Dickey Kerr, a rookie pitcher in 1919 who won two games in the World Series, also spoke publicly about his suspicions. In a 1937 interview with David Bloom of the *Memphis Commercial-Appeal*, Kerr said, "We knew it all the time. A newspaperman tipped me off. But what could we do?"[55] Reserve catcher Joe Jenkins told the *Fresno Bee* in 1962 that the fix rumors were openly discussed inside the clubhouse. He said he noticed Chick Gandil "betting heavily" on the World Series games, but "I didn't think much of it as we used to get good odds and bet all the time."[56]

Outfielder Eddie Murphy expressed similar sentiments in a 1959 interview with Chic Feldman of *The Scrantonian* in Pennsylvania. He said manager Kid Gleason held a team meeting early in the Series, declaring, "I hear $100,000 is to change hands if we lose." But his threats to expose the fix weren't enough to get his team back on track. Murphy also talked about rumors that the Black Sox had thrown games in 1920, too: "We knew something was wrong for a long time, but we felt we had to keep silent because we were fighting for a pennant. We went along and gritted our teeth and played ball. It was tough."[57]

By and large, the "clean Sox" were no longer angry at their teammates for selling out. But they remained disappointed at what might have been: a White Sox baseball dynasty that could have challenged Babe Ruth and the New York Yankees for American League supremacy for years to come.

Hall of Fame pitcher Red Faber said, "Loss of those men ruined our club. If we had kept them, we would have gone on winning pennants, or fighting for them, for years."[58] Added Eddie Collins, "They were the best. There never was a ballclub like that one, in more ways than one."[59]

CINCINNATI REDS INTERVIEWS

To a man, the Reds players had one thing to say whenever they were asked about the tainted World Series: They all insisted they didn't need any help to beat the powerhouse White Sox. "Sure, the 1919 White Sox were good. But the 1919 Cincinnati Reds were better," Hall of Fame outfielder Edd Roush told Lawrence Ritter, author of *The Glory of Their Times*. "I'll believe that till my dying day. … We could have beat them no matter what the circumstances!"[60]

Roush liked to point out that the Reds had a deeper pitching staff and a more well-rounded lineup, which matched up well against the White Sox in a best-of-nine series.[61] "I still don't see why the White Sox were supposed to be such favorites to beat us," Reds third baseman Heinie Groh told Ritter. "I didn't see anything that looked suspicious. I think we'd have beaten them either way; that's what I thought then and I still think so today."[62]

There is reason to believe the Reds were indeed the better team, and there is also some evidence that the conspiring Chicago players called off the fix early in the Series after failing to receive payment from the gamblers. At any rate, the Reds players said they didn't seem to notice anything suspicious—at least on the field. Outfielder Greasy Neale, who went on to become a Hall of Fame football coach in the NFL, told writer Grantland Rice in 1945, "The fellows rumored as the crooks starred all thru the series. … I'll admit, they had to be the greatest artists in baseball history to throw any game outside the first one, for those labeled as crooks looked and acted like great ballplayers. … How could we figure they were crooked?"[63]

Years later, pitchers Dutch Ruether and Slim Sallee said they had a hard time believing the fix was in. "No one ever dreamed there would be anything shady in a World's Series," Sallee told *The Sporting News*.[64] Said Ruether: "In that first game, I got two triples, a single, and a base on balls—a record that's never been beaten. And then I found out they were only foolin'."[65]

By the end of the Series, the Reds could no longer claim to be surprised about rumors of a fix—because one of their own teammates was being offered a bribe to lose, at least according to Edd Roush. Before the decisive Game Eight, Roush said, manager Pat Moran confronted pitcher Hod Eller in the clubhouse. Eller confirmed that he had been approached by gamblers and offered $5,000, but he said he had run them off. Moran cautiously allowed Eller to pitch and the right-hander responded with a stellar performance as the Reds won the game and clinched the Series. Roush first told this story to a New York reporter in 1937 and then repeated it in print many times until his death more than a half-century later.[66] His former teammate, Ray Fisher, corroborated the story in an interview with the *Columbus* (Ohio) *Dispatch* years later.[67] Like many of the interviews mentioned above, Roush's story raises as many questions as it answers, adding a new layer of complexity to our ever-evolving collective knowledge of the Black Sox Scandal.

For decades, the "solid front of silence" was a key part of that story. In his classic history of the American League, published in 1962, historian Lee Allen noted that the "honest players on the team who still survive will not talk," a phenomenon he found "passing strange."[68] Dr. Harold and Dorothy Seymour also claimed "the players, honest as well as accused, have maintained an almost unbroken silence."[69] Few writers or fans have seriously challenged that notion in the years since. But it's clear the players involved in the 1919 World Series were often willing to talk about what happened. Thanks to the power of the Internet, their words are much easier to find today using searchable newspaper archives than they were when Eliot Asinof was writing *Eight Men Out*.

More interviews with White Sox and Reds players almost certainly are waiting to be discovered in the future. Many daily newspapers from Chicago and Cincinnati, let alone all the other places these players lived and worked, haven't been digitized yet. But one thing can now be said for sure: When asked about the scandal, the participants often answered.

"I don't know whether the whole truth of what went on there with the White Sox will ever come out," Edd Roush told author Lawrence Ritter in 1964. "Even today, nobody really knows exactly what took place. Whatever it was, though, it was a dirty, rotten shame."[70] ■

Notes

1. Alexis Stevens, "Sportswriter Furman Bisher dies at 93," *Atlanta Journal-Constitution*, March 19, 2012. Accessed online at http://www.ajc.com/news/sports/sportswriter-furman-bisher-dies-at-93-1/nQSJx/ on November 3, 2015. The author has added emphasis.
2. Gene Carney, *Burying the Black Sox: How Baseball's Cover-Up of the 1919 World Series Fix Almost Succeeded* (Washington, DC: Potomac Books, 2006), 63–64.
3. http://www.blackbetsy.com/theTruth.html
4. Ibid.
5. Latimer is best known as the sportswriter who gave Shoeless Joe his iconic nickname during a minor-league game in 1908.
6. Arnold (Chick) Gandil, as told to Melvin Durslag, "This is My Story of the Black Sox Series," *Sports Illustrated*, September 17, 1956.
7. "'Black Sox' Blast Gandil 'Confession'," *Chicago Tribune*, September 14, 1956.
8. For one early example, see: Frank G. Menke, "Crooked Players Find Themselves Despised By All," King Features Syndicate, *Idaho Statesman*, April 4, 1922. No meaningful effort is made to accurately report on the Black Sox players' whereabouts. Lefty Williams is described as "loafing day after day," Swede Risberg as "idle and seemingly broke." Joe Jackson has "the years stretching before him, barren of baseball hope." The others are described in similar, pathetic terms.
9. James Nitz, "Happy Felsch," SABR BioProject, http://sabr.org/bioproj/person/cd61b579.
10. Eliot Asinof, *Eight Men Out* (New York: Henry Holt, 1963), 284.
11. Eliot Asinof, *Bleeding Between the Lines* (New York: Henry Holt, 1979), 93.
12. Paul Green, "The Later Lives of the Banished Sox," *Sports Collectors Digest*, April 22, 1988, 196–97.
13. Westbrook Pegler, "Control, a Little Riser, Were Cicotte's Secrets," *Kansas City Star*, September 28, 1956.
14. Westbrook Pegler, "Onus of Bad Series Finally Made Happy Felsch Sell His Business," *Butte* (Montana) *Standard*, September 25, 1956.
15. Westbrook Pegler, "Swede Risberg Prospers But He Also Suffered; Son a Prospect," *Butte* (Montana) *Standard*, September 26, 1956.
16. If Asinof discovered any other interviews, they are not part of his collection of research notes which is now available to researchers at the Chicago History Museum.
17. Bob Considine, "On the Line," *Waterloo* (Iowa) *Sunday Courier*, January 12, 1947.
18. John Lardner, "Remember the Black Sox," *The Saturday Evening Post*, April 30, 1938.
19. "Shoeless 'Joe' Jackson Star in Valet Loop Now," *Santa Ana* (California) *Register*, April 7, 1927.
20. "Jackson Applies for Readmission to Pro Baseball," *Florence* (South Carolina) *News*, December 19, 1933.
21. "Baseball Still is 'First Love' of Joe Jackson," *Blytheville* (Arkansas) *Courier News*, March 10, 1937.
22. Shirley Povich, "Say It Ain't So, Joe," *Washington Post*, April 11, 1941.
23. "'Shoeless' Joe Takes Time For Reminiscence," *Blytheville* (Arkansas) *Courier News*, March 9, 1932.
24. As cited in Carney, *Burying the Black Sox*, 62.
25. There is other credible evidence that White Sox officials were aware of the fix as early as Game One and that Charles Comiskey attempted to inform the National Commission about it (only to be dismissed by American League president Ban Johnson with the famous retort, "That's the whelp of a beaten cur!") But Joe Jackson's request to be benched would be the only known instance of a Black Sox player attempting to inform team officials about the fix during the Series. For a detailed analysis of this episode, see chapter 4 of Carney's *Burying the Black Sox*.
26. Scoop Latimer, "Joe Jackson, Contented Carolinan at 54, Forgets Bitter Dose in His Cup and Glories in His 12 Hits in '19 Series," *The Sporting News*, September 24, 1942.
27. "Buck Weaver Asks For Reinstatement," *The New York Times*, January 14, 1922.

28. Ibid.
29. Jack Brickhouse, with Jack Rosenberg and Ned Colletti, *Thanks for Listening!* (South Bend, Indiana: Diamond Communications, 1996), 213–14.
30. James T. Farrell, *My Baseball Diary* (New York: A.S. Barnes, 1957).
31. Pegler, "Control, a Little Riser, Were Cicotte's Secrets."
32. Pegler, "Onus of Bad Series Finally Made Happy Felsch Sell His Business."
33. Pegler, "Swede Risberg Prospers But He Also Suffered; Son a Prospect."
34. Lyria Williams letter to Katie Jackson, October 16, 1956, Legendary Auctions, Summer 2003 catalog.
35. Bob Hoie telephone interview with the author, July 16, 2012. According to Hoie, who spoke with Fred McMullin's daughter-in-law twice in 2002, Fred had supposedly written an account of the scandal that was to be given to veteran Los Angeles sportswriter Matt Gallagher after all the Black Sox players were dead. Years later, when Fred's son Billy asked his mother Delia for the document, she said she had destroyed it.
36. For further discussion on McMullin's role in the scandal, see the author's SABR BioProject biography of McMullin at http://sabr.org/bioproj/person/7d8be958.
37. "Risberg's Silence Costs Him Fortune; Landis Locks Door; It's Too Late Now," *Sioux Falls Argus-Leader*, May 23, 1931.
38. "Diamond Outlaw Asks Baseball Heads to Lift Life-time Suspension," *Lincoln* (Nebraska) *Star*, January 16, 1934.
39. "Reds Rooter Risberg Has Little Hope Now," *Red Bluff* (California) *Daily News*, October 14, 1970.
40. Dwight Chapin, "The Black Sox Scandal: Torn Lives—50 Years Later," *Los Angeles Times*, August 13, 1969.
41. Dwight Chapin, "Gandil Continues to Claim His Innocence," *Los Angeles Times*, August 14, 1969.
42. Joe Falls, "Eddie Cicotte—at 81, He''s Proud of Life He's Led; Family Is, Too," *The Sporting News*, December 6, 1965.
43. Ibid.
44. Edward Prell, "Cicotte Had Great Stuff—Schalk," *Chicago Tribune*, May 9, 1969.
45. Associated Press, "Black Sox Scandal Skeleton Still Rattles," *The Oregonian*, August 10, 1969.
46. *New York World-Telegram and Sun*, June 21, 1955. As cited in Brian E. Cooper, *Ray Schalk: A Baseball Biography* (Jefferson, North Carolina: McFarland & Co., 2009).
47. Asinof, *Bleeding Between the Lines*, 95–97.
48. Ibid.
49. Frank O. Klein, "Catcher Ray Schalk in Huge World Series Exposé," *Collyer's Eye*, December 13, 1919. Schalk was echoing a similar claim made by reporter Hugh Fullerton the day after the World Series concluded.

However, Fullerton's column in the *Chicago Herald-Examiner* on October 10 did not name the seven White Sox players he claimed "would not be there when the gong sounds next Spring." Schalk's interview with *Collyer's Eye* was the first to name them.
50. Oscar C. Reichow, "Ray Schalk Never Hinted At Anything Wrong in Series," *The Sporting News*, January 8, 1920.
51. Ed Burns, "Unforgettable Memory Left With Schalk by Tears of Black Sox When Told by Comiskey of Banishment," *The Sporting News*, November 28, 1940.
52. Rick Huhn, *Eddie Collins: A Baseball Biography* (Jefferson, North Carolina: McFarland & Co., 2008), 179–83.
53. *New York World-Telegram*, July 10, 1943.
54. Jim Leonard, "From Sullivan to Collins," *The Sporting News*, November 1, 1950.
55. David Bloom, "Dick Kerr, Breaking 17-Year Silence, Tells of '19 Series," *The Sporting News*, February 25, 1937.
56. Tom Meehan, "Hanford's Jenkins, Black Sox Innocent, Talks of One Big Smirch On Baseball," *Fresno* (California) *Bee*, May 13, 1962.
57. *The Scrantonian* (Pennsylvania), September 13, 1959.
58. United Press International, "Faber Recalls How Gamblers Were Ruination of White Sox," *Rockford* (Illinois) *Register-Republic*, January 10, 1947.
59. John Lardner, "Remember the Black Sox?" *Saturday Evening Post*, April 30, 1938.
60. Lawrence S. Ritter, *The Glory of Their Times: The Story of the Early Days of Baseball Told by the Men Who Played It* (New York: William Morrow & Co., 1984), 222.
61. The World Series was played in an experimental best-of-nine format from 1919 to 1921.
62. Ritter, 301. For *Glory*, Ritter also interviewed a third member of the 1919 Reds, outfielder Rube Bressler, but they didn't talk much about the 1919 World Series.
63. Grantland Rice, "Sportlight," *Nebraska State Journal*, March 26, 1945.
64. "What's Become of Sallee? Slim's Still Tossing," *The Sporting News*, April 13, 1944.
65. Earl Wilson, "It Happened Last Night," *Uniontown* (Pennsylvania) *Morning Herald*, June 10, 1952.
66. Dan Daniel, *New York World-Telegram*, March 2, 1937. As cited in Susan Dellinger, *Red Legs and Black Sox: Edd Roush and the Untold Story of the 1919 World Series* (Cincinnati: Emmis Books, 2006).
67. Dellinger, 326–27.
68. Lee Allen, *The American League Story* (New York: Hill & Wang, 1962), 100.
69. Harold Seymour and Dorothy Seymour Mills, *Baseball: The Golden Age* (New York: Oxford University Press, 1971), 294.
70. Ritter, 222.

"Playing Rotten, It Ain't That Hard to Do"

How the Black Sox Threw the 1920 Pennant

Bruce S. Allardice

Entering the 1920 season, the defending American League champion Chicago White Sox were not favored to repeat. Almost all experts picked Cleveland, who'd finished second in 1919. The prognosticators cited Chicago's poor performance in the 1919 Series, doubts about the team's pitching depth, the retirement of first baseman Chick Gandil, and suspicions that the Sox had thrown the 1919 Series.[1] Yet after a slow start (they were 29–25 on June 18) the Sox roared back and, by late August, nosed ahead of the Tribe. Loss of a three-game series to Boston at the end of August put the Sox back in second place. They battled the Indians throughout September, until the scandal over fixing the 1919 World Series exploded on September 27, after which the team faded.

Rumors of fixed games surrounded the Sox after the 1919 World Series, and the allegations of crooked play continued through 1920.[2] Yet in all the oceans of ink spilled in discussing the 1919 Series, surprisingly little has been written on the possibility that the Sox threw the 1920 pennant as well. This article presents credible evidence, in testimony and in statistics, that the same players who threw the 1919 Series also threw games (and the pennant) in 1920. At one time or another every "Clean Sox" regular accused their "Black Sox" teammates of throwing games in 1920, and the statistical records back up these accusations.

THE SUSPECT BOSTON SERIES

It is an axiom of law enforcement that criminals exhibit a pattern of conduct—that they repeat their actions until caught. Viewed in this light, it should come as no surprise that the same players who threw a World Series would throw regular season games as well.

After defeating New York 16–4 on August 26, 1920, the red-hot White Sox had a 3½-game lead over Cleveland, with New York four back, and to many observers it appeared that the Sox had the 1920 pennant cinched. Yet they promptly lost seven in a row, including two road games to the third-place Yankees, three straight to fifth-place Boston, and two home games against fourth-place St. Louis. The evidence suggests that the

gamblers may have put pressure on the Sox to blow that lead. In 1919 and 1920, the Sox never lost more than four straight, except for this one stretch against mostly sub .500 teams, and since the Sox were basically injury-free at that point, it's hard to explain this slide. Cicotte's wildness and lack of clutch hitting cost the Sox the second New York game, while in the third, misplays by Risberg and Weaver let in all the Yankees runs. Regarding this game, *Chicago Tribune* sports reporter I.E. Sanborn sourly observed, "Risberg and Weaver were the best players New York had today," while Joe Jackson, thrown out twice on the bases, "ran...like a high school boy." The St. Louis losses featured a lack of clutch hitting, and Cicotte being knocked around.[3]

"Clean" Sox players repeatedly cited the White Sox series with Boston, August 30–September 1, 1920, during that seven-game slide, as the set of games that the crooked players clearly tossed.

The White Sox certainly stunk in those three games at Boston. They lost to the below-.500 Red Sox, 4–0, 7–3, and 6–2, with Williams, Cicotte, and Kerr pitching. All contemporary newspaper accounts noted their poor play. In the opener, the Sox managed only five hits (three by "Clean" Eddie Collins) off Boston's Sam Jones. In the second game, Cicotte got pounded, and Risberg muffed two plays that cost the Sox three runs. In the final game, Kerr was done in by three errors (all by the "Clean" Sox, although Eddie Collins asserted that the error given to Kerr should have been given to Buck Weaver) and lack of clutch hitting. In all, the Sox committed four errors in the three games, and scored only five runs.

Teams—even great teams—are capable of losing three in a row, without any suspicion of foul play. That's baseball. *Chicago Tribune* sportswriter I.E. Sanborn admitted that "there was no accounting for their slump in New York and Boston on any rational basis," but attributed the losses to an ordinary, run-of-the-mill stretch.[4] The Boston newspapers were more critical. *The Herald* noted that "the Chicago club...did not look like a pennant-gaited combination." James

O'Leary of the *Globe* reported "some loose work on the part of the White Sox on a couple of occasions, decidedly out of harmony with their usual smooth-running game." But neither newspaper hinted at foul play. In fact, as the *Boston Globe* admitted a month later, while the White Sox made numerous errors and misplays in this series, "the games…did not create any great stir."[5]

A three-game series provides too small a statistical sample to draw any definitive conclusions. However, the middle-of-the-order White Sox RBI men ("Black" Sox Joe Jackson, Buck Weaver, and Happy Felsch) went 8 for 34 in the series (.235) and drove in only one run with those eight hits. The same three players combined to average two RBIs per game that year, and in those three games they had plenty of opportunities to drive in runs—Eddie Collins, batting in front of them, had seven hits in the series. This would appear to justify comments made by "Clean" Sox players later in the season that the "Black" Sox hitters deliberately failed in the clutch in that series. What is more curious—in no other three-game series in 1920 did the White Sox score as few as five runs—less than two runs per game.

After the scandal broke, Boston sportswriter Jim O'Leary charged that Sox ace Eddie Cicotte threw the second game of the Boston series, under orders from gamblers.[6] Modern Black Sox scholarship points to Cicotte and Chick Gandil as the ringleaders of the 1919 Series fix, conspiring with Boston gambler Sport Sullivan.[7] Cicotte and Sullivan had become friends years earlier when Cicotte pitched for the Boston Red Sox. If he chose, Sullivan could give direct testimony of Cicotte's involvement in the 1919 fix. Thus, more than any other Sox player, Cicotte would be vulnerable if Sullivan exposed the 1919 fix. In addition, if Sullivan pressured Cicotte et al. to throw games, Sullivan could place large wagers on Chicago-Boston games more readily than he could Chicago's games against non-Boston clubs. Given this conjunction of player vulnerability and betting ease, Cicotte's 1920 pitching record against Boston is particularly revealing. In six starts against fifth place Boston, he went 1–4 and gave up 29 earned runs in 48 innings, for an ERA of 5.44. Against the rest of the league, Cicotte was 20-6 with an ERA of 2.85. Against Boston, his ERA, walk ratio, strikeouts and hits per inning were all far worse than when pitching to the rest of the league.[8] The White Sox had a winning record against the Red Sox that year in the other seventeen games. And since the Sox only lost the pennant by two games, Cicotte's four losses against Boston may, by themselves, have cost Chicago the pennant.

Eddie Collins alleged that the crooked players would only win when Cleveland won and would lose when Cleveland lost, so as to maintain the Indians' lead in the standings.

NATIONAL BASEBALL HALL OF FAME LIBRARY, COOPERSTOWN, NY

THE SEPTEMBER SLIDE

This Boston series remains part of a pattern of suspicious conduct by the White Sox in late August and early September. After their August 26 win against New York, they'd played 121 games and only been shut out three times. Yet in the next 19 games, they were shut out five times—more than in the first 121. The big three RBI men batted a combined 13 for 58 (.224) in those five games The pitchers who shut out the Sox during that stretch (Bob Shawkey, Sam Jones, Dutch Leonard, Harry Courtney, and Jose Acosta—not exactly a Hall of Fame set, though Shawkey led the league in ERA that year) had a combined record of 40–54 prior to those games, with three of the four teams being sub-.500. So it wasn't as if the Sox lost to Lefty Grove or the 1927 Yankees.

Eddie Collins and Byrd Lynn later charged that the Black Sox players "tracked" Cleveland during (and after) the Boston series, winning only when Cleveland was winning, and losing when Cleveland lost, so as to not overtake the Tribe. The record bears this out. After the end of the Boston series (September 1), thru September 27, and excluding the three games Cleveland and Chicago played each other, the two teams played on 18 common days. Fifteen of those 18 days, both teams did the same, winning or losing in tandem. This could be some rare coincidence, or it could prove that Collins and Lynn were correct.[9]

Several September games raised some eyebrows. In a September 11 game against Boston, Chicago committed six errors (three by Buck Weaver and Risberg) behind Dickey Kerr, losing a game immediately after Cleveland had lost a game. The *Chicago Tribune* excoriated the Sox play: ""Kerr… was the victim of vile support by some of his teammates… the infield made enough errors... **to have lost a world's series**..." [Emphasis added.] With perhaps unconscious irony, the same day the *Tribune* also ran an article urging baseball to take action against gamblers and clean up the game.[10] Shut-out losses (at home) to the lowly Washington Nationals on September 12 and 14 raised further eyebrows. Lefty Williams was "wild and ineffective" in the former game, while in the latter game Washington's runs were "outright gifts" due to three Sox errors. *The Washington Star* noted something more ominous: "The morale of the White Sox is not what it should be.... It is significant that after returning from the east, where they had lost seven straight games, they were speculating on how much money [they could make in a post-season city series with the Cubs, possible only if they lost the pennant]."[11]

OTHER FIXED REGULAR SEASON GAMES?

Various sources have cited other games that the White Sox might have thrown in 1920. David Fleitz, in his book *Shoeless*, notes a July 25 game in which the Indians defeated the White Sox 7–2, largely due to several botched plays by "Black" Sox enforcer Swede Risberg.[12] Eliot Asinof, author of *Eight Men Out*, points to two earlier losses to Cleveland, on April 27 and May 9.[13] In the former game, a 3–2 loss, Risberg's late inning throwing error allowed the tying run to score. In the latter game, a 4–3 loss, errors by Risberg and Eddie Cicotte helped let in three runs, while lack of clutch hitting foiled their offense. *The Chicago Tribune* sourly commented that the Sox lost the game due to "comical fielding," while the *Cleveland Plain Dealer* added that the Sox were "not at all particular about making their [11] hits produce something."[14]

There are even charges that Chicago threw regular season games in 1919. Later in his life, World Series hero Dickey Kerr charged that his teammates "didn't wait until they got in the [1919] Series to throw games....They threw 'em during the season whenever they got their price."[15] A modern study attempts, with mixed success, to prove a St. Louis-based 1919 regular season fix via statistical analysis, citing Lefty Williams as the prime 1919 game fixer.[16]

TESTIMONY REGARDING THE 1920 FIX

What the players (and others) said—both at the time and later—pointed to a 1920 Fix. Every "Clean" Sox regular, as well as "Black" Soxers Happy Felsch and Eddie Cicotte, agreed that the Sox threw games in 1920.

1. Team star and future Hall of Famer Eddie Collins, on September 2, 1920, told Sox owner Charles

Comiskey that pitcher Eddie Cicotte "wasn't trying" and suggested Comiskey talk to the troubled hurler. To well-connected sportswriter Otto Floto of the *Denver Post*, Collins expanded on this, asserting he told Comiskey after the Boston series that "he was thru (sic) with [the] game if [the] crooks weren't fired."[17] Wrote Floto, "At Boston, Collins noticed for the first time that the scoreboard was the barometer by which the contest was waged. He noticed two outfielders [obviously, Jackson and Felsch] watch every inning and when Cleveland won the Sox would also win. When Cleveland lost the Sox would obligingly lose, for the crooked eight [actually, seven] of the Sox had entered into a combine with the gamblers not to win the pennant for Chicago."

After the scandal broke, Collins said: "We've known something was wrong for a long time, but we felt that we had to keep silent because we were fighting for the pennant."

A few days after the 1920 season ended, Collins charged that the Sox lost the pennant because "two players failed to put forth their best efforts," and added that the two were among the seven indicted.[18] In October, Collins told *Collyer's Eye* that games in 1920 were fixed, and "if gamblers didn't have Weaver and Cicotte in their pocket, then I don't know anything about baseball."[19]

In a 1949 article, Collins was much more specific: "It was in Boston the incident happened that cost us the 1920 pennant. Some gamblers got panicky that we'd win again and they must have got to the players they had under their thumb and ordered the rest of the games thrown...We [the "Clean" Sox] knew

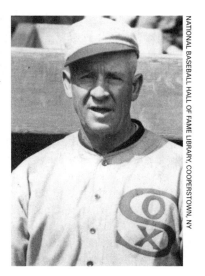

Manager Kid Gleason felt something was wrong with his team but couldn't prove a fix. He ended up bringing the shirking players in for extra workouts.

something was wrong but we couldn't put a finger on it."[20]

Collins also told sportswriter Joe Williams that the Black Sox "threw a dozen games in 1920, or tried to." Williams wrote elsewhere that Collins seemed more bitter over the 1920 fix than the 1919 World Series, and that the 1920 team was so good that, even though "they practically lived with the gamblers," they often won despite themselves.[21]

2. In the *Washington Times*, September 30, 1920, ace pitcher Red Faber complained: "The playing of the Sox on the Eastern trip [i.e., the end of the August 14 – September 1 road trip, where Chicago lost five in a row to New York and Boston] made some of the others believe that something was crooked. It looks like we were double-crossed in the World Series last year and in the pennant race this year…"[22]

Many years later, Faber told Asinof that in 1920 he never knew when some disaster might ruin one of his games. "The hoodlums had some of the boys in their pocket all through the 1920 season, too, throwing ball games right up to the last week of the pennant. I could feel it out there when I pitched—Risberg letting an easy ground ball go by, or Happy Felsch letting a runner take an extra base. You want to scream at them but you don't because you can see how scared they are."[23]

3. In the *Cleveland Plain Dealer*, September 29, 1920, John "Shano" Collins said: "We suspected some of them in the World Series, and we suspected them again because of the way of the play on the last eastern trip. Some of them not only didn't try, but really acted as though they didn't want to win."[24]

He expanded on this in the *Boston Post*: "We fought a losing battle all this year. We had a fine team and we seldom were defeated by any wide margin. We had the strength to stay up there to win if everything had been right, and yet at the critical moment something would always happen. …

"You may remember our last visit this year to Boston. Just before we came there the Red Sox had started a spurt and were beating all comers.[25] This allowed us to creep up to the top, or very near it, for we had been fattening at Cleveland's and New York's expense. And we reached the Hub with a splendid chance to go away out in front.

"Well, we lost all three games; Cicotte was batted out of the box. Our men were hopeless at the bat. The big stickers fell down miserably. I have heard a lot about certain players watching the score board while playing in the Hub and not trying as hard as they might. Well, I'm not going to discuss that. I only know that we lost three straight to the Red Sox, that our defeat put the Indians in first place and that we left Boston with every hope blasted."[26]

4. As recalled later by Eddie Collins, during that crucial Boston series, 1919 World Series hero Dickey Kerr blew up after an error by Buck Weaver, and a botched fly ball that fell between Felsch and Jackson. "When the inning was over Kerr scaled his glove across the diamond. He looks at Weaver and Risberg, who are standing together, and says 'If you told me you wanted to lose this game, I could have done it a lot easier.' There is almost a riot on the bench. Kid Gleason breaks up two fights. That was the end. We lose three or four more games the same way."[27]

5. Outfielder Eddie Murphy later said that during the 1920 season he suspected that the gamblers still held sway over the "Black" Sox, as the team "lost often enough, suspiciously, to cost us the flag." "We knew something was wrong for a long time."[28]

6. Backup catcher Byrd Lynn, in October 1920, got specific: "We lost the pennant because certain players—they are among the eight indicted by the Cook Grand jury—didn't want us to win. … We soon noticed how carefully they studied the scoreboard—more than even the average player does in a pennant race—and that they always made errors

1919 World Series hero Dickey Kerr reportedly lost his temper after errors lost a game in Boston. Collins said, "When the inning was over Kerr scaled his glove across the diamond. He looks at Weaver and Risberg, who are standing together, and says 'If you told me you wanted to lose this game, I could have done it a lot easier.'"

NATIONAL BASEBALL HALL OF FAME LIBRARY, COOPERSTOWN, NY

which lost us the game when Cleveland and New York were losing. If Cleveland won—we won. If Cleveland lost—we lost. The idea was to keep up the betting odds, but not to let us win the pennant."[29]

7. Utility infielder Hervey McClellan, in October 1920, charged that certain players (unnamed) threw the three-game series in Boston, and added, "Several of the players noticed how the score board affected the others, and we felt all along that these men were regulating their play according to the play of other teams."[30]

8. In public, outfielder Nemo Leibold professed ignorance of the 1920 fix. He was quoted in 1921 as saying: "I roomed with Buck [Weaver] throughout the 1919 and 1920 seasons and never had an inkling there was anything wrong." However, during the 1920 season, Leibold told his friend, New York shortstop Roger Peckinpaugh, that something was wrong. As Peckinpaugh later recalled, the clearly upset Leibold told him "Something screwy is going on here. I don't know what it is, but it's something screwy, all right. You guys bear down and you ought to take all four games."[31]

9. When interviewed by investigators after the 1920 season, Buck Weaver said "Black" Sox infielder Fred McMullin offered him a $500 bribe to "lay down" in a game in August of 1920, an offer Weaver refused but did not report to management at the time.[32]

10. Many years later, outfielder Happy Felsch, another of the 1919 fixers, admitted throwing games in 1920 as well, with the colorful observation "Playing rotten, it ain't that hard to do…"[33]

11. Also years later, Red Sox pitcher Joe Wood recalled his friend Eddie Cicotte telling Wood, during the 1920 season, that "We don't dare win" the 1920 pennant.[34]

12. Catcher Ray Schalk usually kept silent about the 1919 fix, but the *Chicago Tribune* on September 26, 1920, alleges Schalk "entertained doubts as to the honesty of two pitchers [obviously Cicotte and Williams]—especially during the last two months [of 1920]."[35]

13. Unidentified "Clean" Sox player, September 29, 1920, while celebrating the "Black" Sox grand jury confessions, told a reporter: "No one will ever know what we put up with all this summer. I don't know how we ever got along."[36]

14. Sox Manager Kid Gleason, on September 29, 1920, the day after the Black Sox confessions, admitted, "I have felt for a long time that some of my players were not going at the speed they should be going." A puzzled Gleason, suspecting another fix but not having proof, brought the players (one being Eddie Cicotte, whom Gleason benched in early September) in for extra workouts.[37]

15. Unidentified Sox players, to *Collyer's Eye*, September 18, 1920 (prior to the confessions), say they're "fed up" with their teammates' "listless efforts."[38]

16. Unidentified Sox player to *The Sporting News*, October 7, 1920, about the 1920 season: "When we started on our last trip east we had every reason to believe we were on the way to win a pennant…. Then Cicotte and Williams seemed to go bad without reason; Jackson, Felsch and Risberg began dumping the ball to the infield every time we had a chance to score runs. Some of us always had believed we were sold out in the [1919] World Series. When the [crooked] players showed they meant to beat us out of getting in on this one we decided to act. Cicotte was told that he would have to win a certain game or he would be mobbed on the field by the honest players on the team—he won it… Between double crossing his gambler partners and taking a licking from his team mates he decided, naturally, to double cross."[39]

17. Unidentified Sox players, per *The Sporting News*, October 7, 1920: "Honest players on the White Sox team are practically unanimous in saying that the cheaters continued to throw down the team all this season. 'We would have won the pennant in a walk,' they say, 'if those fellows had played fair.'"[40]

18. In the *Washington Times*, September 30, 1920, umpire Brick Owens "charged that Eddie Cicotte laid down in the series with Boston [that Owens umpired] a month ago… Cicotte would put lots of stuff on the ball up to the third strike … then he would send over a grooved fast ball without a thing on it. His work could scarcely be detected from the stands, but there was a lot of comment among the players."[41]

Manager Kid Gleason benched Cicotte for 10 days following this Boston start, and another poor performance. The reason the Sox gave for this extraordinary move—benching your ace starter during a hot pennant race—was that Cicotte needed to rest and regroup. However, it is likely Gleason saw the same pattern Owens did. Whatever the reason for the slump (blackmail, bribery, worry, fear that the gamblers would murder him, or just a tired arm), Cicotte won all three of his starts after returning to the rotation.

19. In the same newspaper, another umpire, who refused to be named, charged that the Sox threw a game in Cleveland "last week" that Duster Mails pitched. "Mails pitched for Cleveland," this umpire said, "and he didn't have a thing. But the Sox players didn't hit him, and the Indians won the game."[42]

20. On October 1, 1920, *Boston Globe* sportswriter Jim O'Leary reported on "stories" circulating around Boston that "gamblers who had something on Cicotte" ordered Cicotte to lose the second game of the notorious Boston series, threatening to "break with him and show him up." During that game, O'Leary blurted out: "Why, they're playing just like they did in the World Series!" Chicago sportswriter Oscar Reichow responded: "That's so." O'Leary notes that at the time neither suspected any fix.[43]

21. Roger Peckinpaugh, veteran Yankees shortstop: "You never knew when the White Sox were going to go out there and beat your brains out or roll over and play dead. Somebody was betting on those games [in 1920], that's a cinch."[44]

22. American League President Ban Johnson, in September 1920, admitted that he had "heard statements that the White Sox would not dare to win the 1920 pennant because the managers of a gambling syndicate, alleged to have certain players in their power, had forbidden it." In 1929 Johnson was even more specific: "The Sox would have walked into the 1920 pennant had they played ball, but they were at the mercy of the gamblers."[45]

In sum, every "Clean" Sox regular (Schalk, Shano Collins, Eddie Collins, Leibold, Murphy, Kerr, and Faber), at the time, or later, accused their teammates of laying down in 1920. Known fixer Hap Felsch later admitted as much. Add to that list of accusers two "Clean" Sox backups (Lynn and McClellan), the Sox's

manager (Kid Gleason), umpires, sportswriters, and American League President Ban Johnson, throw in the McMullin bribe attempt and Cicotte's admission, and it becomes clear that once again the fix was in. The accusations focused on the same players that we now know threw the 1919 Series.

MOTIVES OF THE PLAYERS
It is likely the same motives that led to the 1919 scandal (money) also operated in 1920. Famed sportswriter Joe Williams, an intimate friend of Eddie Collins, offered an interesting take on the 1920 fix. He speculated that the "Black" Sox, shortchanged by the gamblers in 1919, "set out to clip the game for all they could before the inevitable [exposure]."[46]

In 1918 the notorious Hal Chase was accused of trying to bribe his Cincinnati teammates. Despite testimony of the players at a hearing conducted by the National League, Chase got off scot free. Two months after the Black Sox Scandal blew open, Chicago sportswriter Hugh Fullerton summed up what the crooked Chicago players thought: "The Chase case gave many players the idea that they could play dishonestly and not be discovered, or if discovered or suspected, would be cleared."[47]

CONCLUSIONS
The overwhelming testimony of "Clean" Sox, "Black" Sox, and neutral observers, is that the Sox threw games—at a minimum three, and perhaps as many as a dozen—in 1920. The statistics support this conclusion. Money was the primary motive, just as it was in 1919. Since they'd dumped the 1919 Series without suffering serious (any?) consequences, there was no reason not to cash in on 1920 as well. Considerable gambler money must have been involved, as low-paid backup Fred McMullen could toss around $500 bribe offers like popcorn. Fear of the gamblers exposing them likely also played a part. ■

Notes
1. See Bruce Allardice, "How Great were the 1919 White Sox?" *SABR Black Sox Research Committee Newsletter* (December 2015), 3–5, for a compilation of the preseason predictions for 1920. The betting odds also favored Cleveland.
2. For example, "Start Quiz to Save Baseball from Gamblers," *Chicago Tribune*, September 5, 1920, which notes a "rumor … that three White Sox are under suspicion, yet are playing in the game regularly."
3. I. E. Sanborn, "Ruth-less Yankees Mop Up Sox, 3–0, for Record Mob," *Chicago Tribune*, August 29, 1920. See the *Tribune*'s August 28–September 5 coverage of the Sox for game descriptions.
4. I. E. Sanborn, "Sox Back, Glum but Grim for Final Flag Dash," *Chicago Tribune*, September 3, 1920.
5. Ed Cunningham, "Red Sox Topple Chicago Hose from League Peak," *Boston Herald*, September 2, 1920; James O'Leary, "Red Sox Topple

the White Sox from Top," *Boston Globe*, September 2, 1920; "White Sox Made Six Errors in Boston Games Which Two Players Say Were Thrown," *Boston Globe*, October 4, 1920. Cf. Rick Huhn, *Eddie Collins: A Baseball Biography* (Jefferson, NC: McFarland, 2008), 171–72. Gary Webster, *Tris Speaker and the 1920 Indians: Tragedy to Glory* (Jefferson, NC: McFarland, 2012), discusses at some length the charge that the White Sox threw this series, and other games.

6. James C. O'Leary, "Recall Defeat Handed Cicotte on Last Visit. Story Circulated in Boston Says Gamblers Brought Pressure of White Sox Hurler to Lose Game to Red Sox in Fenway Park," *Boston Globe*, October 1, 1920.

7. For more on "Sport" Sullivan and the Sullivan-Gandil connection, see Bruce Allardice, "Out of the Shadows: Joseph 'Sport' Sullivan," *SABR Black Sox Research Committee Newsletter* (June 2014), 9–14.

8. All the statistics cited are from www.baseball-reference.com.Cicotte's 1920 breakdown is as follows: .Season: 21–10, 3.26 ERA; vs. Boston, 1–4, 5.43 ERA; vs. other teams, 20–6, 2.85 ERA. By team, Cicotte's won-loss breakdown was: Boston 1–4, Cleveland 0–2, New York 2–2, St. Louis 3–1, Washington 5–1, Detroit 5–0, and Philadelphia 5–0.

9. Cleveland went 17–6 during this stretch, Chicago 18–7.

10. I. E. Sanborn, "Gambling Blot Smirches Game as Moguls Dally," *Chicago Tribune*, September 12, 1920.

11. I. E. Sanborn, "Tale of the Lost Home Run and Sox Defeat, 5–0," *Chicago Tribune*, September 13, 1920. I. E. Sanborn, "Gift Tallies of Sox Hand Cinch to Griffs, 7–0," *Chicago Tribune*, September 15, 1920. Denman Thompson, "Defeats of White Sox Make Griffs Chesty," *Washington Star*, September 15, 1920.

12. David L. Fleitz, *Shoeless: The Life and Times of Joe Jackson* (Jefferson, NC: McFarland, 2001), 213.

13. Eliot Asinof, *Eight Men Out* (New York, Henry Holt, 1963), 145.

14. Irving Vaughan, "Sox Lose First Game of Season to Speakers, 3–2," *Chicago Tribune*, April 28, 1920; Irving Vaughan, "Risberg Spiked as Careless Sox Drop 4–3 Clash," *Chicago Tribune*, May 10, 1920. Irving Vaughan, "Tribe Trims White Sox 4–3 and Takes Undisputed Possession of First Place," *Cleveland Plain Dealer*, May 10, 1920.

15. Joe Williams, "Yanks Have Won Enough Games to Take Pennant," *El Paso Herald-Post*, September 29, 1949.

16. Timothy Newman and Bruce Stuckman, "They Were Black Sox Long Before the 1919 World Series," *Base Ball: A Journal of the Early Game 6* (Spring 2012): 75–85.

17. At the 1924 trial, Comiskey placed this Collins warning not on September 2, but rather the week after the indictments. See William Lamb, *Black Sox in the Courtroom* (Jefferson, NC: McFarland, 2008), 157.

18. Huhn, *Eddie Collins*, 172. Otto Floto, "Collins Told Comiskey He Was Thru With Game If Crooks Weren't Fired," *Denver Post*, October 15, 1920.

19. "Collins Charges 1920 Games Fixed," *Collyer's Eye*, October 30, 1920.

20. Gerry Hern, "The Tipoff on the Black Sox," *Baseball Digest* (June, 1949), 11–12.

21. Joe Williams, "by Joe Williams," Panama (FL) American, March 30, 1951. Seamheads website (www.seamheads.com), # 356.

22. "Umps Say Sox Threw 1920 Pennant," *Washington Times*, September 30, 1920.

23. Eliot Asinof, *Bleeding Between the Lines* (New York: Holt, Rinehart & Winston, 1979), 93.

24. "Sox Traitors Accused of Not Trying to Win '20 Flag," *Canton Repository*, September 29, 1920.

25. Not exactly true, if Collins is quoted correctly. While Boston had taken 4 of 5 from Cleveland early in the week, they'd lost 3 in a row to the Browns immediately prior to the White Sox series, and lost 2 of 3 to New York after the Sox left town. That quotation would better fit the White Sox.

26. Paul H. Shannon, "Collins Shows Crooks Fooled Fellow Players," *Boston Post*, November 27, 1920.

27. Huhn, *Eddie Collins*, 172.

28. Paul Browne, "A Grandfather's Tale: Interviewing Eddie Murphy III,"

SABR Black Sox Research Committee Newsletter (June 2015), 13. John Heeg, "Eddie Murphy," in Jacob Pomrenke (ed.), *Scandal on the South Side: The 1919 Chicago White Sox* (Phoenix, Society of American Baseball Research, 2015).

29. Quoted widely. Cf "Sox Players Charge Mates Threw Games," *Idaho Statesman*, October 4, 1920; "White Sox Players Accuse Teammates," *The New York Times*, October 4, 1920.

30. "Sox Players Charge Mates Threw Games," *Idaho Statesman*, October 4, 1920.

31. Pomrenke, *Scandal on the South Side*, 107. Donald Honig, *The Man in the Dugout* (Lincoln: University of Nebraska Press, 1977), 216. The White Sox played two 4-game series with New York that year—June 16–19, and August 1–4.

32. Gene Carney, *Burying the Black Sox: How Baseball's Cover-Up of the 1919 World Series Fix Almost Succeeded* (Washington, D.C.: Potomac Books, 2006), 332.

33. Asinof, *Bleeding Between the Lines*, 117. Asinof Papers, Chicago History Museum, Box 4, Folder 2. In 1920 Felsch angrily denied throwing 1920 games, calling the charges "bunk."

34. Lawrence Ritter, *The Glory of Their Times*, audio version.

35. "First Evidence of Money Paid to Sox Bared," *Chicago Tribune*, September 26, 1920.

36. "Shadow Lifted, 'Square Guys' of Sox Celebrate," *Chicago Tribune*, September 29, 1920.

37. "Gleason Welcomes Wreck of Team for Good of Baseball," *Chicago Tribune*, September 29, 1920.

38. "Sox Reveal Inside of Big Scandal?," *Collyer's Eye*, September 18, 1920.

39. "When Baseball Gets Before the Grand Jury," *The Sporting News*, October 7, 1920. See also "Believe Pennant Has Been Thrown," *Cleveland Plain Dealer*, September 30, 1920. The game where the "Clean" Sox told Cicotte to win—or else be "mobbed'—presumably occurred in September, after the Boston series. Of the three games he pitched and won that month, the September 19 game appears the most likely, given the timing of the testimony and the state of the pennant race. See "Pitcher Names Bribe Gamblers," *New Orleans States*, September 29, 1920, for an earlier version of the "mobbed" story, which specifies that September 19 game.

40. "When Baseball Gets Before the Grand Jury," *The Sporting News*, October 7, 1920.

41. "Umps Say Sox Threw 1920 Pennant," *Washington Times*, September 30, 1920. Brick Owens and Ollie Chill umpired this series, and the later Cleveland-Sox series. None of this talk of throwing games surprised the newspaper. The next day the *Times* explained further: "Joining the Washington ball club last year, we found it common talk among the Griffmen that some of the Sox had thrown the Series of the year before. On occasion, some of the Chicago players were named as being in on the deal." Louis Dougher, "Looking 'Em Over," *Washington Times* October 1, 1920.

42. "Umps Say Sox Threw 1920 Pennant," *Washington Times*, September 30, 1920. "Jury Refuses to Halt Baseball Probe," *Denver Post*, September 30, 1920. This undoubtedly refers to the September 24, 1920, game where Duster Mails of Cleveland blanked the White Sox 2-0. The White Sox managed only 3 hits (by Eddie Collins, Felsch and Jackson) off the brash southpaw, though Mails walked five. From the box score, it appears the "Clean" Sox also had trouble hitting Mails that day. Brick Owens and Ollie Chill umpired this game.

43. James C. O'Leary, "Recall Defeat Handed Cicotte on Last Visit. Story Circulated in Boston Says Gamblers Brought Pressure of White Sox Hurler to Lose Game to Red Sox in Fenway Park," *Boston Globe*, October 1, 1920.

44. Honig, *The Man in the Dugout*, 216.

45. "Plan Probe of Cohan-Tennes Losses on Sox," *Chicago Tribune*, September 24, 1920; Ban Johnson, "Thirty-Four Years in Baseball—The Story of Ban Johnson's Life," *Chicago Tribune*, March 10, 1929.

46. Seamheads website, #356.

47. Hugh Fullerton, "Baseball on Trial," *The New Republic*, October 20, 1920.

Negro League Baseball, Black Community, and the Socio-Economic Impact of Integration

Kansas City, Missouri as Case Study

Japheth Knopp

This essay will explore the subject of racial and economic integration during the period of approximately 1945 through 1965 by studying the subject of Negro League baseball and the African American community of Kansas City, Missouri, as a vehicle for discussing the broader economic and social impact of desegregation. Of special import here is the economic effect desegregation had on medium and large-scale black-owned businesses during the post-war period, with the Negro Leagues and their franchises serving as prime examples of black-owned businesses that were expansive in size, profitable, publicly visible, and culturally relevant to the community. Specifically, what we are concerned with here is whether the manner in which desegregation occurred did in fact provide for increased economic and political freedoms for African Americans, and what social, fiscal, and communal assets may have been lost in the exchange.

The Kansas City Monarchs baseball club and the Kansas City African American community serve as a focal point for a number of reasons, including access to sources, the stature of the Monarchs as a preeminent team, the position of Jackie Robinson as the first openly black player to cross the color barrier in the modern period, and the vibrancy of the Kansas City black community. Also, Kansas City is unique in that it was the westernmost major metropolis in a border state, straddling the line between North and South and taking on aspects of both.[1] However, in most respects the setting for this essay could have been any urban black area in the United States in this period, with Kansas City being quite representative of the time. St. Louis or Chicago, Newark or Pittsburgh, across the country a general theme emerges of increased political and economic freedoms for African Americans, at least within segregated communities that in many ways were lost after increased contact and competition with white-owned businesses.[2] All of these communities would in this period struggle with the ramifications of "White Flight," decapitalization of urban areas, prejudicial hiring and housing policies, and increased economic competition.[3] The story of black enterprise in America follows a close parallel to what happened to the Negro Leagues.

AUGUST 28, 1945; 18TH & VINE, KANSAS CITY, MO

The headlines of the *Kansas City Call*, the local black newspaper, were still filled with post-war optimism but also with trepidation over continuing economic and civic issues in the months following the end of the war. From the Friday, August 31, 1945, edition we find that the S & D Process Company, an all-black mail order distribution house, had been abruptly closed, laying off its last 60 workers, most of whom were women. At the height of the war the firm had employed some 245 black workers.[4] In the same issue it was announced that the local office of the Federal Employment Practices Commission (which sought to provide more fair hiring and employment standards for minorities, especially in heavy industry and manufacturing) had been closed and was being incorporated in the St. Louis office.[5] The writer had some concerns for what this meant for the black workers in the area.

Perhaps the most troubling news item from this issue was the case of Seaman First Class Junius Bobb, a black sailor arrested for allegedly starting an altercation with a white Marine at Union Station rail depot. At press time the Navy would not disclose details, saying only that the incident was under investigation and that Seaman Bobb would stand trial for assault at Great Lakes Naval Training Center outside of Chicago. According to eyewitnesses, the Marine began the exchange by verbally and physically assaulting Seaman Bobb. The Shore Patrol arrived shortly thereafter and several military policemen began to beat Seaman Bobb with batons in full view of the public. The Marine in question was not arrested. Seaman Bobb's condition was unknown and he was being held incommunicado. The NAACP had announced that they would be providing legal counsel if Seaman Bobb did not prefer a Navy lawyer.[6]

On the whole, however, the general tone of the paper was upbeat and optimistic. While issues involving economic and legal inequality dominated the front page, there were many more stories celebrating success stories from the black community. Local girl Yolanda Meek had been awarded a $5,000 scholarship by the Delta Sigma Theta Sorority.[7] Op-ed columnist Lucia Mallory wrote about the importance of continuing to support the government by buying bonds even after the war had ended, and appealed to her readers to donate clothes and other supplies to the relief effort for victims of war-torn Europe.[8] Even though the local office was being closed, the FEPC was scheduled to hold a meeting October 14 at Municipal Auditorium called "An Industrial Job for all who Qualify," focusing on retaining black employment in the industrial sector after shifting to a peace-time economy.[9]

Many of the same sentiments were echoed in another local black newsletter, which on the front page expressed concern about the unemployment rate of the African American community and what postwar demobilization would mean for the black worker. While employment rates among black workers had doubled between 1940 and 1943, there had already been numerous layoffs in the various wartime industries, where black workers faced a "last hired, first fired" mentality.[10] Companies such as Remington Arms, North American Aircraft, Aluminum Company of America, and Pratt and Whitney Aircraft had increased their employment of black workers by some 200% during the war, 30% of whom were women.[11] What would become of these jobs in peacetime was a major concern. However, the inside fold of the circular contained stories of decorated black service members from the area, making special note of how many of them had been commissioned officers. These consistent themes of concern over civil liberties and economic opportunities intermixed with a sense of community pride and optimism seem to have been pervasive at this time.

This same general pathos is reflected in *The Call*'s sports pages. No fewer than four articles were dedicated to the Kansas City Monarchs of the Negro National League and one of the most storied black teams in baseball history. After dutifully reporting game summaries giving details of two lost games in a doubleheader to the Chicago American Giants by scores of 15–1 and 2–1, the writer moved on to more pleasant aspects of the club. There was a small write-up about the antics of legendary pitcher and showman Satchel Paige, who was equally famous both for his abilities as a player and for his on-field theatrics that dazzled the crowd and added to his already mythic persona. Another item advertised for the upcoming Labor Day doubleheader against the Memphis Red Sox in which ace pitcher and future Hall of Famer Hilton Smith was scheduled to pitch.[12] Somewhat surprisingly, there was no mention of star rookie shortstop Jackie Robinson, who was having one of the finest seasons of any player in the league.[13] While the official announcement would not be made until October, this was the first issue of the Monarchs' local paper following the historic signing of Robinson by Branch Rickey and the Brooklyn Dodgers on August 25, becoming the first black player in the twentieth century to have signed with a major league team.[14]

In the immediate wake of World War II, economic prosperity was permeating all levels of society (though admittedly distributed unequally) and Kansas City's African American community was no exception. Having weathered the Great Depression with unemployment and business failure rates much higher than their white counterparts, businesses were booming in the early postwar period. More than half of all businesses in Kansas City's black section were owned and operated by African American proprietors. While most of these were small-scale service sector operations, there were also banks, insurance agencies, doctors' offices, and law firms. More than 200 local black-owned businesses provided hundreds of jobs and an average weekly salary of $23.81, which was still below the national median, but much improved from just a few years prior.[15] Returning veterans were taking advantage of the Servicemen's Readjustment Act of 1944 and other benefits to open new businesses and purchase their own homes.[16] Employment opportunities for African American women had improved in this area to such an extent that there was a shortage of domestic workers available to work for wealthy white households.[17]

Increased economic opportunities and a sense of empowerment from wartime achievements (combined to a smaller degree with new government programs) fostered a zeitgeist of activism more commonly ascribed to the Civil Rights Movement of a decade later. Instead of maintaining the status quo, there were numerous new groups organized to push for expanded rights in the fields of healthcare, housing, employment, and access to advanced education and other public amenities. Organizations such as the Urban League were becoming increasingly vocal and insistent upon equal opportunity as well as instilling a sense of civic pride in the accomplishments of local African Americans.[18]

The epicenter of the African American community was located around 18th Street between Vine and The Paseo. Businesses of all types, from barber and shoe repair shops to doctors' and lawyers' offices were found in this neighborhood. This section of town was perhaps best known for its night life, with patrons packing clubs with colorful names such as the Cherry Blossom, the Chez Paree, Lucille's Paradise, and the Ol' Kentuck' Bar-B-Q.[19] Kansas City was a regular tour stop for many of the biggest names in blues and jazz from this period. Count Basie and his orchestra, Cab Calloway, Billie Holliday, and Louis Armstrong, among many others, could frequently be found playing the many venues in this district.[20]

And of course, there were the Monarchs, arguably the greatest team of the Negro League era and perhaps one of the finest clubs in baseball history. With perennially winning teams built around future Hall of Famers like Satchel Paige, Buck O'Neil, Cool Papa Bell, and Jackie Robinson, the Monarchs were consistently one of the top drawing teams in baseball (black or white) and nearly always in championship contention. Established shortly after the turn of the century as a barnstorming team, they had been a central element of the black community for years before the establishment of the Negro National League in 1920, and would go on to dominate that circuit for several years before playing as an independent club for a number of seasons and then becoming a charter member of the Negro American League in 1937.[21]

Besides fielding a consistently competitive team, playing in one of the newest and nicest ballparks in the Negro Leagues also helped attract fans. Muehlebach Field, which opened in 1923 and would go through a number of name changes before settling on Municipal Stadium in 1955, was shared by the Monarchs and the Kansas City Blues, the top minor league club in the Yankees farm system. Located on Brooklyn Avenue a few blocks off of 18th Street, the stadium straddled the dividing line between the black and white sections of town and attracted spectators from both. Being as the Monarchs were nearly always in contention for the pennant, Municipal Stadium would host several Negro League World Series, beginning with the first one in 1924. By the 1940s shifting demographics placed Municipal Stadium squarely in the African American area of town and would remain the home of the Monarchs for the rest of their tenure in Kansas City.[22]

The question becomes why, then, if social and economic conditions were improving exponentially in the African American community some ten years before what is nominally considered the beginning of the Civil Rights Era, were circumstances at the culmination of this period (and to an extent, today) practically unchanged, if not worse? The answer lies in how integration occurred, with white-owned businesses able to expand their market share at the expense of black-owned businesses, while at the same time cherry-picking the best-educated and most-qualified black workers and controlling the methods, timing, and public perception of desegregation.

ROLE OF BASEBALL AND BLACK BUSINESSES AS COMMUNITY TOUCHSTONE

One point that has been fairly well developed in the literature is the concept of baseball as community focus. While this model does not apply to African Americans exclusively, one of the most recurring points made in the various histories of the Negro Leagues in particular and black baseball generally was how these teams served a communal purpose. Baseball functioned as a critical component in the separate economy catering to black consumers in the urban centers of both the North and South. While most black businesses struggled to survive from year to year, professional baseball teams and leagues operated for decades, representing a major achievement in black enterprise and institution building.

Kansas City in this period was known not only for its ball club, but also as a hotbed of the jazz scene, and of course for its world famous barbeque. All of these elements merged in the Kansas City black community, centered in the inner-city area of 18th and Vine. According to Monarchs manager and first baseman Buck O'Neil, this was an exciting time and place to be a part of.

> [P]laying for the Monarchs in the late thirties and early forties, staying in the Streets Hotel at 18th and Paseo, and coming down to the dining room where Cab Calloway and Billie Holiday and Bojangles Robinson often ate. 'Course, some of them were having supper while we were having breakfast and vice-versa. 'Good morning, Count,' I'd say. 'Good evening, Buck,' Mr. Basie would say. As somebody once put it, 'People are afraid to go to sleep in Kansas City because they might miss something.'

> Nowadays that downtown neighborhood is kind of sleepy, though we have some plans to wake up the ghosts. But we could never bring it back to its glory days.[23]

While Kansas City may have been somewhat unusual in the variety of activities available and the prominence of its black celebrities, these themes can be found in urban black communities throughout the North during this period. As desegregation gained momentum throughout the postwar era, many black owned businesses were unable to effectively compete with white-owned firms who were now serving, and in some cases employing, African Americans. During the 1950s and 1960s, "White Flight" to the suburbs would continue to draw capital away from urban centers where black communities tended to congregate, leading to large-scale vacancy, plummeting property values, and blighted areas where crime became more frequent. As O'Neil notes, there have been many plans for urban renewal to help reinvigorate these areas. In the case of the 18th and Vine district in Kansas City, these efforts have been largely successful; however, other cities have met with more limited success.

In Jack Etkin's *Innings Ago: Recollections by Kansas City Ballplayers of their Days in the Game*, O'Neil discusses how black teams provided a community focus for groups of African Americans living outside of cities with Negro League teams and in rural areas with small black populations.[24] According to O'Neil, when a team such as the Kansas City Monarchs barnstormed through small towns in the South and Midwest, often the entire black population in the area would turn out, wearing their Sunday best. For these fans, the attraction was perhaps not so much the game itself, but rather the expression of African Americans being treated with something like equality (as in playing on equal terms against white teams) and often demonstrating their ability to compete successfully. For many, these exhibitions were a highlight of the yearly social calendar.[25]

Baseball was of course not the only type of business to serve as a communal focal point. Many businesses, most notably barber shops, beauty parlors, and, perhaps to a lesser extent, night clubs and restaurants also filled this role. The financial stability these businesses provided, in conjunction with a safe and separate space, led to business owners (and beauticians in particular) being leaders and activists in the black community with these shops being at the center, like a base of operations for these activities.[26] With increased competition from businesses outside the black community coupled with decapitalization of inner-city areas, the importance of African American owned and operated businesses as a unique space for organization and communal fellowship began to erode.

ECONOMIC IMPACT OF BLACK BASEBALL

By the early 1920s, with a booming economy generally, and a fast growing and racially aware black population in Northern and Midwestern urban centers, the stage was set for professional African American baseball leagues to successfully develop, and this was certainly the case in the Kansas City community. Between the 1920s and 1950s there would be ten professional black leagues, though the most successful were the Negro National League (NNL) which operated between 1920 and 1931 and then from 1933 through 1948 and the Negro American League (NAL) from 1937 to 1960.[27] It is hardly coincidental that successful organized black baseball began in this period. Black populations in Northern cities boomed during the 1910s with the Great Migration from the South and relatively plentiful job opportunities in defense industries during World War I. This was also the period of Garveyism, the Harlem Renaissance, and the first wave of Black Nationalism. This combination of expendable income, leisure time, and racial awareness all helped to make Negro League baseball popular within the African American community and for the first time profitable for its proprietors. Throughout the 1920s black teams continued to make money, and while paid substantially less than their white counterparts, African American players earned about twice the national median income.[28]

However, by the end of the decade black baseball was in steep decline. The reason for this reversal of fortunes was primarily economic. While national unemployment rates during the Great Depression would peak at about 25% and white baseball saw substantial decreases in attendance, the jobless rate among African Americans was considerably higher.[29] With deteriorating economic conditions, fans attended far fewer games, and teams and leagues began to fail. It was during this period that illegal money, particularly from gambling interests, began to be a major influence in the Negro Leagues. At least two teams were financed entirely by illegal gaming, though it is believed that several other teams may have also been involved.[30] What the true intentions of the gamblers were remains a source of debate. While it is undoubtable that some teams, such as the Newark Eagles owned by Abe and Effa Manly and Gus Greenlee's Pittsburgh Crawfords, served as fronts for laundering money, these owners also claimed to have had a genuine desire to keep their teams afloat and to continue to serve as a community focal point. There is some evidence to support these claims as these owners were well known within the black community and were frequent donors to charities and social causes.[31] Whatever the intent, it is unlikely that the Negro Leagues could have survived the Depression without this influx of capital. Also, the sources of capital and intentions of white owners of major and minor league teams were likely not always completely pure. Several teams were owned by beer barons, and there is much speculation that some of these teams were used as a means of washing monies.[32] While black owners were criticized (sometimes fairly) for being connected with illegal gaming and numbers-running, there were major league owners during the same period who actually owned casinos and horse tracks.[33]

This trend in black baseball was mirrored in African American owned businesses more broadly. In 1932, there were 103,872 black owned businesses in the United States. While most of these were small "mom and pop shops," there had also been growth during the 1920s in larger-scale operations such as insurance companies, publishing houses, and banks. However, even with diversification of business types owned by African Americans, these businesses continued to depend almost exclusively on black customers. With widespread unemployment during the Great Depression (made worse in the African American community due to prejudicial hiring practices), there was less disposable income for black customers to spend. Predictably, black-owned firms began to fail and by 1940 the number of black-owned businesses had declined by 16% to 87,475.[34]

The situation in Kansas City was different and unique in the league, as the Monarchs had a white owner, J.L. Wilkinson, who had long sponsored integrated (both by race and sex) barnstorming teams based out of Kansas City, became one of the charter owners of the Negro National League. While this was a source of conflict for some of the owners, including league founder Rube Foster, Wilkinson's reputation for fairness (plus the fact that he held the lease on the one suitable ballpark) persuaded the owners to accept him into the fold.[35]

After narrowly surviving the 1930s, the Negro Leagues were in resurgence during the first half of the 1940s. Nearly full employment due to the war effort once again gave many African Americans disposable income. For the first time in more than a decade, teams consistently made money, and attendance was at an all-time high. Some teams were assessed as being as valuable as major-league franchises.[36] As the postwar period of economic prosperity set in and all sectors of the population saw rising income levels and standards of living, indications were black businesses, including the Negro Leagues, were finally about to fulfill their potential. This was not to be.

Somewhat paradoxically, for many Negro League teams the years between 1947 and 1950 would be their most financially successful, but this was due almost exclusively to selling the contract rights of their players to white-owned teams in both the major and minor leagues.[37] Whereas the postwar period began very promising for the Negro Leagues with growing attendance, within just a few years most black fans had taken to following their favorite players in the major leagues, and ticket sales fell off precipitously. To complicate matters further, a number of white teams refused to honor the contracts of the Negro Leagues and pirated the players outright without compensating the team owners.[38] At other times owners sold the rights to players at below-market prices, finding it better to get some return rather than risk having the player signed outright. By 1948 only the NAL was still in operation, and it was relegated to minor league status. In 1960 there were only a few teams left and the league disbanded, though some clubs—like the Monarchs—continued to barnstorm. The Indianapolis Clowns were the last Negro League team in business and played their final game in 1988.[39]

WHITE FLIGHT, DECAPITALIZATION, AND THE AFRICAN AMERICAN COMMUNITY

Another important element during this period concerns the decapitalization of urban areas (and especially parts of cities where African Americans tended to congregate) and migration of white families to suburban communities from the late 1940s through the early 1960s. Again, Kansas City serves as a model, with several large industries leaving the center-city area in the 1950s and relocating to suburban areas where most white workers continued to be employed while laying off most of the black workforce. The change began in earnest in the early 1950s with the decline of the railroad industry, chiefly due to competition from automobile and air travel. Union Station, which had been the second busiest rail terminal in America after Chicago and employed large numbers of African Americans in various capacities, declined rapidly and fell into disrepair. Another blow to the economy came with the Great Flood of 1951 which destroyed much of the stockyards located in the West Bottoms section. The stockyards, which were also second nationally to Chicago in size, never fully recovered as the cattle industry moved away from urban centers. With both of these industries went many comparatively well-paid and often unionized jobs.

As in baseball, in many middle- and large-scale industries, black-owned firms were unable to compete with their white counterparts after racial integration. Many skilled black workers were lured away to work at better-paying and more prestigious white-owned businesses. This clearly happened in baseball, where the very best black and Latino players went to the major leagues, forcing the Negro Leagues to try to compete with less talented players.

This was again the case in Kansas City. In 1955 the Philadelphia Athletics moved into Municipal Stadium, where the Monarchs played, and though they were always near the bottom of the American League standings and moved on to Oakland after a number of seasons, this increased competition for entertainment dollars and use of public facilities forced the Monarchs out. In the mid-fifties the Monarchs were sold, and while they retained the name "Kansas City Monarchs," this was a device used as a draw at the gate. The team was headquartered out of Flint, Michigan, until it finally folded in the mid-sixties, only occasionally playing in Kansas City.[40]

"White flight" also affected baseball as new stadiums for almost every major-league team during the 1960s and 1970s were nearly always located away from inner-city areas whereas previous stadiums had been almost exclusively located in downtown areas. This would happen in Kansas City, where the aging Municipal Stadium was abandoned and the Truman Sports Complex—with stadiums for both the new Kansas City Royals and Kansas City Chiefs of the NFL—was built near the interstate many miles away from the city's downtown area and much closer to the predominately white suburbs.

ECONOMIC COSTS OF DESEGREGATION ON NEGRO LEAGUE BASEBALL

While the integration of professional baseball is often seen as a benchmark in the history of civil rights, this did not come without great cost—financial and otherwise—to black baseball and the African American community broadly. Again, this is in keeping with what happened in other large-scale black-owned businesses such as banks, newspapers, and insurance companies.[41] As events unfolded, the best black players were cherry-picked by major-league clubs, leaving the Negro Leagues to try to compete for fan dollars with fewer quality players and less cultural significance.

Of the 73 players who would jump from the Negro Leagues to the majors, eight would be inducted into the Hall of Fame. Between 1947 and 1959, former Negro Leaguers would supply six Rookies of the Year and nine Most Valuable Player winners.[42] Black baseball, like many other African American-owned businesses, now had to compete against white-owned businesses for black clientele and with less talent, capital, and cultural privilege than their white counterparts. The result would be the collapse of the Negro Leagues (and many other black-owned enterprises) which in conjunction

with White Flight left many urban areas much less economically viable and with fewer opportunities for capitalization. From the middle 1950s through the 1970s most major-league teams left their inner-city ballparks for new stadiums closer to the predominately white suburbs, which further removed black fans from the game.[43]

Making matters worse for the black-owned teams was the practice of pirating black players without compensating their former teams. Citing a lack of proper contracts (which is to say, contracts that had been approved for use in the white major and minor leagues), teams simply ignored the vested interests of black clubs and signed the many of the best players outright without any financial consideration of Negro League owners.[44] Denouncing black-owned businesses as being illegitimate and therefore ethical to deal with in an inequitable manner had long been a common practice among white business owners. This view was both obviously exploitative and paternalistic, harkening to the 19th-century stereotypes of black people being unsophisticated and childlike and their efforts being seen as cargo cult-like mimicry of whites rather than legitimate expressions of capitalism.

It is also important to remember that the failure of the Negro Leagues economically impacted many more people than the players on the field. An entire support staff of front-office personnel, groundskeepers, concessionaires, ticket-takers, bus drivers, and so forth were all necessary to put a game on the field. These workers in turn then patronized local businesses. When the teams began to struggle and finally collapsed, many people besides the players also lost their livelihoods. Similarly, as African Americans lost market share of industrial and manufacturing jobs, the service sector also suffered as their regular clientele had increasingly less disposable income. Coupled with increased competition with white-owned businesses, many black-owned urban enterprises began to go under.

ALTERNATIVE PATHS TO INTEGRATION

The manner in which integration in baseball—and in American businesses generally—occurred was not the only model which was possible. It was likely not even the best approach available, but rather served the needs of those in already privileged positions who were able to control not only the manner in which desegregation occurred, but the public perception of it as well in order to exploit the situation for financial gain. Indeed, the very word integration may not be the most applicable in this context because what actually transpired was not so much the fair and equitable combination of two subcultures into one equal and more homogenous group, but rather the reluctant allowance—under certain preconditions—for African Americans to be assimilated into white society.

Another negative aspect of the manner in which baseball was integrated was the unofficial, but common, practice of using racial quotas. Beginning with Rickey's Dodgers, most major league teams—with a few notable exceptions such as Bill Veeck's Cleveland Indians, who became a powerhouse behind several black stars—kept roster spots for African American players to a minimum. Black players were nearly always signed in even numbers, so that their white teammates would not have to share rooms with them on the road.[45] It was not at all unusual to see a black player traded or sent to the minors if there were "too many" black players on the squad.[46] Additionally, while black players often made more money than their white colleagues, this was mostly because almost every black player of the 1940s and 1950s was a star. Slots for journeymen and utility players were the exclusive territory of white players. The message was clear; produce more than the average white player, or leave.

After Jackie Robinson broke the color line, executives and owners from the Negro Leagues met with their counterparts from the major leagues and proposed a number of options for mergers and cooperation. At first it was suggested that the better clubs with large fan bases from the Negro Leagues, such as the Monarchs and Crawfords, be allowed in as expansion franchises.[47] Several of these teams operated in cities without major league teams to compete with, already had large followings and the logistical infrastructure in place, and were perfectly positioned to help the major leagues take advantage of post-war prosperity and newly expendable income. The proposal was unanimously voted down. When this was rejected, the possibility of the Negro Leagues becoming a AAA circuit was raised. This too was summarily dismissed.[48] White owners had no interest in cooperating with their black counterparts, and instead of engaging in a business enterprise which would have most likely proved beneficial for all parties, the major leagues made a deliberate choice to put the Negro Leagues out of business after obtaining their best players and wooing away much of their fan base.

SEPTEMBER 1965; 18TH & VINE, KANSAS CITY

Twenty years later the tone was considerably more pessimistic. The headlines of *The Call* still carried stories about violence and inequality within the black community, but gone was the sense of optimism or increasing opportunity. The lead story from the September 1965 issue (at this point, *The Call* had become a monthly rather than weekly publication) led with a story titled, "Vicious Attack on Farmer: Admits Cutting Man's Tongue Out," in which a young black man killed an elderly black farmer while attempting to keep him from being able to testify against him regarding a crime the older man had witnessed by removing his tongue.[49] Other headlines include, "Three Whites Arrested in Brewster Killing," "Slain Priest Buried in Home Town," "2,200 Still in Jail from L.A. Rioting," and "NAACP Official Injured in Bombing."[50] The paper also ran a two-page summary of a study analyzing the underlying causes of racial violence. The story, titled "New Study Tells Why Riots Occur," examined fifty years of data and concluded that riots occur when whites feel economically threatened and local authorities, particularly the police, are not adequately trained to properly handle the situation.[51] Clearly, racially related violence had by the middle 1960s become a pervasive issue, and other concerns seemed secondary. There are no mentions of scholarships being awarded, mass meetings for employment opportunities, or patriotic calls for donations and privation here.

The sports page is no less bleak. There is no mention of the hapless Kansas City Athletics who were stumbling to another disappointing finish. The only mention of baseball at all was an incident on August 22 when Juan Marichal of the San Francisco Giants beat L.A. Dodgers catcher Johnny Roseboro repeatedly in the head with a baseball bat, leading to a fine and suspension by the National League.[52] Even in baseball, violence seemed to permeate. There was also no mention of the Monarchs, long a source of civic pride, who probably played their last game about this time.[53]

A return visit to what had been the heart of the black community reiterates this theme. Whereas 20 years before, 18th Street was a vibrant center for art and commerce, it had by this time become little more than a ghost town with nearly all the buildings abandoned and left to deteriorate. The first blow came under the guise of reform, when a number of new "blue laws" made it increasingly difficult for the night clubs to operate profitably. Similarly to many other inner-city areas, urban renewal projects that were intended (at least in theory) to help revitalize the area had the exact opposite effect. In the middle 1950s five acres of historic buildings were razed in order to make room for new building projects. However, due to poor financing this area sat vacant for many years and became known as a dangerous place to walk through. With new public accommodation laws came increased competition with other businesses outside of the traditional black section of the city, and many African American owned shops—which generally had less access to capital, and prohibitive conditions attached when it could be found—were in most cases no longer able to operate profitably.[54] By 1964, only two large buildings anchored the area, with the *Kansas City Call* still operating in the same space since 1922 on the east end, and the Lincoln Building housing several professional offices to the west. The corridor between the two comprised a few bars and a handful of shops, with nearly all of the storefronts boarded up in disuse and disrepair.[55]

Municipal Stadium would continue to be used on and off by various teams and for different events until the early 1970s, but little effort or funding was put into maintaining the structure. The primary reason given for moving the Athletics to Oakland was Kansas City's lack of commitment to building a new ballpark.[56] According to owner Charles O. Finley, the neighborhood had become too dangerous for night games, and he blamed the aging and inadequate facility for low attendance numbers (though one might argue that the club being at the bottom of the standings for more than a dozen years contributed more to low turnout). The promise of a new publicly financed stadium helped secure Kansas City an expansion team, the Royals, in 1969 and Municipal Stadium was finally abandoned after the 1972 baseball season.[57] It sat unused and dilapidated until 1976 when it was demolished for being a danger to public safety.[58] Professional baseball had left Kansas City's African American community for the last time.

This seeming trend of negativism within the black community at this time would seem paradoxical, at least in the traditional framework of American history. The Voting Rights Act of 1965 had been signed into law on August 6 of that year, and the Civil Rights Act of 1964, outlawing discrimination based on race, sex, or religion and segregation of public accommodations, was barely a year old. Why then, at a time of such apparent progress, does the record suggest such unfavorable conditions for many in the African American community? One would argue that despite the legal gains made during this period, which were substantial and should not be dismissed, the larger issue was access to economic opportunities. Indeed, the evidence reveals that levels of education and income in the early 1960s were essentially unchanged since World War II.[59] These stagnant levels of earnings and upward are all the more telling being as this period witnessed some of the fastest and most widespread economic growth in American history. Increased competition, lack of capital,

and the withdrawal of industry from inner-city areas all contributed to a rather bleak social and economic prognosis that no legislation could mitigate and which is still with us today.[60]

CONCLUSION

In many ways the story of Negro League baseball in general and the Kansas City black community and ball club in particular provide an excellent example of the economic and social changes occurring in urban African American communities during the post-war era. While on the one hand the end (at least officially) of legal segregation and prejudicial hiring policies was clearly a victory for the cause of progress and many people have undoubtedly been able to succeed and have had opportunities that would not have otherwise been afforded them, it must be remembered that this came at a cost, and many of the long-term issues that have plagued inner-city areas are residual damage caused in large part by the manner in which integration occurred. The reality is that much of the African American community was largely unaffected economically by the successes of the Civil Rights Era. Black workers lacking higher education and job skills, mostly due to an inadequate and unequal education system, remained trapped in low-paying jobs and neighborhoods with increasingly few amenities.[61] While there was growth in this period among the black middle class, these new jobs were almost exclusively in white-owned firms. Large-scale black-owned businesses, unable to find new clients, sources of revenue, and at a competitive disadvantage for the patronage of their traditional customers, failed.

This is not to imply that segregation, economic or otherwise, was in any way beneficial to the African American community. The current face of American society would have been almost unimaginable at the beginning of the Civil Rights Movement. The fact remains, however, that in spite of discrimination and disadvantage, many black entrepreneurs were able to find a niche market and achieve financial success. In the end desegregation happened on what were essentially the terms of the white majority, which in many ways benefited economically from the new arrangement, rather than honest assimilation combining the best qualities of both communities and building a more just and equal society. ∎

Notes

1. Urban League of Kansas City. "The 'Northern City with a Southern Exposure,'" *Matter of Fact: Newsletter of the Urban League of Kansas City, Missouri.* Vol. I; No. 1, July, 1945, 1.

2. Robert H. Kinzer and Edward Sagrin, *The Negro in American Business: The Conflict Between Separatism and Integration* (New York: Greenburg, 1950), 100–1.

3. Thomas J. Sugrue, *Sweet Land of Liberty: The Forgotten Struggle for Civil Rights in the North* (New York: Random House, 2008), 177–79.

4. "All-Black Company Closes Suddenly," *Kansas City Call.* Vol. 27; No. 16, August 31, 1945, 1.

5. "Kansas City FEPC Office Closed," *Kansas City Call.* Vol. 27; No. 16, August 31, 1945, 1.

6. I subsequently did some research on the matter, but was unable to discover the outcome of the trial or what became of Seaman First Class Bobb.

7. "Local Girl Awarded Scholarship," *Kansas City Call.* Vol. 27; No. 16, August 31, 1945, 3.

8. Lucia Mallory, "Keep Buying War Bonds!" *Kansas City Call.* Vol. 27; No. 16, August 31, 1945, 4.

9. "FEPC to Hold Meeting," *The Kansas City Call.* Vol. 27; No. 16, August 31, 1945, 5.

10. Urban League of Kansas City. *Matter of Fact: Newsletter of the Urban League of Kansas City, Missouri.* July, 1945, 1.

11. Census Bureau. *1950 United States Census of Population Report; Kansas City, Missouri* (U.S. Govt. Printing Office; Washington, 1952), 17–19.

12. "Smith to Start Labor Day Double-Header," *Kansas City Call.* Vol. 27; No. 16, August 31, 1945, 9.

13. Statistics for Negro League players are notoriously difficult to find exact figures for. Baseball-Reference.com, usually considered to be authoritative, lists Robinson as having a .414 batting average in 63 games that season, though this is probably incomplete.

14. Frank Foster, *The Forgotten League: A History of the Negro League Baseball* (BookCaps; No city given, 2012), 55.

15. Urban League of Kansas City. "Local Survey Made," *Matter of Fact: Newsletter of the Urban League of Kansas City, Missouri.* Vol. I; No. 6, April–May, 1946, 2.

16. Urban League of Kansas City. "Clinic for Small Business Draws Much Interest," Matter of Fact: Newsletter of the Urban League of Kansas City, Missouri. Vol. I; No. 6, April 1946, 2–3.

17. Urban League of Kansas City. "'You Just Can't Find Good Help Anymore,'" *Matter of Fact: Newsletter of the Urban League of Kansas City, Missouri.* Vol. II; No. 1, August, 1946, 2.

18. Urban League of Kansas City. "It's a Matter-of-Fact that:" *Matter of Fact: Newsletter of the Urban League of Kansas City, Missouri.* Vol. 1; No. 1, July, 1945, 2.

19. Chuck Haddix, "18th & Vine: Street of Dreams," in *Artlog.* Missouri Arts Council. Vol. XIII; No. 1, January–February, 1992, 3.

20. Ibid, 4.

21. Janet Bruce, *The Kansas City Monarchs: Champions of Black Baseball* (University of Kansas Press; Lawrence, 1985), 117.

22. Ibid, 126.

23. Buck O'Neil, *I Was Right on Time: My Journey from the Negro Leagues to the Majors* (Simon & Schuster; New York, 1996), 75–76.

24. Jack Etkin, *Innings Ago: Recollections by Kansas City Ballplayers of their Days in the Game* (Walsworth Publishing; Marceline, MO, 1987), 18.

25. Ibid, 19.

26. Tiffany Gill, *Beauty Shop Politics: African American Women's Activism in the Beauty Industry* (University of Illinois Press; Chicago, 2010), 2.

27. Leslie Heaphy, *The Negro Leagues, 1869–1960* (McFarland & Co; Jefferson, North Carolina, 2003), 224.

28. Ruck, 101.

29. William Sundstrom, "Last Hired, First Fired? *Unemployment and Urban Black Workers during the Great Depression*" in The Journal of Economic History (Vol. 52, No. 2, June, 1992), 485.

30. Bob Luke, *The Most Famous Woman in Baseball: Effa Manley and the Negro Leagues* (Potomac Books; Dulles, Virginia, 2011), 11.

31. ibid, 45.

32. Peter Golenbock, *The Spirit of St. Louis: A History of the St. Louis Cardinals and Browns* (HarperCollins; New York, 2000), 352.

33. Bill Veeck, *Veeck—As in Wreck* (University of Chicago Press; Chicago, 1962), 246-247.

34. Michael Woodward, *Black Entrepreneurs in America: Stories of Struggle and Success* (Rutgers University Press; New Brunswick, NJ, 1997), 18.

35. O'Neil, 77–78.

36. Ruck, 78.

37. Janet Bruce, 118–19.

38. Veeck, 176.

39. Heaphy, 227.

40. Janet Bruce, *The Kansas City Monarchs: Champions of Black Baseball* (University of Kansas Press; Lawrence, 1985), 126.

41. Robert E Weems Jr., *Black Business in the Black Metropolis: The Chicago Mutual Assurance Company, 1925–1985.* (Indiana University Press; Indianapolis, 1996), xv.

42. Ruck, 104–105

43. Lanctot, 395–96.

44. Mitchell Nathanson, *A People's History of Baseball* (University of Illinois Press; Urbana, IL, 2012), 86–87.

45. Nathanson, 99.

46. Ibid, 103–104.

47. Ruck, 115

48. ibid, 116.

49. "Vicious Attack on Farmer: Admits Cutting Man's Tongue Out," *The Kansas City Call*, Vol. 46; No. 22, September 3, 1965, 1.

50. "NAACP Official Injured in Bombing," *The Kansas City Call*, Vol. 46; No. 22, September 3, 1965, 1.

51. "New Study Tells Why Riots Occur," *The Kansas City Call*, Vol. 46; No. 22, September 3, 1965, 1.

52. Bill James, *New Historical Baseball Abstract* (Simon & Schuster; New York, 2001), 253.

53. The exact date has proven impossible to track down after extensive research. By this point the team had been playing out of Flint, Michigan for several seasons, only keeping the name as a source of revenue. It is known that the team played most of the 1965 season and folded near the end of the year. September is a reasonable guess. It is also worth noting that the final game of one of the most storied franchises in the history of baseball may well be lost to us now. Just another example of how quickly and precipitously black baseball fell out of the public eye.

54. Woodward, 26.

55. Haddix, 5.

56. Herbert Michelson, *Charlie O: Charles Oscar Finley vs. the Baseball Establishment* (Bobbs-Merrill; New York, 1975), 125, 127–28.

57. Mark Stallard, *Legacy of Blue: 45 Years of Kansas City Royals History & Trivia* (Kaw Valley Books; Overland Park, KS, 2013), 6.

58. Lawrence Ritter, *Lost Ballparks: A Celebration of Baseball's Legendary Field* (Penguin; New York, 1994), 136.

59. United States Department of Labor. *Home, Education, and Unemployment in Neighborhoods; Kansas City, Missouri,* January, 1963.

60. Andrew Brimmer, "Small Business and Economic Development in the Negro Community," in *Black Americans and White Business.* Edwin Epstein and David Hampton, Ed, (Dickinson Publishing, Encino, CA., 1971).

61. Woodward, 30–31.

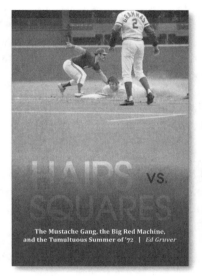
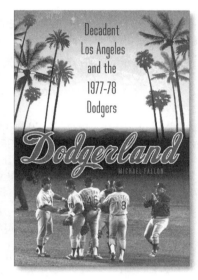
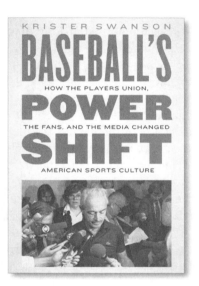

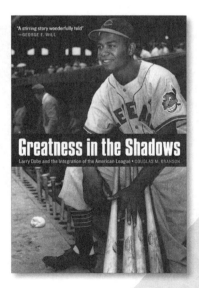

Hype and Hope

The Effect of Rookies and Top Prospects on MLB Attendance

Russell Ormiston

In the Spring 2014 edition of the *Baseball Research Journal*, I authored a study that examined within-season attendance patterns attributable to the homegrown status of the home team's starting pitcher (Ormiston, 2014a). While the analysis failed to find a relationship between homegrown pitchers and game attendance, a control variable in the model—the rookie status of the game's starting pitchers—had an unexpectedly positive and statistically significant effect on attendance. This outcome motivates the current study, as academic research has yet to directly examine the relationship between rookie players and game attendance in Major League Baseball.

The conspicuous absence of research on the attendance effects of rookies is surprising given the celebrated rookie seasons of Mark Fidrych (1976), Fernando Valenzuela (1981), and others who are known to have drawn huge crowds on the days of their starts. What is unclear, however, is whether fan responsiveness is limited to a select few rookie hurlers in history or whether it extends—albeit in a lesser degree—to other key rookies, prospects, and draft picks whose hype may precede them in the major leagues and whose presence may offer hope for a better future for their respective teams.

To address this question, this paper examines the relationship between rookie pitchers and individual game attendance in Major League Baseball between 1969–2013. In particular, this study explores the attendance effects of rookie hurlers' performance, pre-season prospect ranking, and draft pick status in an attempt to understand fan responsiveness to the sport's top up-and-coming players. Utilizing the largest known sample employed in the literature—data from 95,576 MLB games across 45 seasons—this paper offers the potential to detect minute but statistically significant attendance effects attributable to fan responsiveness to the future promise offered by an organization's top prospects and rookie hurlers.

BACKGROUND

While the academic literature on the determinants of MLB game attendance has yet to feature a study specifically examining fan responsiveness to the sport's top rookies and prospects, it is relatively straight-forward to deduce from the existing research that celebrated young starting pitchers may have a sizeable effect on the number of tickets sold. First, many analyses in the literature have implicitly demonstrated that starting pitcher characteristics impact game attendance, as such studies have routinely included control variables for pitchers' performance—often measured by wins and losses—and race/ethnicity (e.g., Hill, Madura and Zuber, 1982; Bruggnik and Eaton, 1996; Raschner, 1999; McDonald and Raschner, 2000; Butler, 2002). While such studies are inconsistent in regard to which variables have statistically significant effects on attendance, there is enough evidence to acknowledge the role that starting pitcher characteristics have on MLB game attendance.

While the studies mentioned above did not particularly focus on the relationship between starting pitcher characteristics and game attendance, this association represented the fundamental question underlying Ormiston (2014b). Developing a pair of metrics to estimate pitchers' star power, this study directly examined the relationship between game attendance and the star power and performance of each team's starting hurlers. The results demonstrated a positive relationship between the star power of both the home and visiting team's starting pitchers and game attendance, an effect that was statistically significant with 99.9 percent confidence. The results also indicated a strong and positive association between attendance and current performance—as measured by Wins Above Replacement (WAR)—of the home team's starting pitcher.

While Ormiston (2014b) demonstrated that a game's starting pitchers can have a considerable effect on game attendance, research exploring fan responsiveness to rookies and prospects has been limited. Outside of the inclusion of a control variable for rookies in Ormiston (2014a), the only known study to focus on this issue—Gittar and Rhoads (2011)—examined whether having one of baseball's top 100 prospects increased minor league teams' season-average attendance. Hypothesizing that local fans would be interested in seeing baseball's next generation of stars before they reached the majors, the study used *Baseball America* prospect rankings and minor-league seasonal attendance data from 1992–2009. The results suggested only a modest attendance effect, as only baseball's elite prospects (top five overall) had any statistically significant effect and that was limited to the triple-A level.

While Gittar and Rhoads (2011) found only a minimal effect of prospects on minor-league attendance, there are reasons to believe that the attendance effects may be stronger at the MLB level. First, due to stipulations in the MLB collective bargaining agreement, elite prospects that burst onto the scene are contractually bound to their respective major league teams for, at minimum, six years. Celebrated prospects, therefore, can offer a fan base considerable hope of a brighter future. In contrast, top-end prospects rarely stay with a particular minor-league team for more than one season before getting promoted to a new level and, thus, cannot offer fans that same potential.[1] Second, the hype surrounding baseball's elite prospects typically reaches its apex when a player is called up to the major leagues, implying that the attendance effect may be largest during a player's first few appearances with his MLB club.

DATA AND MODEL

To examine the potential attendance effects of the rookie and prospect status of both teams' starting pitchers in Major League Baseball, this study utilizes game log data available at Retrosheet.[2] These game logs provide a substantial amount of information on every MLB contest since 1876, including the game's date, location and, starting in 1914, the names of both starting pitchers. This paper focuses on baseball's Divisional Era from 1969–2013, including nearly every game from this period, excluding only those played at a stadium other than a team's normal park in a given season and games in which attendance is not available.[3] This results in an initial sample of 97,572 games, one of the largest data sets employed in the literature to date.

The empirical model employed in this study represents a variation on the approach utilized by Ormiston (2014a, 2014b) and summarized below, with i and t denoting the home team and season, respectively, and g representing the particular game within a particular it home team's season:

$$\ln(\text{Attendance}_{itg}) = \alpha_{it} + \beta_1 \text{PitcherCharacteristics}_{itg} +$$
$$\beta_2 \text{GameCharacteristics}_{itg} +$$
$$\beta_3 \text{GameCompetitiveness}_{itg} + \beta_4 \text{OpponentCharacteristics}_{itg} + \varepsilon_{itg}$$

One of the critical elements to this model is that it utilizes a team-season fixed effects approach, as it includes an indicator variable (α_{it}) to denote each home team's season (e.g., an indicator variable that represents all 81 home games of the 1987 Detroit Tigers). These team-season indicator variables are used to capture all game-invariant characteristics of an individual team's season, including ticket prices, prior years' success and the home city's population and economic vitality. The resulting coefficients in the model, therefore, represent the attendance fluctuations within a particular team-season attributable to available game-variant characteristics.[4,5]

The variables of central importance to this study reside in the PitcherCharacteristics$_{itg}$ vector. In an initial model, this study includes an indicator variable capturing the rookie status of the home and visiting teams' starting pitchers to estimate the average impact of a rookie hurler on attendance.[6] Subsequent models include additional variables designed to examine the moderating attendance effects of the hype and hope generated by a pitcher's pre-season prospect ranking, draft pick status and rookie-season performance. To evaluate a rookie hurler's prospect status, this paper employs the pre-season rankings of *Baseball America*, a leading industry publication, which has produced lists of baseball's overall top 100 prospects (1990–2013) and each MLB team's top 10 prospects (1983–2013) for a significant portion of the time period studied.[7] In addition to prospect rankings, this paper additionally identifies the 13 pitchers who were the number one overall pick—and thus hyped and celebrated in the media—in baseball's annual amateur draft and started at least one MLB game between 1969–2013.[8] Finally, attendance effects driven by pitcher performance—not just rookies—are captured through the use of a hurler's current-season wins above replacement (WAR) total. While using current-season WAR introduces endogeneity into the model, other approaches (e.g., prior season's WAR) underrepresent rookie performance at the time of each start and produce considerable upward bias in the rookie coefficients.

In addition to performance, this study also controls for all starting pitchers' star power at the time of each start as estimated by the age-adjusted star power measure originally introduced by Ormiston (2014a). This value represents a ratio of the linear sum of a pitcher's accomplishments—All-Star Game appearances, no-hitters, post-season awards, etc.—at the time of each start to their "potential experience," or the difference between the pitcher's age and 17.[9,10] While this metric has its flaws—with implications to be discussed later in the paper—it is the best available, objective estimate of star power given that it produces a parabolic arc of stardom for typical pitchers and meets a priori expectations of relative star power across players.[11]

Beyond pitcher characteristics, the specification of the attendance model above is designed to capture all available game-variant information within a particular team-season. First, $GameCharacteristics_{itg}$ includes the month, day of the week, time of the day, and three indicator variables denoting whether a contest was a team's home opener, a doubleheader or at a new stadium that was introduced mid-season. The $GameCompetitiveness_{itg}$ vector encompasses the number of games the home team is over .500 at the time of the game, the difference between the number of games over .500 of the home and visiting club (to measure game uncertainty), the number of games back within the division both clubs are at game time and the average star power of other pitchers in the series. Finally, the $OpponentCharacteristics_{itg}$ vector includes a series of indicator variables to denote an interleague game, an intradivision contest and whether the opposing team was World Series champion or in the playoffs over the last three seasons. This vector also features individual team dummies for each opponent given that some visiting teams (e.g., New York Yankees, Chicago Cubs) will boost attendance regardless of their level of competitiveness.

To estimate this model, censored normal fixed effects regression is utilized in order to account for right-censored attendance data attributable to sellouts, an approach utilized in Meehan, et al. (2007), Lemke, et al. (2010) and Ormiston (2014a, 2014b). In the absence of a published list of MLB sellouts and the fact that the announced attendance at most known sellouts—such as during the streaks of the Cleveland Indians (1995–2001) and Boston Red Sox (2003–13)—does not come close to stadium capacity, this study identifies sellouts by whether game attendance represents 90 percent of capacity. While this likely leads to erroneously labeling some games as sellouts, alternative approaches—such as 95 percent—fail to adequately identify a significant number of known sellouts. The use of the 90 percent threshold results in 25 team-seasons in which the home team is considered to have sold out every game. Since the censored-normal regression approach considers all observations from these team-seasons to be right-censored data, these team-seasons are excluded from the analysis, resulting in an amended sample size of 95,576 games.

RESULTS

Before presenting the regression estimates of the attendance model, Table 1 compares the average attendance in games started by rookies and non-rookies from 1969–2013. On the basis of home team's starting pitcher, average attendance in games started by rookies (24,054) was considerably less than games started by non-rookies (25,718); attendance was also slightly lower in games started by rookie pitchers by the visiting team. While the results of Table 1 may provide initial evidence against a rookie attendance premium in Major League Baseball, a summary approach ignores fundamental differences among rookie pitchers and, perhaps most importantly, the teams that more often employ them.[12]

Table 1. Average Game Attendance by Starting Pitchers' Rookie Status, 1969–2013

	Games Avg.	Attendance
Home Team Starting Pitcher		
Rookie	14,440 (15.1%)	24,054.05
Non-Rookie	81,136 (84.9%)	25,718.19
T-test		14.64***
Visiting Team Starting Pitcher		
Rookie	14,246 (14.9%)	25,254.68
Non-Rookie	81,330 (85.1%)	25,503.91
T-test		2.18**
Total	**95,576**	**25,466.76**

NOTE: Excludes team-seasons in which games are sold out. Statistical significance as follows: *** - p<0.01, ** - p<0.05, * - p<0.10.

As an illustration of the potential attendance impact of rookie pitchers in Major League Baseball, Table 2 presents the average home attendance in team-seasons featuring perhaps the six most celebrated rookie pitchers in the Divisional Era: the half-dozen hurlers who were named All-Stars and won the Rookie of the Year award in the same season. On the surface, the results demonstrate that five of these six hurlers had a considerable impact on game attendance in their rookie campaigns. For example, attendance at Detroit Tigers' home games in 1976—excluding the home opener—was 33,649 in the 18 games started by Mark Fidrych and just 15,147 in games started by other pitchers, amounting to a 122.2 percent increase in attendance to watch the charismatic right-hander. Attendance at the home starts of four other pitchers—Fernando Valenzuela (1981), Dwight Gooden (1984), Hideo Nomo (1995), and Dontrelle Willis (2003)—also exhibited double-digit percent increases when compared to other hurlers on their respective clubs. While the rookie starts of Jose Fernandez (2013) seemed to have little

NATIONAL BASEBALL HALL OF FAME LIBRARY, COOPERSTOWN, NY

Mark Fidrych

27-year-old hurler being named to an all-star team—is associated with a 1.1 percent increase in attendance. Finally, the results reflect a positive and statistically significant relationship between game attendance and the current performance of the home team's starting pitcher, with one additional unit of WAR associated with a 0.40 percent increase in tickets sold.

While the focus of this paper is on the attendance effect of rookie starting pitchers, it is important to note that the remaining coefficients in Model 1 of Table 3 are all of the expected signs, exhibit reasonable magnitude and most are statistically significant, an unsurprising outcome given the large sample utilized in this study. Predictably, the success of the home team—as measured by games over .500 and games back in the division—has a powerful influence on game attendance; for example, each game over .500 for the home team is expected to increase attendance by 1.2 percent. The coefficient on the difference in games over .500 between the home and visiting team is negative and statistically significant; this suggests that games featuring a relative mismatch will likely draw fewer fans compared to a closely-matched contest. The results of Model 1 also demonstrate that fans respond favorably to interleague play, intradivision games, home openers, doubleheaders, recent success by the visiting club, and situations where other star pitchers are starting in a series (perhaps denoting an important series or a star-laden visiting club overall). The coefficients on the visiting team dummy variables are suppressed for space reasons, but the results predictably indicate the highest attendance when the New York Yankees, Los Angeles Dodgers, Chicago Cubs or Boston Red Sox are the visiting team. Finally, attendance is estimated to follow expected patterns by month—peaking from June-August—and by day/time of the game (weekends produce the highest attendance). In sum, the reasonableness of the results match a priori expectations of Major League Baseball attendance and, thus, lend credibility to the methodology used to estimate the attendance effects of rookie starting pitchers.

impact on attendance, an overview of Table 2 implicates a potential relationship between game attendance and select rookie hurlers.

To more carefully examine the impact of rookie starting pitchers on game attendance in Major League Baseball from 1969–2013, Table 3 presents the censored-normal regression estimates of the model described above. Model 1 demonstrates that, all else equal, a rookie starting pitcher for the home team is expected to increase game attendance by 0.83 percent—about 208 fans given an average crowd of 25,000—with the effect statistically significant with at least 95 percent confidence. A rookie starting pitcher for the visiting team is posited to have little, if any, effect on game attendance, as the coefficient is minimal ($\beta = -0.0028$) and is not statistically significant at any reasonable level. Consistent with prior studies, the results of Model 1 also demonstrate that the star power of both teams' starting pitchers significantly affect game attendance, with the coefficients suggesting that an additional 0.1 in star power—equivalent to a

Table 2. Average Home Attendance, Team Seasons with All-Star Pitchers who won Rookie of the Year, Excluding Home Openers, 1969–2013

Year	Team	Rookie	Rookie Pitcher Games	Rookie Pitcher Avg. Att.	Other Pitchers Games	Other Pitchers Avg. Att.	% Change
1976	Detroit	Mark Fidrych	18	33,649	61	15,147	122.2
1981	Los Angeles (NL)	Fernando Valenzuela	11	48,241	44	40,941	17.8
1984	New York (NL)	Dwight Gooden	16	28,659	64	23,585	21.5
1995	Los Angeles (NL)	Hideo Nomo	14	42,858	57	37,113	15.5
2003	Florida	Dontrelle Willis	15	21,643	65	14,625	48.0
2013	Miami	Jose Fernandez	15	19,329	65	19,415	-0.4

Table 3. The Effect of Rookie Starting Pitchers on ln(Game Attendance), 1969–2013

	MODEL 1	MODEL 2	MODEL 3
Home Team Starting Pitcher			
Rookie	0.0083**	0.0062	
	2.02	1.58	
Rookie: All-Star & ROY		0.2910**	0.2973**
		2.20	2.24
Rookie: WAR > 5			0.0724**
			2.48
Rookie: 3 < WAR < 5			-0.0084
			0.74
Rookie: 1 < WAR < 3			0.0083
			1.29
Rookie: WAR < 1			0.0060
			1.17
Age-Adjusted Star Power	0.1076***	0.1060***	0.1060***
	7.57	7.48	7.45
Wins Above Replacement	0.0040***	0.0037***	0.0037***
	5.01	4.99	4.76
Visiting Team Starting Pitcher			
Rookie	-0.0028	-0.0040	
	-0.74	-1.07	
Rookie: All-Star & ROY		0.1827***	0.1797***
		-3.02	2.98
Rookie: WAR > 5			0.0514*
			1.76
Rookie: 3 < WAR < 5			0.0089
			0.78
Rookie: 1 < WAR < 3			-0.0102
			1.56
Rookie: WAR < 1			-0.0046
			1.01
Age-Adjusted Star Power	0.1051***	0.1048***	0.1056***
	-9.65	-9.62	9.74
Wins Above Replacement	0.0002	0.0001	-0.0001
	-0.36	-0.13	-0.15
Game Competitiveness			
Home Team: Games Back in Division	-0.0050***	-0.0050***	-0.0050***
	4.63	4.63	4.63
Visiting Team: Games Back in Division	-0.0008	-0.0008	-0.0008
	1.42	1.42	1.41
Home Team: Games Over .500	0.0118***	0.0118***	0.0118***
	17.91	17.9	17.92
Difference: Home Team Games Over .500 Minus Visiting Team Games Over .500	-0.0038***	-0.0038***	-0.0038***
	12.06	12.06	12.07
Opponent Characteristics			
Interleague Game	0.1103***	0.1103***	0.1103***
	13.14	13.14	13.14
Intradivision Game	0.0283***	0.0283***	0.0283
	7.81	7.81	7.81
World Series Champions, Last Season	0.0770***	0.0771***	0.0772***
	6.74	6.75	6.76
World Series Champions, Two Seasons Ago	0.0475***	0.0476***	0.0475***
	4.33	4.34	4.33
World Series Champions, Three Seasons Ago	0.0312***	0.0316***	0.0312***
	2.84	2.88	2.85
Playoffs, Last Season	0.0487***	0.0488***	0.0488***
	10.07	10.11	10.09

	MODEL 1	MODEL 2	MODEL 3
Playoffs, Two Seasons Ago	0.0287***	0.0289***	0.0289***
	6.05	6.09	6.100
Playoffs, Three Seasons Ago	0.0203***	0.0202***	0.0203***
	4.08	4.06	4.09
Game Characteristics			
Home Opener	1.0698***	1.0670***	1.0702***
	55.34	55.30	55.34
Doubleheader	0.3331****	0.3333***	0.3333***
	26.08	26.13	26.14
New Stadium, Midseason	0.6872***	0.6872***	0.6879***
	5.22	5.22	5.19
Month: March/April	-0.0913***	-0.0917***	-0.0919***
	6.00	6.03	6.04
Month: May	0.0548***	0.0544***	0.0543***
	4.20	4.17	4.16
Month: June	0.2232***	0.2227***	0.2226***
	18.78	18.76	18.75
Month: July	0.3291***	0.3289***	0.3288***
	31.02	31.02	31.02
Month: August	0.2750***	0.2749***	0.2748***
	31.88	31.87	31.87
Month: September/October	Base	Base	Base
Day and Time: Monday, Day	0.2373***	0.2352***	0.2352***
	7.45	7.34	7.34
Day and Time: Monday, Night	-0.0327***	-0.0336***	-0.0338***
	2.84	2.90	2.91
Day and Time: Tuesday, Day	0.0711	0.0777	0.0771
	1.25	1.35	1.34
Day and Time: Tuesday, Night	0.0119	0.0125	0.0125
	1.14	1.19	1.18
Day and Time: Wednesday, Day	0.0362*	0.0356*	0.0356*
	1.88	1.85	1.85
Day and Time: Wednesday, Night	Base	Base	Base
Day and Time: Thursday, Day	0.0802***	0.0799***	0.0800***
	4.08	4.09	4.09
Day and Time: Thursday, Night	0.0222	0.0211	0.0212
	1.55	1.46	1.46
Day and Time: Friday, Day	0.1301***	0.1291***	0.1290***
	2.90	2.88	2.88
Day and Time: Friday, Night	0.2495***	0.2486***	0.2485***
	11.40	11.33	11.32
Day and Time: Saturday, Day	0.3792***	0.3777***	0.3776***
	14.70	14.50	14.52
Day and Time: Saturday, Night	0.4404***	0.4394***	0.4396***
	17.02	16.88	16.91
Day and Time: Sunday, Day	0.2795***	0.2794***	0.2796***
	15.40	15.39	15.38
Day and Time: Sunday, Night	0.1827***	0.1825***	0.1821***
	5.01	5.00	4.99
Star Power, Other Home SP in Series	0.0611**	0.0612**	0.0614**
	2.57	2.57	2.58
Star Power, Other Visiting SP in Series	0.0706***	0.0714***	0.0717***
	4.31	4.36	4.38
Visiting Team Dummy Variables	Yes	Yes	Yes
Observations	95,576	95,576	95,576
Right-Censored Observations	11,908	11,908	11,908
Pseudo R-squared	0.5561	0.5564	0.5564

NOTE: Results are presented with the coefficient on first line and the absolute value of t-statistic on the second line. Standard errors clustered on team-season. Significance: * - $p<0.10$, ** - $p<0.05$, *** - $p<0.01$.

Returning to the primary question of this study, the results of Model 1 indicate a positive and statistically significant relationship between game attendance and rookie starting pitchers for the home team. However, there is concern that this overall impact is largely driven by the "manias" that surrounded many of the six celebrated hurlers identified in Table 2. To test these distributional concerns, Model 2 includes an indicator variable capturing the rookie-season starts of these six pitchers. The results of Model 2 confirm that these celebrated hurlers had a considerable impact on game attendance during their rookie seasons, with their starts increasing home and road attendance by 33.9 ($\beta = 0.2910$) and 20.1 ($\beta = 0.1827$) percent, respectively, over the standard rookie premium, with both effects being statistically significant with at least 95 percent confidence.[13] Perhaps more importantly, the coefficient on the rookie status of the home team's starting pitcher declines in magnitude and is no longer statistically significant at any reasonable level, thereby confirming that the significant relationship found in Model 1 was largely driven by a celebrated few rookie hurlers.

Given the implication that fan responsiveness to rookie starting pitchers is limited to only a select few hurlers, Model 3 expands the analysis by separating all other rookie pitchers—besides the six previously identified—into one of four categories based on their rookie-season wins above replacement value. The results demonstrate a positive and statistically significant attendance premium exists for rookie pitchers—both at home and on the road—beyond the six celebrated rookie hurlers discussed earlier, but the effect is limited only to the starts of rookie pitchers who posted a WAR of 5.0 or larger in their rookie season. Beyond this select group, however, the results fail to demonstrate any significant relationship between rookie pitchers and game attendance.

The pattern demonstrated in Table 3 suggests that fan responsiveness is limited to rookie starting pitchers who display a particular caliber of excellence with their on-field performance. While this effect may be indicative of fans reacting to the hope generated by an exceptional rookie pitcher, responsiveness to on-field performance ignores the potential influence of hype that often accompanies top prospects as they ascend through an organization's farm system and make their initial appearances with the home club. To those ends, Table 4 presents the results of a re-estimated attendance model substituting rookie performance variables with those denoting a first-year pitcher's draft status and pre-season prospect ranking. Given collinearity concerns attributable to the limited number of pitchers

in some categories, a rookie pitcher's amateur draft status, team prospect ranking and overall prospect ranking are all tested separately across the three different time periods within which data are available.

Within Table 4, Models 1 and 2 examine fan responsiveness to starts made by former No. 1 overall draft picks in their rookie seasons between 1969–2013. The results indicate a positive attendance effect when the home team is starting a former top amateur draft pick; while the effect is only statistically significant with 90 percent confidence, the estimates indicate an expected attendance increase of 13.0 ($\beta = 12.25$) percentage points over the typical rookie premium. However, when compared to the base results in Model 1, the identification of former No. 1 draft picks in the model reduces the magnitude and statistical significance of the rookie coefficient similar to the effects demonstrated in Table 3. In contrast, former No. 1 picks have no statistically significant attendance effect when starting games on the road.

To examine the potential attendance effects of pre-season prospect rankings during a pitcher's rookie season, Models 3 and 4 utilize *Baseball America*'s organizational prospect rankings. Given that such rankings have been published annually since 1983, Model 3 re-estimates the basic model since that time. The results indicate a deterioration in the magnitude and statistical significance of the rookie premium. This, by itself, is not surprising given that recent studies have demonstrated that fan responsiveness to many game-specific characteristics have declined precipitously over time (Beckman et al., 2011; Ormiston, 2014b). Nevertheless, the results of Model 4—which includes an indicator variable denoting that a rookie starting pitcher was the organization's top pre-season prospect—fail to find any relationship between prospect ranking and game attendance; while the coefficient is negative for such pitchers in both home and road starts, the magnitude is miniscule and the effect is not statistically significant at any reasonable level.

While the results of Model 4 fail to demonstrate a statistical relationship between a pitcher's prospect ranking and game attendance, this could be attributable to the fact that the caliber of an organization's top prospect can vary wildly across teams depending on the strength of the clubs' respective farm systems. Therefore, to estimate the attendance effect attributable to baseball's most highly-regarded prospects—regardless of team ranking—Models 5 and 6 re-estimate the attendance model for games between 1990–2013, during which time *Baseball America* published annual pre-season top 100 prospect rankings within the sport.

Table 4. The Effect of Starting Pitcher Prospect Status on Game Attendance, 1969–2013

	1969–2013		1983–2013		1990–2013	
	MODEL 1	**MODEL 2**	**MODEL 3**	**MODEL 4**	**MODEL 5**	**MODEL 6**
Home Team Starting Pitcher						
Rookie	0.0083**	0.0071*	0.0053	0.0058	0.0052	0.0040
	2.02	1.73	1.39	1.43	1.29	0.91
No. 1 Overall Draft Pick		0.1225*				
		1.65				
Team Top Prospect				0.0046		
				0.43		
Prospect Rank: Nos. 1–10						0.0120
						0.70
Prospect Rank: Nos. 11–25						0.0087
						0.58
Prospect Rank: Nos. 26–50						0.0073
						0.52
Prospect Rank: Nos. 51–100						-0.0040
						0.37
Age-Adjusted Star Power	0.1077***	0.1075***	0.0787***	0.0788***	0.0628***	0.0629***
	7.57	7.58	5.52	5.53	3.78	3.79
Wins Above Replacement	0.0040***	0.0040***	0.0036***	0.0036***	0.0036***	0.0036***
	5.01	5.02	5.34	5.36	4.85	4.79
Visiting Team Starting Pitcher						
Rookie	-0.0028	-0.0029	-0.0028	-0.0021	-0.0007	-0.0024
	0.74	0.77	0.72	0.51	0.18	0.53
No. 1 Overall Draft Pick		0.0158				
		0.43				
Team Top Prospect				-0.0061		
				0.59		
Prospect Rank: Nos. 1–10						0.0144
						0.91
Prospect Rank: Nos. 11–25						0.0100
						0.69
Prospect Rank: Nos. 26–50						0.0014
						0.10
Prospect Rank: Nos. 51–100						0.0020
						0.18
Age-Adjusted Star Power	0.1051***	0.1048***	0.0937***	0.0936***	0.0801***	0.0803***
	9.65	9.63	8.19	8.20	6.67	6.68
Wins Above Replacement	0.0002	0.0002	0.0007	0.0007	0.0007	0.0006
	0.36	0.37	1.06	1.08	0.94	0.88
Observations	95,576	95,576	68,256	68,256	53,512	53,512
Pseudo R-squared	0.5561	0.5561	0.6295	0.6295	0.6944	0.6944

NOTE: Results are presented with the coefficient on first line and the absolute value of t-statistic on the second line. Coefficients on control variables have been suppressed. Standard errors clustered on team-season. Significance: * - $p<0.10$, ** - $p<0.05$, *** - $p<0.01$.

Separating these rankings into four categories, the results fail to uncover any statistically significant relationship between the overall prospect ranking of either team's starting pitcher and game attendance.

The results of Table 4 may offer initial evidence that fans are unresponsive to the hype associated with a pitcher's prospect ranking, however this analysis has examined the attendance effect of this ranking on all of a pitcher's rookie-season starts. If an attendance effect of "hype" exists, it should theoretically be most prevalent in a prospect's Major League debut, or the point at which a player's performance is most uncertain—and thus susceptible to hyperbole—to a team's general fan base. As the player demonstrates his level of ability in an MLB uniform, that uncertainty dissipates and fan responsiveness may be limited to the performance-based effects presented in Table 3.

To address this question, the effects of amateur draft status and prospect ranking on game attendance during a rookie's Major League debut are presented in Table 5. The results of Model 1 indicate that the debut of a former No. 1 overall draft pick is expected to increase attendance by 47.8 percent ($\beta = 0.3910$), however this effect falls outside a 90-percent two-sided statistical significance test. Further, the estimated effect is particularly sensitive to each particular debut given that only six No. 1 draft picks made their debut as starting pitchers in their home park; of particular importance, removing the debut of David Clyde in 1973 reduces the estimated coefficient by more than two-thirds. This sensitivity is even more prevalent when looking at the attendance effects of No. 1 draft picks on the road. While the results suggest a negative and statistically significant effect, there was only one former No. 1 pick who debuted in a road start (Mike Moore) during the second game of a doubleheader in Oakland on April 11, 1982. While game attendance was quite small for a Sunday doubleheader, it is likely that this was attributable to omitted variable bias—it was Easter Sunday—rather than fan avoidance of the debut of a former No. 1 draft pick.

While there are not enough observations to draw significant conclusions in Model 1, this is not as much of a concern in Model 2 as there were 40-plus debuts by a team's top prospect both at home and on the road between 1983–2013. The results suggest that the debut of a home team's top prospect as a starting pitcher increases game attendance by 7.2 percent ($\beta = 0.694$), however this effect falls outside the bounds of a 90-percent, two-sided statistical significance test. Unsurprisingly, the debut of a team's top prospect on the road had no effect on game attendance.

As discussed earlier, the lack of a statistically significant effect in Model 2 may be due to the variable caliber of teams' top prospect. Using *Baseball America*'s top 100 prospect lists to isolate the sport's most highly-regarded prospects between 1990–2013, the results of Model 3 demonstrate that the Major League debut of a top 10 starting pitching prospect is expected to increase attendance by 13.8 percent ($\beta = 0.1289$), an effect that is statistically significant at a 90 percent confidence level. While this result—found across 17 pitchers—suggests that fans are responsive, on some level, to the hype of baseball's most exceptional prospects, these results fail to indicate that this responsiveness extends beyond the sport's top 10 prospects or to debuts made by a visiting team's top prospect.

DISCUSSION

Despite volumes of academic research on the determinants of sports attendance, research on fan responsiveness to the promise offered by emerging young players has been conspicuously incomplete. This paper has attempted to address this question by examining within-season fluctuations in game attendance in Major League Baseball from 1969–2013 attributable to rookie starting pitchers. The results demonstrate some fan responsiveness to rookie hurlers, however such effects are limited to exceptional cases, namely the era's most elite rookie performers and the Major League debuts of the sport's top 10 prospects. Other rookie pitchers—regardless of caliber—exert little influence on game attendance.

While the results of this paper may be initially underwhelming, the analyses offer potentially powerful insight into the psyche of professional sports fans. As demonstrated in this paper—and discussed more thoroughly in Ormiston (2014b)—the current performance and star power of the home team's starting pitcher can have a substantial effect on game attendance. In comparison, fan responsiveness to the future promise offered by most highly-regarded prospects and rookie pitchers is minimal. While this result may be partially attributable to fan inattentiveness to the home team's farm system, the difference in magnitude between these effects provides a clear—if unsurprising—demonstration of fans' time preferences when deciding to attend

Fernando Valenzuela

Table 5. The Effect of Starting Pitchers MLB Debut on Game Attendance, 1969–2013

Home Team Starting Pitcher	MODEL 1 1969–2013	MODEL 2 1983–2013	MODEL 3 1990–2013
Rookie	0.0081** 1.98	0.0051 1.33	0.0044 1.11
Debut, No. 1 Overall Draft Pick	0.3910 1.37		
Debut, Team Top Prospect		0.0694 1.42	
Debut, Prospect Rank: No. 1–10			0.1289* 1.74
Debut, Prospect Rank: Nos. 11–25			0.0024 0.04
Debut, Prospect Rank: Nos. 26–50			0.0410 0.69
Debut, Prospect Rank: Nos. 51–100			0.0480 1.27
Age-Adjusted Star Power	0.1075*** 7.57	0.0787*** 5.53	0.0629*** 3.79
Wins Above Replacement	0.0040*** 5.01	0.0036*** 5.33	0.0036*** 4.84
Visiting Team Starting Pitcher			
Rookie	-0.0028 0.75	-0.0026 0.67	-0.0008 0.20
Debut, No. 1 Overall Draft Pick	-0.2018*** 11.54		
Debut, Team Top Prospect		-0.0466 0.76	
Debut, Prospect Rank: No. 1–10			0.0690 0.76
Debut, Prospect Rank: Nos. 11–25			0.0131 0.28
Debut, Prospect Rank: Nos. 26–50			0.0160 0.36
Debut, Prospect Rank: Nos. 51–100			-0.0358 0.72
Age-Adjusted Star Power	0.1050*** 9.64	0.0936*** 8.19	0.0801*** 6.66
Wins Above Replacement	0.0003 0.38	0.0007 1.06	0.0007 0.95
Observations	95,576	68,256	53,512
Pseudo R-squared	0.5561	0.6295	0.6944

NOTE: Results are presented with the coefficient on first line and the absolute value of t-statistic on the second line. Coefficients on control variables have been suppressed. Standard errors clustered on team-season. Significance: * - $p<0.10$, ** - $p<0.05$, *** - $p<0.01$.

a game, a topic that has yet to be broached in the academic literature. Future research is encouraged to build upon this work, potentially examining whether roster composition among losing clubs—the choice of employing past-their-prime veterans or unproven young players—affects seasonal attendance.

As a second insight to be gleaned from this paper, the results consistently demonstrate that fan responsiveness to celebrated rookies and the debuts of top prospects was considerably stronger when such players pitched for the home team. Up until this point, research on attendance patterns in the National Basketball Association (Berri and Schmidt, 2006) and Major League Baseball (Ormiston, 2014b) have noted that the attendance impact of star players appeared to be more significant on the road. While this latter outcome may be surprising on the surface, consider that a home team's fans in MLB can reasonably count on 15–20 home starts per season by their club's favorite pitcher, making each individual game less of an event. In contrast, if a star—or well-hyped rookie prospect—takes the hill for the visiting team, it may represent the only opportunity for the home city's fans to see that player in action all season. The results of this paper run counter to the findings of these two prior studies, further supporting the hypothesis that the advanced home team premium for celebrated rookies and prospects can be attributable to the hype and hope generated by these players. Future research is encouraged to examine how emerging, young offensive talent (or players in other sports) affects game attendance given potential differences between the effects of starting pitchers and everyday players.

Before concluding, it is necessary to identify a number of concerns with the analyses of the current paper. First, as alluded to in the study, many of the rookie and prospect categories exhibiting statistically significant attendance effects include a limited number of pitchers. This leaves the results especially sensitive to outliers; as such, future researchers are cautioned about the robustness of these effects moving forward. Further, many of the hurlers with the most substantial effects on team attendance pitched decades ago and it is unclear whether these exceptional outcomes would occur today, as evidenced by the lack of any effect attributable to Jose Fernandez with the 2013 Miami Marlins and the decline in fan responsiveness to game characteristics noted in Beckman, et al. (2011) and Ormiston (2014a).

Finally, there are concerns that the rookie effects identified in this paper are somewhat biased due to measurement error in the star power variable. As discussed in Ormiston (2014b), the age-adjusted star power variable only recognizes "star power" when a pitcher achieves a tangible accomplishment (e.g., All-Star Game, no-hitter). While this is not an issue for most rookie pitchers—whose lack of star power would be adequately estimated—it is likely that this measure would underestimate the star power of an elite rookie pitcher, especially in his first few starts. While the magnitude of this potential bias is unclear, concerns are somewhat attenuated due to the use of the current-season wins above replacement value (to fully capture the effects of a dominant performer) and the fact that fan responsiveness to visiting team rookie pitchers is near zero given that Ormiston (2014b) demonstrated the positive and considerable relationship between game attendance and the star power of the visiting starting pitcher. Future research is strongly encouraged to devise alternative measures of star power given that readily available measures—such as fan voting for the All-Star Game—are unavailable for pitchers. ∎

References

Beckman, E.M., Cai, W., Esrock, R.M., & Lemke, R.J. (2011). "Explaining Game-to-Game Ticket Sales for Major League Baseball Games Over Time," *Journal of Sports Economics*, online only.

Berri, D.J., & Schmidt, M.B. (2006). "On the Road With the National Basketball Association's Superstar Externality," *Journal of Sports Economics*, 7, 347–58.

Bruggink, T.H., & Eaton, J.W. (1996). "Rebuilding Attendance in Major League Baseball: The Demand for Individual Games" in L. Hadley & E. Gustafson (Eds.), *Baseball Economics: Current Research*. Praeger Press.

Butler, M.R. (2002). "Interleague Play and Baseball Attendance," *Journal of Sports Economics*, 3, 320–34.

Gittar, S.R., & Rhoads, T.A. (2011). "Top Prospects and Minor League Baseball Attendance," *Journal of Sports Economics*, 12, 341–51.

Hill, J.R., Madura, J., & Zuber, R.A. (1982). "The Short-Run Demand for Major League Baseball," *Atlantic Economic Journal*, 10, 31–35.

Lemke, R.J., Leonard, M., & Tlhokwane, K. (2010). "Estimating Attendance at Major League Baseball Games for the 2007 Season," *Journal of Sports Economics*, 11, 316–48.

McDonald, M., & Rascher, D. (2000). "Does Bat Day Make Cents? The Effect of Promotions on the Demand for Major League Baseball," *Journal of Sport Management*, 14, 8–27.

Meehan, Jr., J.W., Nelson, R.A., & Richardson, T.V. (2007). "Competitive Balance and Game Attendance in Major League Baseball," *Journal of Sports Economics*, 8, 563–80.

Ormiston, R. (2014a). "Do Fans Prefer Homegrown Players? An Analysis of MLB Attendance, 1976-2012," *Baseball Research Journal*, 43, 108–17.

Ormiston, R. (2014b). "Attendance Effects of Star Pitchers in Major League Baseball," *Journal of Sports Economics*, 15, 338–64.

Rascher, D.A. (1999). "A Test of the Optimal Positive Production Network Externality in Major League Baseball" in J. Fizel, E. Gustafson, & L. Hadley (Eds.), *Sports Economics: Current Research* (27–45). Westport, CT: Praeger.

Notes

1. This attendance effect may be offset at the minor-league level if a prospect is only expected to play for a particular minor-league team for a limited duration, thereby drawing crowds hopeful to see the player before he is promoted to another team.
2. The Retrosheet game-by-game database can be found at www.retrosheet.org/gamelogs/index.html.
3. These special cases involve games moved to neutral sites due to inclement weather, temporary stadium construction, or other reasons (e.g., games played outside the US and Canada). This also excludes the "home games" played by the Montreal Expos in San Juan, Puerto Rico.
4. Analyses examining the attendance effects of each game's starting pitchers are generally unencumbered by endogeneity concerns given that the names of the starting hurlers are announced to the public, often a few days ahead of time, such that fans can ascertain ahead of time whether a particular pitcher will—or will not—be playing in a given game.
5. Team-based variable pricing initiatives are not included due to a lack of data availability.
6. Consistent with the standards employed by Baseball America, this paper defines a rookie pitcher as a hurler with no more than 50 career innings pitched or 30 career games played prior to the season in question.
7. The overall top 100 prospect lists can be found at www.baseballamerica.com/ today/prospects/rankings/top-100-prospects/all-time. The top 10 prospect lists by organization were gathered from www.baseballamerica.com/majors/top-10-prospect-rankings-archives (1983-2000) and from the annual publication Baseball America Prospect Handbook (2001-2013).
8. The 13 pitchers who were number one overall picks and started at least one game in the majors are David Clyde, Floyd Bannister, Mike Moore, Tim Belcher, Andy Benes, Ben McDonald, Paul Wilson, Kris Benson, Bryan Bullington, Luke Hochevar, David Price, Stephen Strasburg and Gerrit Cole. Another pitcher, Matt Anderson, was the number one pick in the 1997 draft, but made all 257 of his MLB appearances in relief. Two other number one overall picks—Brien Taylor (1991) and Mark Appel (2013)—had not appeared in an MLB game during the time period studied.
9. In more detail, the numerator of the star power variable equals the linear sum of the number of times a pitcher has been named to the All-Star Game, the number of Cy Young awards won, the number of Most Value Player awards won, the number of no-hitters started, the number of All-Star Game MVP awards, the number of post-season MVP awards, whether the pitcher won the Rookie of the Year and whether the pitcher had won 300 games. The denominator equals a pitcher's age (as of July 1st of the given year) minus 17.
10. To compute the star and wins above replacement data, information on award winners and WAR were drawn from Baseball-Reference.com. Data on no-hitters were located on Retrosheet.org. All-Star Game information was drawn from MLB.com.
11. As an example of how this estimate meets expectations, note that this system rates Dwight Gooden, Fernando Valenzuela, and Tom Seaver as reaching the highest level of star power between 1969-2013, a reasonable outcome.
12. As an example, the average game-time winning percentage of a team starting a rookie hurler (.480) is significantly lower than that of a team starting a non-rookie pitcher (.503).
13. Demonstrating the sensitivity of the results to individual players, removing Mark Fidrych's rookie-season starts from the model reduces the home team coefficient on these celebrated hurlers from 0.2910 to 0.1550, representing a 47 percent decline; the visiting team coefficient falls from 0.1827 to 0.1261, a 31-percent decline. Both effects, however, remain statistically significant at a 95 percent confidence level.

The Roster Depreciation Allowance

How Major League Baseball Teams Turn Profits Into Losses

Stephen R. Keeney

Under current generally accepted accounting principles, I can turn a $4 million profit into a $2 million loss, and I can get every national accounting firm to agree with me.[1]
—Paul Beeston, President of the Toronto Blue Jays

Major professional sports are big businesses. And owners of sports teams generally run them accordingly, seeking to strike a balance between costs—including taxes—and revenues which maximizes profits. As Paul Beeston's words show, sports franchises are even more profitable than leagues and owners like to admit. MLB Commissioner Bud Selig testified before Congress in 2001 that baseball teams were losing hundreds of millions of dollars per year.[2] The Congressional committee was skeptical, as was Forbes.com, which concluded that MLB teams likely had an operating profit of around $75 million.[3]

But if Paul Beeston can turn profits into losses under basic accounting principles, then perhaps Selig and Forbes were both technically "right." How can this be? One way is tax breaks. Taxing sports franchises is a challenge because the business model and profitability depend heavily upon intangible assets: things that create value but cannot be physically touched, such as television and trademark rights.[4] The issues and regulations regarding valuation of franchises are so complex that sports analysts often fail to fully understand them.[5]

This article discusses one such tax issue: the Roster Depreciation Allowance. The topic has been discussed in simple terms in the popular press, as in this quotation from *Time*: "Owners get to deduct player salaries twice over, as an actual expense (since they're actually paying them) and as a depreciating asset (like GM would for a factory or FedEx a jet)."[6] It has also been discussed in the academic field with in-depth mathematical and economic language and analysis.[7] This article presents a middle ground, delving into the history of the Roster Depreciation Allowance and presenting an understanding of the application and consequences of the Roster Depreciation Allowance that is more nuanced than the popular press but accessible to those without a strong background in mathematics or economics.

The Roster Depreciation Allowance (RDA) is a tax law that allows a purchaser to depreciate (or, more accurately, to amortize) almost the entire purchase price of a sports franchise. Depreciation is when a company takes the decrease in value of a tangible asset over a certain period of time as an economic loss in its accounting. If a landscaping company buys a riding mower, the company will take a certain percentage of that mower's cost each year for a certain number of years as a loss, which counts against the company's profits. The loss is economic because the company isn't actually losing any money on the mower; but because the mower is worth less than it was when the company bought it, companies are allowed to count that loss against their revenues for accounting purposes. By lowering the revenues and subsequently the profits of the company, depreciation lowers the company's taxable income.

The accounting principles behind depreciation are fairly simple. For every transaction, one account must increase, and one must decrease, both by the same dollar amount. When a company spends $1,500 on a riding lawn mower, assuming they pay in cash or an equivalent rather than with a loan, the company's bank account decreases by $1,500. But now the company owns a mower worth $1,500, so its asset account—the value of the stuff and money it owns—must go up by the same $1,500. That part is simple enough. But after the company uses the mower for several years the mower's value will be reduced to zero.[8] When the mower's value hits zero, the company's asset account would have essentially been reduced by $1,500 because they have $1,500 less stuff. But to keep their books balanced, there must be an equal increase somewhere else. That increase comes in the "depreciation expenses" category, which increases a company's expenses (the money a business spends conducting its business) just as if the company had paid money to an

A young Bud Selig paid $10.8 million to buy the player contract rights of the entire roster of the Seattle Pilots, even though the roster's total salaries were only $607,400.

employee. The concept of depreciation simply allows the company to make those adjustments in smaller increments, say 10% per year for 10 years, instead of all at once.

The IRS puts out several rules and regulations which determine the percentage of the purchase price of any given item that is depreciable, over how many years the depreciation is spread, and what methods of depreciation are allowed. Amortization, as used here, is simply depreciation for intangible assets.[9] If a company buys an intangible asset, like a patent, it is amortized rather than depreciated, but the same basic process applies. To avoid confusion the rest of this paper will refer to the amortization that takes place under the RDA as depreciation.

The RDA is one of several "gymnastic bookkeeping techniques" businesses and sports franchises use to minimize tax liabilities.[10] The RDA is a depreciation of almost the entire purchase price of a sports franchise over 15 years. This means that each year for 15 years, the purchaser (or purchasers) of a professional sports franchise can take a tax deduction based on the purchase price of the franchise. The current RDA allows sports franchise purchasers to depreciate almost 100 percent of the purchase price over the first 15 years after the purchase; a tax deduction of about 6.67 percent of the purchase price per year.[11]

The RDA is not exactly unique because many businesses depreciate the costs of both tangible (physical, like lawn mowers) and intangible (not physical but still profitable, like patents) assets. But it is unique in that it deals with sports franchises. Unlike riding lawn mowers or patents, which are essentially worthless at some point in time, the value of sports franchises continue to increase. While depreciation generally allows companies to count the loss of value of their assets as

costs of operation, the RDA allows companies to count losses on an asset whose value continues to rise.

The current RDA is fairly straightforward, but has not always been that way. Before the first RDA became law in 1976, nobody—not owners, lawyers, accountants, courts, or the IRS—could accurately depreciate the sports franchise as an asset with any consistency.[12] Because high barriers to entry mean that buying a sports franchise was and still is a relatively uncommon event, it took lawmakers a while to figure out what to do.

Before moving into the history of the RDA, it is important to understand a few key concepts. The first is the concept of franchise rights. Franchise rights refer to the full panoply of rights associated with being a franchise in a major sports league, such as rights to revenue sharing, rights to trademarks, trade names, licenses, and other intellectual property, rights to regional exclusivity, and all the other rights that come from being a member of the league. The second concept is the distinction between player contracts and player contract rights. Player contracts state how much a player will make over how many years, and will set out what the player has to do to earn that money. In short, player contracts are about a player's salary. Player contract rights refers to the ownership of the right to enforce the contract and the duty to abide by it. So even though a player may have a $3 million per year salary, if he brings in $4 million in revenue, a person may only pay $500,000 for the contract rights, because he will pay the salary and the price of the contract rights for a total of $3.5 million in exchange for $4 million in revenue. But if the same $3 million player brings in $10 million in revenue a year, then someone may pay $5 million for his contract rights, for a total salary plus purchase price of $8 million in order to gain that $10 million in revenue. In an example that will be examined later, when Bud Selig bought the Seattle Pilots in 1970, he said that he paid $10.8 million to buy the player contract rights of the entire roster, even though the roster's total salaries were only $607,400.[13]

Two key court cases came about in the late 1920s which dealt with how baseball teams treated the costs of player contracts. The case of *Chicago Nat'l League Ball Club v. Commissioner*[14] dealt with the Chicago Cubs' 1927 and 1928 corporate tax returns and the case of *Commissioner v. Pittsburgh Athletic Co.*[15] dealt with the Pittsburgh Pirates' 1928–30 corporate tax returns. Until 1928, the Pirates had been taking a tax deduction for the difference between all the player contracts they bought and all the player contracts they sold in a given year. But now both teams, the Cubs starting in 1927 and the Pirates starting in 1928, had begun taking the entire amount paid for player contracts in a given year as tax deductions in that same year.[16]

The reserve clause played a key role in these decisions because it essentially created a perpetual team option contract. Both teams argued that since all player contracts were technically only one-year contracts, they had useful lives of one year and thus the full amount was depreciable in the year in which they were purchased. The IRS argued that the amounts paid for player contracts should be deducted over a period of at least three years because the reserve clause essentially gave the contracts a useful life equal to a player's entire career. In both cases, the court relied on non-baseball precedent to say that even though a contract has an option to extend its duration, the life of the contract itself was not necessarily changed by the option. So in both cases, the team won.

An early version of the RDA was enacted just over a decade later. When sports entrepreneur Bill Veeck bought the Cleveland Indians in 1946, he persuaded Congress and the IRS to act. Veeck argued that the amount of the purchase price that went towards buying the rights to the player contracts should be treated as a depreciable asset.[17] Sports teams could then "double dip" by taking the RDA depreciation for the purchase price of the contracts—how much the new owners paid to old owners for the ability to enforce the contracts—and then deducting the salaries actually paid each year to players as labor costs. Moreover, unlike most assets which can only be depreciated once, the RDA applies anew each time a franchise is purchased.[18] This new, clear version of the rules increased the value of franchises, and Veeck quickly capitalized by selling the Indians in 1949.[19]

With the purchase price of player contracts now a depreciable asset, team buyers began doing what the Chicago court could not: determining how much of the purchase price was for the franchise rights (league membership, regional exclusivity, revenue sharing and licensing rights, etc.) and how much was for the player contracts. The IRS's stated position was that the price of the franchise rights was not depreciable because it did not have a determinable life (the NFL, NBA, or MLB and their franchises could potentially live on and be profitable forever), but the price of the player contracts was depreciable because they had a determinable life (the contract was only valuable for however many years the player was bound to the club).[20] While the franchise rights are the more valuable part of team ownership, buyers wanted to make as much of the purchase price depreciable as possible.[21] So buyers began allocating huge percentages of the purchase price to the player contracts and away from the franchise rights.

The NFL granted an expansion franchise in 1965 which became the Atlanta Falcons.[22] The new owners tried to depreciate both the cost of the contracts of the 42 players acquired via the expansion draft and the cost of the Falcons' franchise right to a share of the NFL television revenues.[23] The IRS asserted deficiencies, arguing that the owners allocated too much of the purchase price to the player contracts and not enough to the franchise rights.[24] The IRS also argued that the "mass asset rule" should apply to prevent the Falcons from dividing the purchase price between the franchise rights and the player contracts. The "mass asset rule" prevents depreciation of intangible assets of indeterminate life (such as rights to television revenue) if they are inseparable from intangible assets of determinable life (such as player contracts). The IRS argued that it was impossible to separate the costs of becoming an NFL franchise and the costs expended to acquire the players on its roster, and that therefore the "mass asset rule" should apply.

The court disagreed. It held that the "mass asset rule" did not apply because the player contracts 1) had their own value separate from the franchise rights, and 2) had a limited useful life which could be ascertained with reasonable accuracy.[25] So the court allowed the Falcons to separate and depreciate the cost of player contracts from the rest of the intangibles.[26] The court also held that the television rights bundle could not be depreciated because it was of indeterminable length, running as long as the franchise is part of the NFL.[27] Thus, franchise owners benefitted the most when they attributed more of the purchase price to player contracts instead of to the franchise rights, so that's exactly what they started doing.

Former MLB commissioner Bud Selig took the practice of allocating costs towards player contracts in order to maximize depreciation deductions to new heights when he bought the Seattle Pilots in 1970. Selig bought the Pilots for $10.8 million.[28] He allocated 94 percent of the purchase price (or about $10.2 million) to the purchase of player contracts, even though the contracts themselves were only for $607,400 worth of salaries, according to Baseball-Almanac.com.[29,30] The remaining purchase price was allocated to the equipment and supplies ($100,000) and the value of the franchise ($500,000).[31] The court upheld this allocation.[32]

In response to Selig's allocation (but before the decision upholding it came down) the IRS and Congress acted to prevent such allocations in the future. Congress enacted Section 1056, which regulated the tax treatment of player contracts. Subsections (a)–(c) dealt with the "basis" of player contracts.[33] "Basis" is a tax term describing the amount of money "put into" an asset—minus any depreciation deductions taken—by the owner. This determines the amount of taxable profit/loss the owner will realize on a subsequent sale of the asset.[34] Subsection (d) creates a presumption that no more than 50 percent of the purchase price of a sports franchise could be allocated to player contracts, unless the purchaser establishes to the IRS that a higher percentage is proper. This amount could then be depreciated over a five-year period (rather than over the lives of the individual contracts). This law created the 50/5 rule: 50 percent of the total purchase price of the franchise could be depreciated over five years.

The 50/5 rule streamlined sports franchise book-keeping by making all the purchased contract rights one large, depreciable asset. This may have been an attempt to get courts to stop evaluating the reasonableness of the contract rights purchase price first and allocating the remainder to franchise rights second.[35] However, since it created only a presumption and not a rule, the IRS continued to struggle against franchise buyers who argued that more than 50% of the purchase price was for the player contracts.[36]

Around the turn of the century, Congress drastically changed the RDA. In 1993, Congress had passed a tax law called Section 197, which gave all businesses the ability to depreciate the purchase price of intangible assets, but specifically excluded sports franchises.[37,38] So the 50/5 rule in Section 1056 continued to apply to professional sports franchises. Then Congress passed the *American Jobs Creation Act of 2004*. As part of this Act, Section 1056 was repealed, and the purchase price of sports franchises became subject to the 15-year depreciation rules applicable to other intangible assets under Section 197.[39] "Section 197 allows an amortized deduction for the capitalized costs of [things listed in Section 197]."[40] These intangibles include "workforce in place" (player contract rights), as well as "any franchise, trademark, or trade name."[41,42] Thus, the specific exclusion of sports franchises from intangible assets was ended.[43] Under this new 100/15 rule, almost the full purchase price of a franchise is depreciable over 15 years.[44]

The RDA is perhaps best understood through hypotheticals. An analysis of the 2004 rule gives the following example:

Buyer (B) pays Seller (S) $350 million for an MLB franchise. $40 million represents the costs of all tangible assets (uniforms, bats, balls, mascot costumes, etc.) and the intangible assets which are not the franchise itself or the player contracts (such as a stadium lease). The remaining $310 million is a depreciable asset, just as if B had bought a factory or patent.[45]

As this example illustrates, not all intangible assets are depreciable under the RDA, such as the stadium lease[46] mentioned above. This leaves room for the old-fashioned disputes about allocation, but the amount of money in contention is much smaller.

For an example of the difference between the old and new incarnations of the RDA, consider the following: Assume that an investor, or a group of investors, purchased a sports franchise for $150 million total. Under the old 50/5 rule, the franchise would be able to depreciate $75 million (50 percent) over five years, or $15 million dollars per year. That means that $15 million worth of revenues are not taxed. Assuming a tax rate of 35 percent, that $15 million in revenue would have generated income tax of $5.25 million.[47] Multiplied by five years means $26.25 million in tax savings for the franchise.

Now, let's use the same hypothetical for the current RDA. A purchaser or group of purchasers buys a sports franchise for $150 million, with $100 million of that being for the franchise and player contract rights.[48] Under the 100/15 rule, the franchise can depreciate $100 million over fifteen years, or about $6.67 million per year. That means that $6.67 million of revenues per year are not taxed. Assuming a tax rate of 35 percent, the franchise owners gain approximately $2.33 million in taxes, which they would have had to pay the IRS without the RDA. Multiplied by fifteen years, that equals about $35 million in tax savings.

These examples have two caveats. One is that, in the examples above, if an owner buys a team for $150 million he will almost certainly allocate far more than $100 million to the franchise and player rights ($100 million is only 67 percent of $150 million, but remember Bud Selig allocated 94 percent to player rights alone). Thus, the tax advantages to the owners under the current rules would be even greater than the example illustrates. The last ten times a major sports franchise (NHL, NFL, NBA, or MLB) was sold, the prices ranged from $170 million to $2.15 billion, with five of those ten between $200 and $600 million.[49] So, if a team were purchased for $400 million and the owners allocated $376 million to player rights and other depreciable intangibles ($376 million is 94% of the purchase price, which Bud Selig got away with), they could depreciate just under $25.1 million per year, which at a 35 percent tax rate would be savings of $8.77 million per year to the owners.

The second caveat is that nothing in this paper discusses changes to the depreciable amount. Theoretically, a franchise would acquire and sell the rights of individual players each season, and would thus have to realize gains or losses on each sale, and likely apply the RDA to each new player contract it acquires, depending on how it does its accounting. Since these examples are illustrative only, we are only dealing with the initial purchase of all player contracts the franchise owns at the time of the sale.

This is a good point to provide greater context for the numbers we've been discussing to see the real impact of the RDA and the 2004 changes. As discussed earlier, the RDA creates tax savings for owners. But these breaks are only temporary. We have to remember the concepts of depreciation and basis discussed above. When you depreciate an asset, your basis in that asset decreases. If you sell that asset, you are taxed on the portion of that income which exceeds your basis. Remember that lawn mower from our landscaping company from before? Let's say the company

buys a lawn mower for $1,500. Its basis in the lawn mower is $1,500. The company then depreciates $150 (10%) per year for six years, for a total depreciation of $900. The company's basis in the lawn mower is decreased by that $900 of depreciation, so that the company's basis is now $600. So after owning the lawn mower for six years, the company now sells it to someone else for $750. The company will have to pay tax on the difference between the $750 it received for the lawn mower and its $600 basis in the lawn mower, which is $150 of taxable income.

The same is true of sports franchises under the RDA. For every dollar a franchise takes as depreciation, they will have to pay taxes on another dollar of profit from the sale of the franchise. So the RDA itself does not really affect the dollar amount of taxes paid by a franchise. But it does do two other things. First, because the amount of the depreciation allowed was increased from 50% of the purchase price to almost 100% of the purchase price, it allows more revenue to go untaxed (see Table 1). Second, by using the RDA and other perfectly legitimate accounting methods, franchises make revenue disappear from the profit line. As stated, this untaxed revenue will eventually be paid back.

Table1. Pre-vs.Post-2004 RDA Taxable Amounts

Pre-2004 RDA Purchase Price: $150m					Post-2004 RDA Purchase Price: $150m				
Year	Deduction ($)	Basis ($)	Revenue ($)	Rev. Taxed ($)	Year	Deduction ($)	Basis ($)	Revenue ($)	Rev. Taxed ($)
1	7.50	142.50	5.00	(2.50)	1	10.00	140.00	5.00	(5.00)
2	7.50	135.00	5.08	(2.43)	2	10.00	130.00	5.08	(4.93)
3	7.50	127.50	5.15	(2.35)	3	10.00	120.00	5.15	(4.85)
4	7.50	120.00	5.23	(2.27)	4	10.00	110.00	5.23	(4.77)
5	7.50	112.50	5.31	(2.19)	5	10.00	100.00	5.31	(4.69)
6	0.00	105.00	5.39	5.39	6	10.00	90.00	5.39	(4.61)
7	0.00	105.00	5.47	5.47	7	10.00	80.00	5.47	(4.53)
8	0.00	105.00	5.55	5.55	8	10.00	70.00	5.55	(4.45)
9	0.00	105.00	5.63	5.63	9	10.00	60.00	5.63	(4.37)
10	0.00	105.00	5.72	5.72	10	10.00	50.00	5.72	(4.28)
11	0.00	105.00	5.80	5.80	11	10.00	40.00	5.80	(4.20)
12	0.00	105.00	5.89	5.89	12	10.00	30.00	5.89	(4.11)
13	0.00	105.00	5.98	5.98	13	10.00	20.00	5.98	(4.02)
14	0.00	105.00	6.07	6.07	14	10.00	10.00	6.07	(3.93)
15	0.00	105.00	6.16	6.16	15	10.00	0.00	6.16	(3.84)
Total			83.41	45.91	Total			83.41	(66.59)

Sale Price ($)	Basis ($)	Taxable ($)			Sale Price ($)	Basis ($)	Taxable ($)		
200.00	105.00	95.00			200.00	0.00	200.00		

Total Taxable Income Pre-2004 ($)					Total Taxable Income Post-2004 ($)				
Sale	95.00				Sale	200.00			
Revenue	45.91				Revenue	(66.59)			
Total	140.91				Total	133.41			

*All numbers are in millions of dollars
**Assumes $5 million in revenue per year increasing 1.5% per year, purely for illustration

President of the Toronto Blue Jays Paul Beeston reportedly said, "Under current generally accepted accounting principles, I can turn a $4 million profit into a $2 million loss, and I can get every national accounting firm to agree with me."

These tax breaks create a type of deferred-tax situation—a situation where companies can use accounting to delay paying current taxes due until a later date—because they allow the franchise owners to keep more money now and make up for taxes due later. Because every $1 of depreciation decreases basis by $1, at a 35% tax rate the owners are saving $.35 now, but will have to pay that $.35 back later if they sell the franchise. Of course, these savings the owners get are going to be generating more income for them while the total they owe the IRS will stay the same, effectively acting as an interest-free loan from the government to the owners.[50] This article is not trying to decry some perceived injustice in the existence of the RDA—but it is something sports fans should be aware of when they are considering financial numbers put out by both the media and the teams themselves.

Congress placed sports franchises under the general law for intangible asset depreciation in 2004 for several reasons. First, it made the rules more uniform across industries. Second, the clearer rules were meant to minimize disputes regarding proper allocation, and in turn to reduce the IRS's administrative and enforcement costs.[51] Finally, supporters argued that it would increase tax payments by about $381 million over ten years.[52] While the deductible amount doubled, the amortization time period tripled, which would increase tax bills in the short term. As the above hypotheticals show, while the amortizable amount increased from 50 to almost 100 percent, the dollar amount amortized each year decreased; meaning that in the early years the teams would have more taxable income. While the 50/5 example above allowed an annual deduction of $5.25 million, the 100/15 example only allowed an annual deduction of $2.33 million, increasing the team's taxable income for the first five years. Of course, after those five years, as the depreciation continued to apply, the

increased percentage meant that even more money was safe from taxation than before.

By doubling the amount of tax deductions a team could take—provided, of course, that the new owners hang on to the team for the full 15 years—the new RDA increased franchise values. Higher depreciation totals meant more tax deductions and more untaxed profits for owners in the long run. Experts in the field theorized that the average values of sports franchises would increase by five percent.[53] One economic report argued that average value would in fact increase by 11.6 percent.[54]

Further, for many teams, even the lower depreciation amounts exceed taxable income for each of the 15 years, allowing the owners to pass the paper losses on to their personal income tax liability.[55] For example, a Los Angeles group of investors bought the Dodgers for $2.15 billion in 2012.[56] Thus, it can take over $143 million per year as a deduction, which is a tax savings of just over $50 million per year for the owners, again assuming a 35 percent tax rate.[57] The elongated time frame means that the Dodgers' new owners can extend the tax benefits to their private income taxes as business losses for ten years longer than under the old rules, but more importantly the extended coverage of the new RDA , from 50% to almost 100% of purchase price, allows them to almost double the total deductible amount.[58] If Paul Beeston could turn a $4 million profit into a $2 million loss, just imagine how much profit the Dodgers' owners could turn into losses with $143 million in deductions.

There have been several examples in recent sports history that illustrate the effects of the RDA on the business of sports. In 1974, before the modern rules, only 5 of 27 professional basketball teams reported a profit.[59] This history of paper losses has continued under the new rules. In 2011, with the Collective Bargaining Agreement between the league and players expiring, the NBA stated that 22 of its 30 teams were losing money.[60] As a lockout loomed, NBA players argued that the "losses" suffered by teams were paper rather than real.[61] As a former director of the MLB Players Association once said, if "[y]ou go through *The Sporting News* of the last 100 years, and you will find two things are always true. You never have enough pitchers, and nobody ever made money."[62]

Forbes reported in August 2013 that the Houston Astros, who had finished with the worst record in Major League Baseball each year from 2011 through 2013, were on pace to make $99 million in profit in 2013—the most of any team in baseball history.[63] The Astros responded that their numbers were not near

Bill Veeck successfully argued to Congress and the IRS that when he bought the Indians in 1946, the amount of the purchase price that went towards buying the rights to the player contracts should be treated as a depreciable asset. Sports teams could then "double dip."

that amount. The difference is because the Astros, unlike *Forbes*, included non-cash losses, such as the RDA, in its calculation.[64] Current Astros owner Jim Crane bought the team in 2011. Between then and 2013, he cut player salaries from $77 million to $13 million.[65] According to the *Sports Business Journal*, Crane paid about $700 million for the team.[66] This means that the Astros would get about $46.7 million per year in paper losses associated with acquiring player contracts, despite paying actual salary amounts as low as $13 million. If you multiply the $46.7 million per year deduction by 35 percent, the RDA allows the team to keep about $16.3 million dollars per year which it would have had to pay in taxes. That's more than enough to double the salary of the entire 2013 roster. So, with the help of the RDA, the Astros are taking a large paper loss as well as decreasing labor expenses, greatly increasing their profit margin. If you subtract the $46.7 million in depreciation losses from the *Forbes* projection of $99 million in profits, it's easy to see why the Astros claimed the numbers were so far off. It's also easy to see how such vastly profitable businesses as sports franchises can say they are not making money with a straight face.

If you were to get on the public address system at any ballpark in America during a baseball game and ask for a show of hands on how many people are interested in how their teams account for depreciation of intangible assets, among the sea of boos you would probably find no hands up. But the people who run the teams are very interested in limiting their tax liability. It allows them to either pocket more money in profits or to pay better players to win more games. And as fans and society continue to take an increasingly academic look at professional sports, the Roster Depreciation Allowance is a crucial consideration in the economics of professional sports. The next time you

see an article about the financial condition of your favorite team, you'll know that there is much more going on in the books than meets the eye. ∎

Notes

1. Dan Alexander, "Can Houston Astros Really Be Losing Money Despite Rock-Bottom Payroll?," Forbes.com, August 29, 2013, http://www.forbes.com/sites/danalexander/2013/08/29/can-houston-astros-really-be-losing-money-despite-rock-bottom-payroll.

2. Richard Sandomir, "Selig Defends His Plan of Contraction to Congress," December 7, 2001, http://www.nytimes.com/2001/12/07/sports/baseball-selig-defends-his-plan-of-contraction-to-congress.html.

3. Michael Ozanian, "Is Baseball Really Broke?," April 3, 2002, http://www.forbes.com/2002/04/01/0401baseball.html.

4. See Robert Holo and Jonathan Talansky, "Taxing the Business of Sports," 9 Fla. Tax Rev. 161 (2008): 184 (discussing current issues in taxing sports at the entity level).

5. See Tommy Craggs, "Exclusive: How an NBA Team Makes Money Disappear [UPDATE WITH CORRECTION]," Deadspin.com, June 30, 2011, http://deadspin.com/5816870/exclusive-how-and-why-an-nba-team-makes-a-7-million-profit-look-like-a-28-million-loss (misconstruing the nature of the allowance and implying that it is of unlimited duration rather than the current 15-year limit); and Larry Coon, "Is the NBA Really Losing Money?," ESPN.com, July 12, 2011, http://sports.espn.go.com/nba/columns/story?columnist=coon_larry&page=NBAFinancials-110630 (asserting the pre-2004 law of the Roster Depreciation Allowance as current in 2011).

6. Gary Belsky, "Why $1.5 Billion for the Dodgers Might be a Bargain," Time.com, March 9, 2012, http://business.time.com/2012/03/09/why-1-5-billion-for-the-dodgers-might-turn-out-to-be-a-bargain/.

7. N. Edward Coulson and Rodney Fort, Tax Revisions of 2004 and Pro Sports Team Ownership, available at http://econ.la.psu.edu/~ecoulson/veeck.pdf.

8. The mower may have "scrap value" which a company may account for, but for practical and illustrative purposes we will assume the mower becomes worth $0 at the end of its useful life.

9. Amortization is a general name for the spreading out of payments over a long period of time into equal amounts. In terms of loans such as mortgages and car loan, amortization refers to spreading out the total debt into equal regular payments rather than paying it all at once at the end of the loan period. In terms of business assets, amortization refers to the process of spreading the cost of an intangible asset's depreciation into equal parts over a period of time, and taking the depreciation as a paper loss at regular intervals.

10. Ron Maierhofer, No Money Down: How to Buy a Sports Franchise, A Journey Through an American Dream (Dog Ear Publishing, 2009), 27.

11. 26 U.S.C. § 197.

12. 26 U.S.C. § 1056, effective January 1, 1976 through 2004. See http://law.justia.com/codes/us/1996/title26/chap1/subchapo/partiv/sec1056 and http://uscode.house.gov/view.xhtml?req=granuleid:USC-prelim-title26-section1056&num=0&edition=prelim.

13. "1969 Seattle Pilots Roster," Baseball-Almanac.com, http://www.baseball-almanac.com/teamstats/roster.php?y=1969&t=SE1. The $607,400 team total salary comes from adding together the salaries listed on the page cited.

14. Chicago Nat'l League Ball Club v. Commissioner, 1933 WL 4911 (B.T.A.) (1933), affirmed sub nom Commissioner of Internal Revenue v. Chicago Nat'l League Ball Club, 74 F.2d 1010 (1935).

15. Commissioner of Internal Revenue v. Pittsburgh Athletic Co., 72 F.2d 883 (1934).

16. The distinction between player contract rights and player salaries is key here: the teams were deducting the costs of acquiring the rights of the player as business expenses, and also claiming the salaries paid to players as labor costs.

17. See Jason A. Winfree & Mark S. Rosentraub, *Sports Finance and Management* (Boca Raton, Fl.: CRC Press, 2012), 428–29 (discussing the history of the RDA), and Coulson, supra note 7 (discussing Bill Veeck's role in creating the RDA and the economic consequences).

18. Winfree, *Sports Finance*, 429.

19. Ibid.

20. Ibid, at 197. See also, Rev. Rul. 71-137, 1971-1 C.B. 104.

21. Talansky, "Taxing…Sports," 193.

22. "Atlanta Falcons Team Page," NFL.com, http://www.nfl.com/teams/atlantafalcons/profile?team=ATL.

23. See Laird v. U.S., 556 F. 2d. 1224, 1226-1230 (5th Cir. 1977) (upholding the Falcons' allocation of purchase price).

24. Ibid.

25. Ibid, 1232–33.

26. Ibid.

27. Ibid., 1235–37.

28. See Selig v. U.S., 740 F. 2d. 572, 574 (7th Cir. 1984) (upholding the allocation made by Selig).

29. Winfree, Sports Finance, 429.

30. "1969 Seattle Pilots Roster," Baseball-Almanac.com, http://www.baseball-almanac.com/teamstats/roster.php?y=1969&t=SE1.

31. Selig, 740 F. 2d. at 575.

32. Talansky, "Taxing…Sports," 189 (one commentator referred to the opinion as one that "reads more like a Ken Burns paean to baseball than a legal opinion" because the court talked as much about the history of baseball in America as it dibid about the applicable law).

33. 26 U.S.C. § 1056.

34. For example, if you buy a house for $200,000 and make $50,000 in upgrades, your basis in the house is $250,000. If you are a landlord and you have depreciated $100,000 of the same house on your books, your basis is $150,000 ($250,000–$100,000). If you sell the house, your taxable income is the amount you got for the house minus your basis.

35. Talansky, "Taxing…Sports," 193.

36. Ibid., at 197.

37. 26 U.S.C. § 197.

38. "Notes,"26 U.S.C. § 197, Cornell Law, https://www.law.cornell.edu/uscode/text/26/197.

39. Talansky, "Taxing…Sports," 200.

40. 26 C.F.R. § 1.197-2.

41. 26 U.S.C. § 197(d)(1)(C)(i).

42. 26 U.S.C. § 197(d)(1)(F).

43. Talansky, "Taxing…Sports," 196. See also, *Complete Analysis of the American Jobs Creation Act of 2004*, Chapter 300 Cost Recovery, "315 Professional Sports Franchises are Made Subject to 15-Year Amortization; Special Basis Allocation and Depreciation Recapture Rules for Players Contracts are Repealed," 2004 CATA 315, 2004 WL 2318514 (briefly explaining the history of allocation debates between purchasers and the IRS).

44. The regular rules for depreciation of tangible assets continues to apply to all tangible things the new owners get, such as uniforms, bats, balls, equipment, etc.

45. See Complete Analysis, note 33 (paraphrases, not quoted).

46. Intangibles like the stadium lease, which are not related to franchise rights or player contracts, may be depreciable under other sections of the tax code, but they are not included in the RDA and their treatment is outside the scope of this paper.

47. I chose a 35% tax rate because it is the second-highest personal income tax rate and the highest corporate income tax rate. The actual tax rate—that rate the entity should pay under the tax code—will depend upon how the ownership entity is taxed (whether pass-through like a partnership or as an entity like a corporation), the net income of the individuals or entity, and whether the income is taxed at the much lower capital gains tax rate. The effective tax rate—the percent actually paid in taxes—will depend upon the expenses and deductions of the individual team or owners, and several other factors which may be too numerous to use in an illustrative example.

48. In both examples the team is purchased for $150 million, but in the post-2004 example the depreciation is based on $100 million rather than $150 million. This is because the pre-2004 50/5 rule applied to the total purchase price paid for the franchise, while the post-2004 100/15 rule applies only to the portion of the purchase price paid for intangible assets like franchise rights, player contract rights, and trademarks.

49. Dan Primack and Daniel Roberts, "American Sports Teams: All Worth More Than You Think," Fortune.com, http://fortune.com/2014/06/05/american-sports-teams-all-worth-more-than-you-think/.

50. This situation is very similar to a tax deferment. For more on tax deferments, see Stephen Foley, "The $62 bn Secret of Warren Buffett's Success," *Financial Times*, FT.com, March 4, 2015, available at http://www.ft.com/cms/s/2/9c690e44-c1d2-11e4-abb3-00144feab7de.html#slide0, and Joshua Kennon, "Using Deferred Taxes to Increase Your Investment Returns," available at http://beginnersinvest.about.com/od/capitalgainstax/a/Using-Deferred-Taxes-To-Increase-Your-Investment-Returns.htm.

51. Ibid.

52. Talansky, "Taxing…Sports," 202, and Coulson, "Tax Revisions of 2004," at 1.

53. Talansky, "Taxing…Sports," 203, and Coulson, "Tax Revisions of 2004," abstract.

54. Ibid., at 18.

55. Depending on what type of business entity owned the team. Most teams are owned by partnerships, which generally allow the tax benefits to pass through to the owners' individual income tax liabilities.

56. Sean Leahy, "Bankrupt to Big Bucks: The New Economics of the Los Angeles Dodgers," San Diego State University Sports MBA '13, http://sandiegostatesmba13.blogspot.com/2012/09/bankrupt-to-big-bucks-new-economics-of.html.

57. Ibid.

58. Alexander, "Can Houston Astros Really Be Losing Money." In fact, the last 6 World Series winners combined have made less than $99 million.

59. Talansky, "Taxing…Sports," 192-193.

60. Coon, "Is the NBA Really Losing Money?"

61. Coon, "Is the NBA Really Losing Money?"

62. Talansky, "Taxing…Sports," 184, n. 71.

63. Dan Alexander, "2013 Houston Astros: Baseball's Worst Team is the Most Profitable in History," Forbes.com, August 26, 2013, http://www.forbes.com/sites/danalexander/2013/08/26/2013-houston-astros-baseballs-worst-team-is-most-profitable-in-history/.

64. Alexander, "Can Houston Astros Really Be Losing Money."

65. Alexander, "2013 Houston Astros."

66. Daniel Kaplan, "Crane's $220M Loan from BofA to Finance Purchase of Astros has 'Recession-Era Structure,'" SportsBusinessDaily.com, June 6, 2011 http://www.sportsbusinessdaily.com/Journal/Issues/2011/06/06/Finance/Astros.aspx.

Revisiting the Hines Triple Play

Richard Hershberger

On May 8, 1878, the National League club of Providence hosted their counterparts from Boston. In the eighth inning Providence turned a triple play, initiated by center fielder Paul Hines. Was it the first unassisted triple play, or was the play completed by Providence second baseman Charlie Sweasy? This has long been a subject of debate, to the present day. This article will reexamine the question, considering contemporaneous game accounts and the rules of 1878.

The undisputed facts are as follows: Boston had two men on base, Ezra Sutton on second and Jack Manning on third. The batter, Jack Burdock, hit a soft line drive—probably what would later be called a Texas Leaguer—over the shortstop's head. It was obvious that the shortstop wouldn't catch the ball, so Sutton and Manning took off running. Hines charged in from center field, making a spectacular shoestring catch. His momentum carried him forward and he kept running to third base and stepped on the bag. Charlie Sweasy, the second baseman, then called for the ball. Hines threw the ball to Sweasy, who stepped on second base.

The running catch was the first out. There is agreement that Manning was at or near home plate when Hines tagged third base, making another out. The dispute is whether Hines's tag of third also put out Sutton. There are two questions. In legal terms, there is a question of fact and a question of law.

The question of fact is on which side of third Sutton was when Hines tagged the base. Was he with Manning near home plate, or was he between second and third? If the latter, then the third out unquestionably was made by Sweasy tagging second, with Hines getting an assist.

The question of law arises if Sutton was past third base. Under the 1878 rules, did Hines's tag of third base put him out, or was it Sweasy's tag of second?

THE HISTORICAL DEBATE

The contemporaneous accounts reached, as will be shown below, different conclusions, but there was little further discussion at the time. The historical debate began in earnest about ten years later, and dealt almost entirely on the question of fact. The main exponent of the play's being unassisted was Tim Murnane. He had been the Providence first baseman in the game. After he retired from the playing field he became a sportswriter for the Boston Globe. He recounted the famous play, crediting Hines for making it unassisted.

This provoked a response from William Rankin, a veteran sportswriter with the New York Clipper. Rankin was cantankerous and contrarian. He delighted in debunking baseball myths. His typical technique was to use the Clipper files to correct others' reminiscences.[1] He approached the Hines triple play in his usual manner. He consulted the Clipper's biographical sketch of Hines in the December 5, 1879, issue, which included a description of the play:

> In the Providence-Boston game, at Providence, R.I., on May 8, 1878, the Bostons wanted one run to tie the score, and had men on second and third bases, with none out and Burdock at the bat. He made a seemingly safe hit just over the short stop's head, which was captured on the fly close to the ground by Hines, after running at terrific speed, and, keeping straight on, he touched third base, and then completed a brilliant triple play by throwing the ball to second base before the respective occupants of the bases could return.[2]

Rankin reprinted this, pointing out that it showed that the triple play was not unassisted.[3]

Murnane responded with his own recollection:

> The writer at the time played first base in the same game for Providence, and a short statement might convince The Clipper that the play was made. Manning and Sutton were on third and second respectively. There was one out [sic: should be "no one out"] and Burdock was at the bat. One run was needed to tie the score in the eighth inning. Burdock hit a short line fly that

96

would have touched the ground about twenty feet back of second base. The base runners, seeing the impossibility of any one getting the hit, went for home. Sutton had touched third before Hines had the ball, which he got within a few inches of the ground. He had nearly lost his balance, and was past second base before he got straightened up. Hague stood on third base ready to take the ball when Hines sent it to him, but Sutton, who was near the home plate, saw there was no chance to get back, and Hines kept on running until he stood on third base. As the men were forced, all three were out. Every one seemed to be mixed up, and Hines walked down the line to second, touched the base and tossed the ball to Tommy Bond, the Boston pitcher. As the men never attempted to go back when Hines touched third base, he had accomplished a triple play.[4]

Rankin responded by referring to the *Clipper*'s original game account, in the May 18, 1878, issue, which confirmed the 1879 version, and concluded that Murnane was simply wrong.[5] Murnane confirmed his version with Hines himself. This led to the final piece of the puzzle, so far as Rankin was concerned. This came the following summer, when Ezra Sutton, the runner from second, who was still playing professional ball, gave his version:

> Hines is wrong; for at the time I had not reached third base, as he claims, but was fully twenty feet away from that point when the ball was caught.[6]

This set the terms of the dispute. Murnane, backed by Hines, claimed that Sutton was past third base when it was tagged. Rankin, backed by Sutton, claimed that he was not. Other participants in the game chimed in on either side. Most articles over the next few decades simply restated one position or the other, or left the conclusion open. Minor variants crept in, such as a claim that Hines, after tagging third, ran down and tagged Sutton.[7] Another variation: Hines caught the ball, then tagged second before running to and tagging third base.[8] The essential question remained the location of Sutton when Hines tagged third.

The argument for the unassisted version was gradually bolstered by interviews with other participants in the game. The most thorough of these was reported by Smith D. Fry in 1913 for *Baseball Magazine*. Fry began with Nicholas Young, the former president of the National League, who had in 1878 been the league secretary. Young claimed that he had never heard of

Paul Hines might have, or might not have, made a historic unassisted triple play in 1878.

HINES, CENTRE FIELD, WASHINGTON.

any doubt expressed about the play being unassisted, which if true suggests he hadn't been paying attention. In any case the source of his authority is unclear. There has never been any suggestion that he was present at the game. Next, Fry interviewed Charley Snyder and Doug Allison, the two catchers in the game, then Hines himself, and finally he corresponded with umpire Charley Daniels. They all agreed that Sutton had been past third base. Daniels added that he called out, "Three out. Side out," before Hines threw the ball to Sweasy. Allison has the variant that Tom Carey, the shortstop, took the ball from Hines and threw it to Sweasy, and as Sweasy tagged second base he and Carey shouted to the crowd, "Just for good measure."[9]

This is how the debate has remained to this day. A recent example is an essay "Three in One?" by Kathy Torres in the SABR publication *Inventing Baseball*.[10] Another is a post entitled "Paul Hines and the Unassisted Triple Play" by John Thorn on his blog *Our Game*.[11] Torres is noncommittal, while Thorn (the official historian of Major League Baseball) affirms his belief that the play was unassisted. MLB.com, on the other hand, does not include the play from its list of unassisted triple plays, implicitly rejecting the claim.[12]

THE CONTEMPORANEOUS ACCOUNTS

What did the newspaper accounts at the time say about the play? A review was made of eleven accounts (two of which are duplicated, appearing in identical form in two additional newspapers). Six are from Boston newspapers: the *Daily Advertiser*, *Globe*, *Herald*, *Journal*, *Post*, and *Evening Transcript*. Two are from Providence papers: the *Journal* (duplicated in the *Providence*

Bulletin) and the *Press* (duplicated in the *Providence Star*). Two are from Cincinnati papers, the *Commercial* and the *Enquirer*. These were all published the day after the game. The last is from the weekly *New York Clipper*, the closest thing to a baseball newspaper of record at this time, from the issue of May 18, 1878.

The accounts that reach the necessary level of detail agree that Sutton was past third. Several are silent on the question, but none suggest that he was between second and third. The *Globe* unequivocally wrote "...Hines kept on to third, which both Manning and Sutton had passed running home on the fly..." The *Daily Advertiser* stated that Manning and Sutton "started for home, and never looked behind them until they reached there" while the *Commercial* said of them "both of whom had reached home plate." In no account is there any suggestion that Sutton loitered between second and third or that he made an attempt to return after he had passed third.

The question would seem to be answered. The evidence is overwhelming that Sutton was indeed past third base. In retrospect, the competing version with Sutton between second and third never made much sense. This was a slow-developing play, with Hines running in from center field all the way to third base, then throwing to second. If Sutton had been cautiously lingering midway between second and third he would have had ample time to get back to the bag. If he had passed third base and was scrambling to return to second he would have had to run past Hines on his way back. This scenario would require special pleading such that the play was even more remarkable than as reported.

THE CONTEMPORANEOUS INTERPRETATIONS

With the facts of the play established, the next question is: was this considered an unassisted play? The *Boston Globe* clearly states that it was: "Hines kept on to third, which both Manning and Sutton had passed running home on the fly, and there stopping, made a triple play with no assistance." But at the same time the account in the *Providence Journal* expressly states that the throw to second is what retired the last runner and completed the triple play: "[Hines] touched third, thus, unassisted, putting out both Burdock and Manning, and then threw swiftly to Sweasey, retiring Sutton, and completing a brilliant triple play..."

The opinion that the play was assisted was the more widely held. Of the eleven accounts, seven unambiguously indicate that the throw to second completed the play. Three of the four that count the triple play as unassisted were Boston papers: the

Globe, *Journal*, and *Post*, with the *Cincinnati Enquirer* the one other paper holding this position. These positions are often stated in the narrative descriptions of the game, and are reflected in the box scores. Figure 1 shows the box score from the *Providence Journal*. Note that Hines is credited with fielding four outs and one assist and Sweasey has one out and two assists, and that the summary assigns credit for the triple play to Hines and Sweasey. Compare this with Figure 2, showing the box score from the *Boston Globe*. Hines here has five outs and zero assists while Sweasey has zero outs and three assists.

There also were two near-contemporaneous discussions of the matter. The *New York Clipper* and the *Chicago Tribune* at this time included weekly question-and-answer sections. Some unnamed persons in Providence made a bet on whether or not the triple play was unassisted. They appealed to a "local authority" who ruled that "the ball must be thrown to second." The loser in this decision then appealed to the *Clipper*, appearing in the May 18, 1878, issue:

[Question:] A player is on 3d and another on 2d, no one out. The batsman strikes a high ball towards centre-field, on which the men on bases run home. Centre field catches the ball on fly, and runs to third base, both of the runners having run home. Are not both of them out by the catcher of the fly-ball touching third base before they returned to that base without his throwing the ball to second base? [Answer:] Certainly they are.[13]

This in turn provoked an appeal to the *Tribune*, appearing in the May 19, 1878, issue:

[Question:] ...Now will you please pass on the matter, and quote the rule, if there be one, to cover the matter? Answer—The thing is simple enough. Sec. 12 of Rule 5 reads: "Any player running the bases on fair or foul balls caught before touching the ground must return to the base he occupied when the ball was struck, and retouch such base before attempting to make another or score a run, and said player shall be liable to be put out in so returning, as in the case of running to first base when a fair ball is hit and not caught flying." The man who was on second base must return to that base, it being the one he occupied "when the ball was struck," and he can be put out by holding the ball on that base (not some other base) before he gets back. So far as putting the man out is concerned, the ball might as well be held on the manager's nose as on the third base. It would affect as much one way as the other.[14]

THE RULES QUESTION

The question of fact turns out to be a garden path. Sutton certainly was past third. There was no disagreement at the time. Where opinions differed was how to score the play. Was Sutton out at third, or at second? Here we turn to the rules. The relevant rule in 1878, as the *Tribune* noted, was Rule V Section 12:

> Any player running the bases on fair or foul balls caught before touching the ground must return to the base he occupied when the ball was struck, and retouch such base before attempting to make another or score a run, and said player shall be liable to be put out in so returning, as in the case of running to first base when a fair ball is hit and not caught flying [i.e. a fielder with the ball need only tag the base, not the player].[15]

Can the runner be put out only from his original base, or can he be put out the same way at an intermediate base he has passed? The rule does not explicitly say.[16] There is room to interpret it both ways, hence the disagreement between newspaper accounts.[17]

What was the official ruling in 1878? Unfortunately, we don't know for sure. The home club's official scorer would send a score sheet to the NL secretary. Should a rules interpretation be necessary, the league secretary would be the next step up, followed by the league president, board of directors, and ultimately the annual league convention.

No interpretation above the club scorer was believed necessary at the time. Baseball had not yet reached a stage in its development where people felt questions such as this needed necessarily to be authoritatively answered. There was no question but that it had been a triple play, so neither club had any argument to appeal to a higher authority. The score sheet was not disputed and would therefore be the operative document. Sheets from this era, however, do not survive.

It would be typical for the official scorer to also be a local baseball reporter. Lewis Meacham of the *Chicago Tribune*, for example, was the Chicago club's official scorer. The *Tribune*'s box scores can stand in as a proxy for the official score sheet for games played in Chicago. But this only works if the identity of the official scorer is known, and what paper he wrote for. This is not the case here. The Providence club has received comparatively little attention from modern

AUTHOR'S COLLECTION

The box score from the Providence Journal *of May 9, 1878. Hines is credited with four outs and one assist, while Sweasy is credited with one out. The summary credits the triple play to both.*

The box score from the Boston Post *of May 9, 1878. Hines is credited with five outs and zero assists, while Sweasy is credited with zero outs.*

researchers, so it is possible that this information could be uncovered in the future. What is known at this point is that the Providence papers examined here all agreed that the triple play was only completed when the ball was thrown to Sweasy.[18]

INTERPRETING THE LATER DEBATE

How can a debate that has gone on for so long have been so beside the point? This is not hard to understand. Murnane, writing for the *Boston Globe*, had access to the *Globe*'s archives, one of the papers that reported the play as unassisted. It is likely that Murnane didn't even realize that there had been any other interpretation. Rankin, working from the *Clipper*'s archives, knew that it had reported the play as being completed by the throw to second. He too most likely did not know that it had been reported any other way. They were talking past each other. Rankin resolved this by accepting the implicit assumption about the rules interpretation, and recasting the dispute as being about the fact of where Sutton was. This was only possible because the *Clipper*'s account was ambiguous on this point. By casting the argument this way Rankin and Murnane were no longer talking past each other: they were merely disagreeing about what happened, with neither realizing that this was not the right question.

There also is the issue of incentives. The later debate was an extended exercise in chewing the fat: a topic for mid-winter discussion once discussion of the previous season had been exhausted but before there was much to talk about for next season. The incentive is to tell a good story. An unassisted triple play is a better story than a more conventional play.

An illustrative example is an interview of George Wright from 1915 in *The Sporting Life*. Wright had been with the Boston club in 1878. The interview rambles, with Wright telling old war stories. When he gets to the Hines play he tells how when Burdock hit the ball "it was obvious to the coacher on third base that it was going over the head of the shortstop. Consequently the coach signaled wildly for the two runners to go home." Then when Hines makes the catch the coach "was dumbfounded. He never thought for a second that Hines would try for the play, in fact he did not realize what had happened until it was all over. Then comes the denouement: "I know—because I was the coacher on third."[19] Wright had nothing to prove to anyone, so he was happy to turn this into a story he told on himself: a story which is much better if in relation to an epic play.

Another example is the account by the umpire, Charlie Daniels. The 1915 *Baseball Magazine* article was not the first time he had told this story. A similar version appeared four years earlier.[20] His contribution became part of the standard version. The problem is that Daniels was not, as he would recall it, the umpire at this game. That was John A. Cross. It is entirely possible that Daniels was present. The National League at that time maintained a list of approved umpires, with the names submitted by the various clubs. Daniels was based out of Boston, and Cross out of Providence. He might well have made the short journey to Providence to watch the game. Daniels also had a much longer umpiring career, extending through the 1880s, while Cross's career was brief and unremarkable. Daniels was part of the baseball community, telling and retelling the story of this memorable play he had witnessed. It was natural for his hearers to assume he had been the umpire. After enough retellings, he came to remember it that way, too. We need not take Daniels to have been a conscious liar, but neither should we take at face value the details of his version, with his instantaneous call of three outs while the ball was still seemingly in play.

There were only two people with an incentive to tell the story differently. The standard version has Sutton making a base running blunder. It is natural that he would favor a different version, where he was put out presumably through no fault of his own. Then there was Rankin, the driving force behind skepticism about the play. Rankin was a natural contrarian, so for him the incentive was to debunk the generally favored version.

The incentives also favored an argument about a concrete fact rather than an abstract rules debate. It is easy to make and to understand an argument about where the runner was. It is much harder to make and understand an argument about rules interpretation.

As much as anything, the lesson to be taken away is that not only do stories improve in the telling, but people forget what the issues were at the time of the events described.

CONCLUSION

The conclusion here is sadly unsatisfying. The best story would be to show conclusively that Hines had indeed made an unassisted triple play. We could remove the asterisk from the record, and tell the young ones the story of Hines's amazing play. The next best story would be to show conclusively that Hines had in fact not made an unassisted triple play. This would tidy up the record, and Rankin was not entirely wrong about the pleasures of contrarianism. What we have here is perhaps the worst outcome. The available evidence shows that the most common opinion at the time was that the play was not unassisted; that the official scorer most likely shared this opinion; but the evidence is not conclusive. The only hope for a final resolution is if the official scorer of the Providence club should be identified, and should he be a newspaper reporter, and should his account be available. Until then, the asterisk must remain. ■

Notes

1. For an example of Rankin going awry with this technique, see Richard Hershberger, "The Creation of the Alexander Cartwright Myth," *Baseball Research Journal* Vol. 43 No. 1 (Spring 2014), 13–21.
2. *New York Clipper*, December 5, 1879.
3. *New York Clipper*, January 26, 1889.
4. Quoted in the *New York Clipper* February 9, 1889.
5. Ibid.
6. *New York Clipper*, June 29, 1889.
7. *Cleveland Leader and Herald*, January 22, 1889.
8. Alfred Spink, *The National Game*, National Game Publishing Co., St. Louis: 1910, 262.
9. Smith D. Fry, "The Most Sensation Play in Baseball," *Baseball Magazine*, October 1913, 69–72.
10. Bill Felber, ed., *Inventing Baseball: The 100 Greatest Games of the 19th Century*, SABR Inc: Phoenix, AZ, 18–19.
11. John Thorn, Our Game blog, MLB.com, http://ourgame.mlblogs.com/2015/05/05/paul-hines-and-the-unassisted-triple-play.
12. MLB.com, http://mlb.mlb.com/mlb/history/rare_feats/index.jsp?feature=unassisted_triple_plays.
13. *New York Clipper*, May 18, 1878.
14. *Chicago Tribune*, May 19, 1878.
15. *Constitution and Playing Rules of the National League of Professional Base Ball Clubs*, Rule V Section12 (Chicago: A.G. Spalding and Bro., 1878).
16. As a point of information, the modern rules clarify this question. Rule 5.09(c)(1) (Rule 7.10(a) prior to the 2015 reorganization of the rules) reads: "Any runner shall be called out, on appeal, when… after a fly ball is caught, he fails to retouch his original base before he or his original base is tagged." Sutton would not be out at third under the modern rules, as it was not his original base. One way to look at the question is as whether the modern language is an alteration or a clarification of the older rule.
17. Thorn in his blog post cites 1878's Rule V Section 15, "Any base-runner failing to touch the base he runs for shall be declared out if the ball be held by a fielder, while touching said base, before the base-runner returns and touches it." This is not the relevant rule. It applies to a runner rounding the bases and missing a base. There is no hint that Sutton missed third base.
18. There is some indirect evidence hinting that the *Providence Dispatch* might have been the de facto organ of the club, and its baseball reporter the club's scorer. Unfortunately the daily edition appears not to have survived, and the Sunday edition has detailed reports only from the previous Saturday.
19. *Sporting Life*, November 20, 1915.
20. Hartford (CT) Courant, June 9, 1911.

Analyzing Coverage of the Hines Triple Play

Brian Marshall

In 1878 a triple play by Providence's Paul Hines did-n't attract any extraordinary attention other than the excitement of a triple play that saved the day for Providence. The Hines play gained notoriety in baseball folklore when it was labeled by some as the first unassisted triple play in National League history. The rules of the time, recorded stats, and likely events of the game itself are detailed by Richard Hershberger elsewhere in this journal. I began my own analysis by comparing and reviewing prominent articles about the play and discovered troubling discrepancies in the later accounts which fatally undermine their credibility.

Not surprisingly, the Providence newspapers had the most detailed coverage of the game. The following comes from the *Providence Morning Star* dated Thursday Morning, May 9, 1878.

> The score now stood Providence 3, Bostons 0. O'Rourke got his base on called balls. Manning sent a little grounder between first and second, which Sweasy hastily picked up and threw wild over Murnan's head, O'Rourke scoring on this un-fortunate error and Manning taking third. Sutton got first on a muffed ball by Murnan. Burdock then struck what everybody considered was a clean base hit, about two rods back of short stop's position, the men on bases having confidence enough to come home. Here a phenomenal and surprising play was made; Hines made a difficult and brilliant running catch of the ball, putting out the striker; the momentum acquired carried him near to third base, which he stepped on, thus forc-ing out Manning; Sweasy then signalled for the ball, which Hines threw to him, putting out Sut-ton. This triple play, saving two and perhaps more runs, created tempestuous enthusiasm, the crowd rising en masse, cheering and waving hats.[1]

Word for word the same coverage is found in the *Providence Evening Press* dated Thursday Evening, May 9, 1878.[2] The *Providence Journal*—as published in the *New York Clipper*— reported the game as follows:

O'Rourke obtained his first on called balls. Manning batted a slowly rolling grounder between first and second bases, which Sweasy picked up and hastily tossed to Murnan. It was tossed over his head, and O'Rourke ran like a deer around the bases and scored a run while Manning succeeded in reaching third—a most distressing error to the Providence spectators. Murnan muffed Sutton's fly, and then Burdock struck the ball, lifting it over Carey's head sufficiently far to warrant the base runners, and even the anxious crowd, in prophesying that it was a base hit, Manning and Sutton speeded to the home plate, while fear and trembling possessed the hearts of the breathless spectators. But Hines, meantime, had espied the ball, and running at the top of his speed from far centrefield, captured it ere it touched the ground, ceased not his running until he had touched third, thus, unassisted, putting out both Burdock and Manning, and threw swiftly to Sweasy, retir-ing Sutton, and completing a brilliant triple play, amid the wildest shouts and demonstrations of delight imaginable.[3]

Boston newspapers tended to be not as detailed. The *Boston Evening Transcript* dated Thursday Morn-ing, May 9, 1878 published:

In the eighth inning there was great excitement, when, through errors of the Providence club, O'Rourke scored and Manning and Sutton were on bases. Burdock struck a fly—just beyond Carey—which Hines caught after a long run, ran to third base and put out Manning and threw to second, putting out Sutton and making a triple play.[4]

The *Boston Herald*—as published in The *New York Clipper* read:

The game was a very exciting one, particularly in the eighth inning, when by errors of Providence alone O'Rourke scored and Manning and Sutton were on bases. Burdock struck a fly just back of short stop, which Hines seized after a long run, ran to third, put out Manning, and then threw to second in time to put out Sutton, making a triple play amid the utmost excitement.[5]

The *New York Clipper* itself ran the following:

In the eighth inning O'Rourke made the first run for the visitors off errors, leaving Manning and Sutton on bases. Burdock's fly back of short was captured by Hines after a sharp run, he putting out Manning at third, and throwing to second in time to put out Sutton.[6]

Nineteen months later, the triple play gained attention via a secondary mention, in a December 1879 biographical sidebar about Paul Hines in the *New York Clipper*:

As an outfielder he has but few if any equals, and the wonderful and brilliant running-catches made by him are too numerous to mention in detail, and we can only cite the following instance, culled at random: In the Providence-Boston game, at Providence, R. I., on May 8, 1878, the Bostons wanted one [sic] run to tie the score, and had men on the third and second bases, with none out, and Burdock at the bat. He made a seemingly safe hit just over short-stop's head, which was captured on the fly close to the ground by Hines, after running at terrific speed for more than fifty yards, and, keeping straight on, he touched third base and threw the ball to second before the respective occupants could return, thus making one of the most brilliant of the few triple-plays yet chronicled.[7]

This article was the first mention of the Boston runners being on second and third at the time of Burdock's hit. According to the *Clipper*, the trailing runner (whom we know to be Ezra Sutton) was at second, not first.

Almost a decade later, in fall 1888, chronicler Tim Murnane, who had played in that Boston-Providence game, alluded to the play being unassisted, and by spring 1889 Hines himself was making the claim. Sutton disputed Hines in a *Clipper* article dated June 29, 1889:

It is now a question of veracity between Paul Hines and Ezra Sutton as to whether the former

is to be credited with making a triple play unassisted. Hines claims that in a game between the Boston and Providence teams, May 8, 1878, in Providence, he accomplished the feat. Manning and Sutton were on third and second bases respectively in this game, when Burdock hit an apparently safe fly ball, but Hines, after a desperate run, caught the ball, and continued on to third, which he touched, and now he claims that as Manning and Sutton had both passed that base, he should be credited with making a triple unassisted. Hines says he can prove the feat by everyone present at the game. As Sutton was one of the base runners, we will give his version as follows: "Hines is wrong; for at the time I had not reached third base, as he claims, but was fully twenty feet away from that point when the ball was caught." Thus by touching third base Hines only made a double play, but by throwing the ball to Sweasy at second base, he completed a triple play, and this and Sutton's statement agree exactly with the account of the game as it appears in the files of THE CLIPPER.[8]

A *Clipper* article dated March 23, 1901, took issue with Murnane's assertion as well:

This stood unimpeached until the Fall of 1888, when Tim Murnan made the astonishing assertion that the records were all wrong and that Hines completed the triple play alone. It is singular that he should have waited so long before making such an absurd statement.[9]

The 1901 article also quoted Alfred H. Wright, who wrote the 1879 Hines bio sidebar in the *Clipper*:

It was Hines who told me about him running at terrific speed for more than fifty yards, he seeming particularly anxious about having the distance specified." Then why did not Hines also tell Mr. Wright that he had completed the play unassisted and have it inserted in his sketch, so it would have been an undisputed fact, and not have waited until he had been coached by Murnan [sic] in the Spring of 1889 before making the claim to that performance?[10]

Two months later *The Sporting News* published an article entitled "That Fake Triple Play" on the subject, quoting numerous players:

Jim O'Rourke, the Boston center fielder:

It is with pleasure I give you my recollections of this phenomenal catch by Paul Hines. I won't attempt in language to particularly describe the impressions made upon us by this catch. Its effect was electric. You can imagine enough. Why, the circumstances of that catch are as fresh in my mind today as if it happened but yesterday. I can picture Hines coming down the little slope from center field toward third base like a deer, reaching at full length, catching the ball within an inch of the ground, and not stopping until he landed on third base, from which he returned the ball to second base, thereby completing a triple play, the brilliancy of which I never since recalled. My dear friend, Tim Murnan, must be under a misapprehension when he says Hines completed the triple play unassisted.[11]

Charlie Sweasy:

In answer to your query I would state that I assisted Hines in making the triple play mentioned, viz.: The ball was struck by Burdock to short left field. Hines started for it on the dead run, and succeeded in catching it, but nearly stumbled. Regaining his feet he kept on running to third base, reaching it before Manning succeeded in returning, thereby putting Manning out. Sutton, who had reached third base, seeing Hines coming with the ball, started back to second base. Hines, after touching third base, started to catch Sutton, but Sutton, being a good swift runner as well as Hines, he saw that could not catch him and threw the ball to me at second base in time to put Sutton out. This is my recollection of the play.[12]

Sweasy's comments imply Ezra Sutton was likely on first base, rather than second, if Sutton had only reached the area of third shortly before Hines. If Hines ran about fifty yards to make the catch and then traveled to third, and with thirty yards between bases, Hines and Sutton traveled about the same distance. Therefore a sprinting Sutton would have gone first to third. Had he been on second base, it is highly probable he would have rounded third base before Hines's arrival.

Tommy Bond, the Boston pitcher, provided a short response saying that the events of the triple play were as stated in the *Providence Journal*. Bond's short comment was followed by Sutton's:

Would say to reply that my letter published in the *Clipper* in June 1889 in reference to the triple play is correct in every detail. I reproduce it here: "I notice that Paul Hines, in writing the *Boston Globe*, says; 'Sutton was near the home plate when I touched third base, putting out both Manning and Sutton, and completing a triple play.' Hines is wrong, for at the time I had not reached third base, as he claims, but was fully twenty feet away from that point when the ball was caught. Hines touched third base, putting out Manning, and then threw the ball to Sweasy at second base, putting me out. The two men made the triple play.

Jack Manning, the Boston right fielder, added:

As I remember the triple play you refer to, it happened just as the papers stated at the time. With two men on base, one on second and the other on third, Burdock hit a fly over the shortstop's head, which everybody thought was safe, and both men started for home. Hines, after a hard run, caught the ball close to the ground and kept on running to third base, putting out the man who had occupied that base before he could return. He [Hines] started for Sutton, who was trying to get back to second base, when somebody shouted to him to throw the ball and he threw to Sweasy, who was playing second base at the time, thereby completing the triple play, which was a dandy, giving Hines two put outs and an assist.

Last was Doug Allison, the Providence catcher:"All I can say is Hines put out only two men unassisted and threw the ball to Sweasy at second base, this getting an assist."

The following year, *The New York Times* published an article when Harry O'Hagan managed an unassisted triple play that included a statement from Sweasy:

Charles J. Sweasy, who covered second base for the Providence team during the game, made a statement showing conclusively that Hines did not make the play unassisted, Sweasy said:

I assisted Hines in making the triple play mentioned so largely in the public prints. The ball was struck by Burdock to short left field. Hines started for it on a dead run, and succeeded in catching it, but nearly stumbled. Regaining his feet, however, he kept on running to third base, reaching that station before Manning could return, thereby putting Manning out.

Sutton, who had reached third, seeing Hines coming with the ball, started back to second. Hines touched third and started to catch Sutton, but, Sutton being a good sprinter, Hines saw that he could not catch him, and threw the ball to me at second base in time to catch Sutton before he reached it.

This statement of Second Baseman Sweasy, who assisted in the play, disposes of Hines's [sic] claim to have accomplished a triple play unassisted.[13]

Sweasy's comments in that 1902 *Times* article effectively replicate his previous comments in *The Sporting News*.

By then Tim Murnane was President of the New England League and edited the first guide of the National Association of Professional Baseball Leagues, published by Spalding. The guide included not only not only the stats, rules, schedules, and a catalog of Spalding sporting products section, but a few sections of general interest, one of which was titled "Hines' Great Triple Play."[14] Three players involved in the game, George Wright, Jack (John) Manning, and Murnane himself, were quoted. The article opens, "On June 8, 1878, at Providence, R. I., Paul Hines accomplished a triple play unaided." Of course, what Murnane meant to say was May, not June.

George Wright, who was the captain of the Boston club, said:

I was coaching back of third base at the time. The score was 2 to 1 in favor of Providence, and I was anxious to get in two runs, as it practically meant the game. Burdock hit the ball and my whole attention was turned to the runner coming from second, as it looked like a perfectly safe drive. As the runner came to third I coached him home, never dreaming of a catch. When I saw that Hines had actually reached the ball and was still running towards me I commenced to realize that both men were out. As Manning never looked to the right or left, but was headed for home until the boys stood up and waved him back, it was too late, and I remember as if it was but yesterday how Hines ran up and stood on third base with the ball still in his hand, completing a triple play.[15]

Wright's comments are riddled with inaccuracies. The score was 3–0 going into the bottom of the eighth inning, not 2–1, and became 3–1 once Jim O'Rourke scored. The second issue is twofold: a) a runner on second base and b) the implication of it being Manning on second base. It was impossible for the runner on second base to be Manning given Boston's batting order. And Wright's account of Hines standing on third base holding the ball contravenes all the many descriptions of the throw to Sweasy.

The next player to comment was Jack (John) Manning:

I was taking a big lead off second base. As Sutton was on third, I felt sure that my run would win the game. When Burdock hit a low liner to the left of second I took my cue from the coacher at third and turned for home, figuring that I must beat out a throw. I was over half way home when I noticed the Boston players on the bench jumping about and yelling for me to go back. There was a mix-up. Hines was standing on third base with the ball, while his own players were yelling for him to throw it to second.[16]

Again, Manning could not have been on second base while Sutton was on third since Sutton batted after him. A second matter is the description of Burdock's hit being a "low liner." A low liner to the left of second base would not have allowed Hines enough time to run under it to catch it, and contradicts accounts that described the hit as "over the head" of the short stop. The other critical point about the Manning comments is that they were night and day different in every regard—who was on second, who was on third, the type of hit that Burdock made, and where the runners were when Hines reached third—from his comments in *The Sporting News*.

Lastly, Tim Murnane:

The writer was playing first base in that game for Providence, and was in a perfect place to see the play and here is how he saw it: With Sutton on third, Manning at second and Burdock at the bat. Hines made a move to play a deep field, and then edged in, as Burdock was placing the ball very cleverly at the time, and a safe hit meant mischief to Providence, as there was no one out and the score was 2 to 1, with the game about over. Thinking that Hines was well out, Burdock chopped one to short left center that looked like a 50 to 1 shot, and away went Sutton and

Manning. At third base George Wright, with cap in hand, waved Manning in. When the ball was hit Hines was under a full head of steam like a flash, and being a remarkably quick starter he saw there was a dying chance to save the day. It was a bit down grade from center field where he was playing, the ground bare of grass and quite hard. The players speed was unusually fast. With a long reach the ball was taken six inches from the ground about fifteen yards back of second base, five yards to the left of the base. This angle headed Hines towards third base, and never fully regaining his feet until he struck the base line, while keeping his eye on the runners, he ran down the line with the ball raised to throw, and Hague was standing at third for the ball but finding that both of the runners were close to the home plate he jogged to the base and stood there fully fifteen seconds while the crowd howled like mad and the players were lost in the excitement. As Hines stood at third Sweasy was at second calling for the ball, wanting to make sure thing of it, as Manning had started back, Hines walked down the baseline about five yards and tossed the ball to Sweasy, who called for an out at second, wholly unnecessary, but yet in a way to mystify the scorers of that time, and the result was that the play was never accurately reported.[17]

The Murnane article is a wonder because all three of the players made two identical errors— reporting the score as 2–1, that Sutton was on third and Manning at second—easily disproved by a glance at the boxscore. It was as if they had agreed to report in a coordinated fashion yet the three of them didn't even have the basic facts straight. In the final paragraph Murnane states, "I have taken a great deal of time and trouble to see that justice has been done Mr. Hines."

In 1915 George Wright again presented his version of the play, this time in *Sporting Life*:

I was on the Boston team at the time and we came down to Providence to play. At the time the triple play was made by Hines there were Boston men on second and third bases. The batter hit a Texas Leaguer and it was obvious to the coacher on third base that it was going over the head of the shortstop. Consequently the coach signaled wildly for the two runners to go home. Hines came in with a burst of speed from center field, made a remarkable scooping catch of the ball just as it was about to touch the ground, and ran all

the way to third base. The man on third was home and the man who had been on second had crossed third and was nearly half way home. So by touching the third bag Hines forced out two. The coacher on third was dumbfounded. He never thought for a second that Hines would try for the play, in fact he did not realize what happened until it was all over. I know—because I was the coacher on third.[18]

Interestingly Wright did not mention the score at the time nor the names of the runners. One can only speculate he had become aware of the errors he made in the Murnane article.

The Hines triple play was also recounted in *Baseball Magazine* in 1913.[19] Smith D. Fry was writing in Washington and therefore consulted baseball people from the Washington, DC area, including Paul Hines himself, as well as Nick Young, Charlie Snyder, Doug Allison, and umpire Charlie Daniels. Fry also mentions Senator Nelson W. Aldrich who actually saw the game and was a resident of Washington at the time the article was being researched.

The first person Fry consulted was "Uncle Nick Young" who was Secretary of the National League at the time the play was made. "Everybody in the baseball world knew that Hines made that triple play unassisted," Young declared. "No baseball authority ever denied it." Although Young was a resident of Washington and his prominent history with the league should have lent credibility to his words, it appears that Young did not actually witness the play.

Fry spoke with both catchers from the game, Doug Allison for Providence and Pop Snyder for Boston. "I certainly saw Paul Hines make his great triple play, unassisted," said Snyder.

Paul Hines swept like a whirlwind from deep center into short left field, and he caught that ball. I should say about knee high or lower. The ball was going like a rifle shot, but Paul gripped it, held it as one man out of a thousand could have done, and ran on to third base. Both of our runners had gone past third base and were congratulating themselves on having made runs. It was a triple play, unassisted, and was so declared by the umpire.

The most glaring aspect about Snyder's comments has to do with position of the base runners at the time when Burdock came to bat and the fact that the base runner on first made it all the way around to score, meaning he covered two hundred and seventy feet. It simply isn't probable that a base runner would cover ninety yards in the same time that it took Hines to cover some sixty yards or so to reach third base. That would imply that the base runner, not running in a straight line and having to touch second and third bases, was able to cover a third more distance than Hines, who was running in a relatively straight line, in the same amount of time.

Doug Allison provided the following:

Yes, I was catcher for the Providence Grays that year. I was behind the bat when Burdock came to the plate. Boston's second baseman, Sutton, made a single to begin the inning. Then Manning, who was Boston's pitcher and also center fielder, was the next batter, and he also made a single. That put Sutton on second and Manning on first. Burdock was a dangerous batter. When he came up I signaled Paul to get out into deep field for him, and he did so. But I noticed that Paul was shifting toward left, guessing the batter well. Well, Burdock hit the second ball that was pitched, and he smashed it out into left field. It looked to like a sure enough home run, clearing the bases. But as I saw Burdock rushing around the paths I also saw Paul Hines come tearing in from deep center to short left. He speared it about knee high in short left, back of third. He stumbled and almost fell, but kept on running and veering around, he kept on until he reached third base. There he halted and held up the ball. We only had one umpire in those days, and Charley Daniels, one of the best, was umpiring that day. He saw what Paul was up to, ran out toward him, and was not more than ten feet away when Paul perched on third base with the ball aloft in his hand. Daniels called out his decision: 'Three out, Side out.' And that crowd went wild.

Then, as I remember it, Carey, our shortstop, took the ball and threw it to Sweeney [sic], our second baseman, and he touched second base as they both shouted to the crowd: "Just for good measure."

Allison has Sutton batting before Manning and also stated the umpire was Charlie Daniels when it wasn't, it was John A. Cross. Lastly Allison mentioned "Carey, our shortstop, took the ball and threw it to Sweeney" which contradicts his own comments in *The Sporting News*. The mention of Carey was a first, and was the

mention of "Sweeney" simply a slip from "Sweasy?" Paul Hines himself said:

"It was at Providence, Rhode Island, May 15 [sic], 1878. I knew that Burdock was a dangerous batter. I knew also that he was inclined to pull 'em [sic] out into left field. Believing that any long knock into left field would be gathered in by our left fielder, I figured that Burdock might knock one into the field too short for the left fielder and too far out for either the third baseman or the shortstop. While I was guessing the batter and moving toward left field (as 'Doug' Allison told you he saw me), Burdock got his hit. I was on the move in a dog trot while our pitcher, Corey, was winding up. When ball and bat cracked I was under way instantly; and instantly I saw where the ball was going. I barely got there in time to grip the ball somewhere between my knee and ankle. It was so near my ankle that I almost fell and broke my neck. Although I came near falling, I managed to keep my balance by keeping up the momentum until I could swerve about toward third base. As soon as stepped on the base I held up the ball. Umpire Charley Daniels was quite near. The umpire called so that he could be heard all over the field; 'Three out, Side out.' Somebody motioned me to go to second base. You know, my hearing is deficient, and I depended largely on signs in those days. Well, I ran down and touched second. Then Carey, our shortstop, and Sweeney, our second baseman, took the ball, and danced around with it, cutting up monkey shines."[20]

The Hines recollection was vastly different than that presented in the *New York Clipper* dated December 6, 1879.[21] Hines mentioned Charlie Daniels as the umpire, Carey, and Sweeney as the second baseman as Allison had done, implying there was a degree of collusion in their recollections.

How about Charlie Daniels, the apparent umpire according to Hines and Allison? He told Fry:

Well, well, well, so they are still trying to deny dear old Paul that famous triple play unassisted. I was the umpire on that occasion and was connected with the National League, and the American Association many years afterward, and in active association with the game between twenty-five and thirty years; most of the time I was umpiring.

On the occasion of the famous play by Paul Hines, Ezra Sutton was on second base and someone else was on first base. Burdock, at the bat, hit a fly which travelled rainbow fashion to left field. There was a light wind blowing, and carrying the ball a little toward second base, but back of it. When the second baseman saw Paul tearing in after the ball, he wisely got out of the way.

Sutton made home, from second base, and the other man was near the home plate, when Hines caught the ball about a foot from the ground, almost turned a somersault, and rushed to third base, where he stood and held up the ball. Of course I did my duty then and made the decision; "Three out. Side out."

According to the published boxscores for the May 8, 1878, game the umpire was John A. Cross. Retrosheet lists what individual games each man umpired during a given season. Cross is listed as having umpired the May 8, 1878, game while Daniels is not.[22,23] I am at a loss to explain why Daniels would claim credit for being the umpire in a game for which he was not.

The final paragraph of the *Baseball Magazine* article states: "These statements of fact, told without rhetorical effort or other display, but merely with historic intent, should settle for all time the right of Paul Hines to the fame of making the first and greatest triple play, unassisted, ever made in the national game. Every true sportsman likes to give 'honor to whom honor is due.'"[24]

Knowing that the article is filled with contradictory and incorrect statements, coupled with apparent collusion much like the Murnane article of 1902, one cannot take the final paragraph at face value. According to Murnane, his article of 1902 was supposed to settle for all time that Paul Hines made the first "unassisted" triple play in in National League history. To Mr. Fry and Mr. Murnane, I say, "So gentlemen, which is it? Who has the true story?" It's a rhetorical question because the answer is neither of them. Why, because the play wasn't unassisted at all; it was assisted and both Murnane and Fry, who tried to use the players, and others, as a means to gain perceived credibility, in a coordinated effort to make their story appear factual in the eyes of the baseball community. In the end both Fry and Murnane not only stumbled over themselves but lost any credibility they might have gained from using the players, and others, to begin with. After analyzing all the information to write this paper it is evident to this writer that the triple play from the game played on May 8, 1878, involving Paul Hines, was an assisted triple play and not an unassisted triple play. ■

Author's Note

Team names and the spelling of player names, not from quoted material, was based on that as listed on baseball-reference.com.

Additional References

Kathy Torres, "Three in One?" in *Inventing Baseball: The 100 Greatest Games of the 19th Century* (Phoenix, AZ: Society for American Baseball Research, Inc., 2013.) 108–09.

John Thorn. "Paul Hines and the Unassisted Triple Play," MLB.com Blogs, Our Game, posted May 5, 2015.

Notes

1. "After That Pennant: Providence, 3; Boston, 2: Hines Saves Us By a Triple Play," *Providence Morning Star*, Thursday Morning, May 9, 1878, 1.
2. "After That Pennant: Providence, 3; Bostons, 2: Hines Saves Us By a Triple Play," *Providence Evening Press*, Thursday Evening, May 9, 1878, 1.
3. "Baseball: That Triple Play," *New York Clipper*, March 23, 1901, 80.
4. "Base Ball," *Boston Evening Transcript*, Thursday Evening, May 9, 1878, 5.
5. "Baseball: That Triple Play," *New York Clipper*, March 23, 1901, 80.
6. "Baseball: Boston vs Providence," *New York Clipper*, May 18, 1878, 59.
7. "Paul A. Hines, Centre-fielder," *New York Clipper*, December 6, 1879, 293.
8. "Baseball: Stray Sparks From The Diamond," *New York Clipper*, June 29, 1889, 261.
9. "Baseball: That Triple Play," *New York Clipper*, March 23, 1901, 80.
10. Ibid.
11. "That Fake Triple Play: Players Who Were in the Game Say Sweasy Helped Hines," *The Sporting News*, Volume 31, Number 8, May 4, 1901, 7.
12. Ibid.
13. "The Greatest Play Ever Made In Baseball: How O'Hagan Put Out Three Men Unassisted on Monday Last," *The New York Times*, Sunday, August 24, 1902, 23.
14. T. H. Murnane, Editor. "Hines' Great Triple Play," in *Official Guide of the National Association of Professional Base Ball Leagues for Season of 1902*. New York, NY: A. G. Spalding & Bros., 1902, 53–56.
15. Ibid.
16. Ibid.
17. Ibid.
18. "A Real Old-Timers Talk of Early Days: The First Unassisted Triple Play," *Sporting Life*, Volume 12, Number 20, November 20, 1915, 6.
19. "The Most Sensational Play in Baseball: How Neal Ball Became Famous in Day—A Greater Feat by an Old-Time Star—Paul Hines and His Wonderful Triple Play of 1878," *Baseball Magazine*, Volume 11, Issue 6, October 1913, 69–72.
20. Ibid.
21. "Paul A. Hines, Centre-fielder," *New York Clipper*, December 6, 1879, 293.
22. Retrosheet Web Page: Umpire John Cross, 1878. Accessed March 15, 2016: http://www.retrosheet.org/boxesetc/C/Pcrosj901.htm.
23. Retrosheet Web Page: Umpire Charles F. Daniels, 1878. Accessed March 15, 2016: http://www.retrosheet.org/boxesetc/D/Pdanic901.htm
24. "The Most Sensational Play in Baseball: How Neal Ball Became Famous in Day—A Greater Feat by an Old-Time Star—Paul Hines and His Wonderful Triple Play of 1878," *Baseball Magazine*, Volume 11, Issue 6, October 1913, 69–72.

Notes Related to Cy Young's First No-Hitter

Brian Marshall

Next to a perfect game, the no-hitter may be the most alluring event in baseball, attracting the attention of researchers, historians, and fans alike. Historians are keen to understand every detail related to a no-hitter—easily done for recent games, but not for the games of the nineteenth century. We were told in the movie *Field of Dreams* that "the one constant through all the years has been baseball," and while that may be true in general, it certainly isn't true in terms of the level of detail. The information resources of the time were typically only the newspapers that covered the game, and their attention to detail not only varied but information often wasn't complete. Case in point are the various articles published regarding Cy Young's first no-hitter, which provide conflicting, incorrect, and incomplete information. Given the stature of Cy Young in the history of Major League Baseball, anything that advances our know-ledge of such a significant performance in his career is of interest. This article compiles the first known "play-by-play" for this game in order to clarify the proceedings on an inning-by-inning basis. The intent is not to discuss Cy Young's pitching but to clarify the events of the no-hitter and improve the historical record.

Denton True (Cyclone, Cy for short) Young pitched three no-hitters in his career, one of which (May 5, 1904) was the first perfect game in American League history and also the first in the majors at the present pitching distance.[1,2] His first occurred on September 18, 1897, while pitching for the Cleveland Spiders, in the first game of a doubleheader against the Cincinnati Reds.[3,4,5,6]

That Saturday was fair, about 70 degrees, with brisk northerly winds for the first game of a doubleheader at League Park in Cleveland, Ohio.[7] The game started at one o'clock local time with the Reds at bat. The game featured six future Hall of Famers in Cy Young, Jesse Burkett, and Bobby Wallace for Cleveland, and Jake Beckley, Bid McPhee, and Buck Ewing for Cincinnati. Ewing was the manager of the Reds at the time.

Often the detailed information in the lower portion of the boxscores of the late nineteenth century mentioned the number of bases on balls and strikeouts for a given pitcher, but didn't always identify the batters that they applied to. To add even more spice to the mix, the game write-ups could be misleading. Take, for example, the small blurb ahead of the game boxscore in *Sporting Life* which states, in reference to the Cincinnati baserunners: "Only four men got to first, all on errors." While it is true that only four men reached first base, it is inaccurate that they all reached on errors. One of them reached on a base on balls as indicated right below that same boxscore: "First on Balls—By [sic] Young 1, by Rhines 4."[8] This sort of contradiction was not uncommon in the published material of the time. The article covering the game often did not jibe with the boxscore statistics.

To identify which players struck out and walked in the game, I not only studied the newspaper boxscores, I also solicited the ICI (Information Concepts Incorporated) data.[9] The *Cleveland Leader* newspaper coverage proved to be extremely useful in that it not only filled in the holes, but brought my attention to a set of errors in the boxscore.[10] All of the boxscores that I had seen—both published at the time and afterward—indicate eight hits for Cleveland and 30 at bats. These totals are correct but there was an error in how the hits were credited to two of the Cleveland players, Cupid Childs and Cy Young. The boxscores incorrectly list Childs with two hits, not one, while Young actually had one hit not zero. (See the corrected boxscore on page 114.) The *Leader* states the following:

> In the fourth Pickering walked, Belden beat a pretty bunt, Zimmer sacrificed, and on Young's infield drive Pick was caught at the plate. Burkett's single scored Belden. Young was out trying for third on it.[11]

The description of Young's hit as an "infield drive" may have been a play on words since the *Cincinnati Enquirer* referred to the hit as a "tap."[12] Young's fourth-inning hit could have been a fielder's choice, much like Belden's could have provided the situation

NATIONAL BASEBALL HALL OF FAME LIBRARY, COOPERSTOWN, NY

Cy Young

for a fielder's choice. Unfortunately, the newspaper articles do not specify who fielded Young's hit, nor do we know where the infielders were standing at the time, which makes it difficult to say whether Young could have reached first base prior to the throw getting there. We also do not know whether the ball would have been fielded cleanly in time to make the throw to first, not to mention that it may have been a situation where the only put-out that was possible was at home plate. Since Pickering was not forced at home, that was possibly a tougher play since the tag had to be applied, while Young at first would have required no tag. Young did, in fact, reach first base—hence it is presumed the play to get Young out at first was not a given and Young should be credited with a hit. In comparing the Belden hit in the fourth with the Young tap, it is possible the hits may have been similar in nature with the only difference being there was a play at the plate associated with the Young hit while there was a possible play at second base associated with the Belden hit. I constructed an inning-by-inning play-by-play for the game which documents each of the plate appearances as well as each of the outs. (See play-by-play on page 115.)

The play-by-play confirms that Childs had one hit, a double in the first inning, not two, which presents

a dilemma regarding the Young hit. If Young's hit is considered a valid hit then two corrections must be made to the boxscore: 1) the hits for Childs would change from two to one and 2) the hits for Young would change from zero to one.

I was able to validate each of the other hits for Cleveland. Belden and O'Connor each had two, Childs one—the only extra base hit in the game, and Burkett, Young, and Pickering each had singles for a total of eight Cleveland hits. I also reviewed the ICI game-by-game data sheets for both Childs and Young to understand how ICI assessed them. As expected, their data were consistent with that of the typical newspaper boxscore: two hits in three at bats for Childs and zero hits in three at bats for Young. At the very least, if Young's hit is not considered a valid hit, it is still necessary to change the Childs hits, reducing Cleveland's hits to seven, not eight.

The game coverage in the newspapers does not indicate any double plays, which further validates Childs having only one hit. Otherwise there would have to have been an additional Cleveland batter. The *Cleveland Leader* game coverage was another example of the boxscore not reflecting the written coverage of the game. For whatever reason, the boxscore data didn't reflect the written account of the game. Possibly the person who wrote the game coverage wasn't the person who compiled the boxscore.

I was also interested to validate the number of at bats for Cincinnati in relation to the number of baserunners. The play-by-play made this a very simple job since Cy Young only faced 29 batters, equivalent to plate appearances. In fact, Young never faced more than three batters in a single inning except in the sixth, when he faced five batters. Of the 29 plate appearances, one of them was walked, Billy Rhines in the sixth inning, which meant there were only 28 actual at bats. Regarding the Cincinnati baserunners, there were only four of them throughout the whole game. Three reached on errors—Bug Holliday twice and Tommy Corcoran once—and as mentioned Rhines was walked. Holliday reached on errors in the fourth inning and sixth. In the fourth he was put out when he tried to steal second base and in the sixth he was left on base. Corcoran reached on an error in the fifth inning, stole second base, and was put out trying to steal third. Only two Cincinnati baserunners managed to reach second base and none got as far as third. Two Cincinnati baserunners were left on base, Rhines and Holliday, both in the sixth. In comparison, the play-by-play stated Cleveland only left four men on base, not five as the published boxscores indicate. The men left on base were McKean in the first inning as the result of an error, Belden and Zimmer in the second inning after being walked, and Burkett in the fourth inning as the result of a hit.

Some drama ensued regarding whether the two times Holliday reached base should have been scored as hits or as errors by Bobby Wallace, third baseman for Cleveland. The *Cleveland Leader* stated the following:

Only four visitors reached first base during the game. Rhines drew the lonely gift, a very bad throw by McKean, after a very easy chance gave Corcoran a life, and Holliday was twice safe on errors by Wallace. One was a slow grounder which Bobby got his hands on, but let roll past him to left field, and the other was a sharp-hit drive which Wallace grabbed in wonderful style, but threw wild to first, pulling O'Connor five feet off the bag. Had the throw been good, Holliday would have been an easy out. This last chance was the only approach to a hit which the Reds got, and it was by no means near enough to mar Young's great record.[13]

The *Cleveland Plain Dealer* reported it thus:

That Cy's arm was in old time form this result shows and nobody ever saw better ball pitched since ball pitching began. The nearest thing to a base hit was a sort of scratch that Wallace would have taken had he not considered it too easy; as it was it got through him. Again Holliday hit a hard one at Wallace but he knocked it down. It fell at his feet and he had plenty of time to throw the runner out but his throw took O'Connor off the bag. Besides these cases there was not even a suspicion of a hit and besides this pitching record the game was featureless, at least all other features faded into insignificance.[14]

The *Cincinnati Enquirer* used the exact wording as that in the *Cleveland Plain Dealer*, formatted slightly differently, while the following is from a separate section entitled "Coming Home":

Holliday says Young's record was not so much, and that the Cincinnati team should have been given two hits. One of the errors given to Wallace was a very close decision. One ball went through Wallace's legs on bad bound [sic]. It was a slow ball and Wallace touched it. Wallace admitted after the game that he should have had it.[15]

Cy Young pitched three no-hitters in his career, which spanned five major league teams.

The *Cincinnati Commercial Tribune* stated the following:

Holliday was the only man who made even a suspicion of a hit, and he never got to second. He hit a couple of hot ones to Wallace, but Bobby should have had both of them. He stopped a good drive, but threw it wild, and then allowed a slow one to get through him.[16]

The *Sporting Life* dated September 25, 1897, ran the following article:

FORGOTTEN HOW TO BAT

The Reds appear to have forgotten all they ever knew about the use of the bat. They didn't try to bunt; they didn't try to place hits over the infielders' heads; they didn't even try to "chop the ball"—a trick that a Baltimore critic asserts the Birds invented last year. Instead they stood up very a la the Quakers and banged wildly away at the ball in a desperate effort apparently to knock it into the next county. As a result the number of pop flies sent up to the infielders was as many in each game as the put-outs usually credited to a first baseman.

"CY'S" GREAT PITCHING

This weakness was very apparent in Friday's game, when Wilson pitched, but it was even more glaringly shown in the first game Saturday, when Cy Young made his great record of shutting out the Reds without a base hit. The rail splitter had remarkable speed, and kept the ball over the heart of the plate, but the visitors did not make even an effort at scientific work, thus making the great pitcher's work much easier.

MANLY WALLACE

During this game the nearest approach to a hit was made in the seventh [sic], when Holliday hit to Wallace. The ball went straight at Bobby, but the little third baseman let it go through his hands, and roll into the field. It could have been given a hit if for any reason it was desired to boost Bobby's fielding average, but Wallace is not seeking that kind of glory. "It was my error, and it was an inexcusable one," said Wallace after the game. "I was playing in the right spot for Bug, and the ball came straight at me, but in some way got through me. I should feel guilty if that was charged up against "Cy" as a hit after his wonderful work.[17]

The Browning book stated the following:

Critics carped that Cy Young got a break from the official scorer on a ball that Bobby Wallace threw away. Others, however, disagreed, and Wallace himself declared the error call to have been correct. In any case, Young's first no-hit effort—also the first by anyone in four years in the major league—was a brilliant accomplishment against a fine Cincinnati team.[18]

There is mention in the literature record of the hits by Holliday being originally scored as hits then later changed to errors. The following passage is from the Westcott and Lewis book:

The only sour note in the no-hitter was the fact that Holliday was credited with singles on the two balls Wallace failed to field cleanly, but the hits were changed to errors in the eighth inning.[19]

Regarding the mention of the errors being changed in the eighth inning, none of the articles published at the time of the game made any such mention or hinted that that was the case. That doesn't mean it didn't happen, it just means it wasn't common knowledge that it happened. Whether or not the scorer actually did credit Holliday with hits initially then, apparently in the eighth inning, changed the scoring to indicate errors for Wallace may not be as intriguing as it may appear, or even very significant for that matter. In the game today, and while watching a telecast, it is not uncommon for a play to be scored one way at the time it occurred then later in the telecast the announcer will say that the scoring on the play had been changed. It happens and we simply accept it regardless of our personal opinion, so why should we be surprised that a scorer may have changed the scoring on a play back in 1897? Another perspective is that the game was played in Cleveland and it is possible there may have been some home team bias from a scoring perspective. The Kermisch article suggests that Cy Young's first no-hitter may not have been a genuine no-hitter, based on comments by none other than Cy Young himself.[20]

The Young no-hitter of 1897 was actually an improvement on his best one-game performance during the 1896 season, when he pitched the National League's only one-hit game on July 23 against the Philadelphia Phillies.[21,22,23] That game came within one out of being a no-hitter when Ed Delahanty, playing first base and batting third in the order, managed a clean hit to short right field in the ninth after Cooley and Hallman had flied out. The *Philadelphia Public Ledger* said that "Cooley had been robbed of the first hit of the game by Burkett."[24] It is purely speculative, although plausible, that, due to the Delahanty reputation, the outfield may have been playing back, which allowed the ball to land in short right field.

A general note related to Cy Young's perceived value in 1897, although probably not surprising to readers, was that there had been some dickering for Young's services. The *Baltimore Sun* stated the following:

BOSTON, Aug. 26.—The Boston club has been after Pitcher Willis, of the Syracuse club, but would not pay $3,000, the price asked for him. The directors are crazy to get Pitcher Cyrus [sic] Young, of Cleveland, and it would not be surprising if $10,000 were paid for him, so anxious is Boston to win the pennant.[25]

One aside: I found it interesting that while in the modern game it is common for broadcasters to talk about pitch speed and pitch total, those same metrics were apparently also of interest to some in the nineteenth century. Regarding the pitch total there was mention in *Sporting Life*: "In a full-nine inning game a League pitcher will average 115 pitched balls."[26] And regarding pitch speed, the *Providence Sunday Star* stated that a Pud Galvin pitch had been measured at $2/5$ of a second with a Longines chronograph, which calculates to a speed of 93.75 miles per hour based on a catcher distance of five feet behind home plate.[27]

In summary, this article has presented a number of areas where information about Cy Young's first no-hitter was lacking, conflicting, or incorrect, as follows:

Sporting Life: the game write-up is in conflict with boxscore.

The *Cleveland Leader* newspaper coverage: the game write-up is in conflict with boxscore.

The *Cleveland Leader* newspaper coverage: Childs 2 or 1 hits, Young 0 or 1 hits.

The *Cleveland Leader, Cleveland Plain Dealer, Cincinnati Enquirer, Cincinnati Commercial Tribune*, and *Sporting Life*: the game articles lacked sufficient detail regarding play description, leaving play interpretations ambiguous.

The *Cleveland Leader, Cleveland Plain Dealer, Cincinnati Enquirer, Cincinnati Commercial Tribune*, and *Sporting Life*: these outlets inconsistently reported the issue regarding Wallace's errors/Holliday's possible hits.

Westcott and Lewis's book and Kermisch report that hit(s) were changed to error(s) during the course of the game. ■

Author's Note
Team names and the spelling of player names was based on that as listed on Baseball-Reference.com.

Notes
1. David Southwick. "Cy Young" in *New Century, New Team: The 1901 Boston Americans*, edited by Bill Nowlin. Phoenix, AZ: Society for American Baseball Research, Inc., 2013, 173–77.
2. Bill James and Rob Neyer. *The Neyer/James Guide to Pitchers: An Historical Compendium of Pitching, Pitchers, and Pitches.* New York, NY: Fireside, a division of Simon & Schuster, Inc., 2004, 484.
3. "Young's Record: It May be Tied but Never Can be Beaten: A Shutout in Runs and Hits," *Cleveland Plain Dealer*, Sunday, September 19, 1897, 8.
4. Game Coverage, *Cincinnati Commercial Tribune*, Sunday, September 19, 1897, unknown. From SABR web site; Research Resources, Newspaper Scans.
5. "Cy Young's Great Feat: He Shut Out Cincinnati Without Allowing the Reds a Hit," *Baltimore American*, Sunday, September 19, 1897, 10.
6. Young's first no hitter was the first in the National League (NL) since 1893 when Bill Hawke, then with the Ned Hanlon-led Baltimore Orioles,

managed the feat on August 16 against the Washington Senators. The key significance of the Hawke no hitter in 1893 was the fact that it was the first at the then new pitching distance of 60.5 feet which is the same distance used in the game today.
Additionally there was another common factor between the Hawke no hitter in 1893 and the Young no hitter in 1897 and that had to do with the fact that Dummy Hoy played at center field, on the losing side, in both games. Hoy was with the Washington Senators in 1893 and with the Cincinnati Reds in 1897.
7. The weather information is from the *Cleveland Plain Dealer*, Sunday, September 19, 1897, 1.
8. "The World of Baseball: The League Race: Games Played Saturday, Sept. 18," *Sporting Life*, Volume 30, Number 1, September 25, 1897, 3.
9. Information Concepts Incorporated. *The Baseball Encyclopedia: The Complete and Official Record of Major League Baseball.* New York, NY: The Macmillan Company, 1969. 2337. Incidentally, for those who aren't familiar with ICI, David Neft was the man behind ICI and it was the ICI research and resultant data that formed the basis for the Macmillan Baseball Encyclopedia of 1969.
10. "Not a Hit: Young's Great Feat Against the Reds Yesterday," *Cleveland Leader*, Sunday, September 19, 1897, page unknown.
11. *Cleveland Leader*, "Not a Hit."
12. "Not One Hit Off "Cy" Young," *Cincinnati Enquirer*, Sunday, September 19, 1897, 2.
13. *Cleveland Leader*, "Not a Hit."
14. "Young's Record: It May be Tied but Never Can be Beaten: A Shutout in Runs and Hits," *Cleveland Plain Dealer*, Sunday, September 19, 1897, 8.
15. Cincinnati Enquirer, "Not One Hit."
16. Game Coverage, *Cincinnati Commercial Tribune*, Sunday, September 19, 1897, unknown. From SABR web site; Research Resources, Newspaper Scans.
17. "Cleveland Chatter: Patsy's Boys Playing in Their Old Form Once More: "Cy" Young's Great Pitching," *Sporting Life*, Volume 30, Number 1, September 25, 1897, 4.
18. Reed Browning. *Cy Young: A Baseball Life.* Amherst, MA: University of Massachusetts Press, 2000. 283. (Appendix Two: Cy Young's Greatest Games, Number 3, September 18, 1897, 222–23.
19. Rich Westcott and Allen Lewis. *No-Hitters: The 225 Games, 1893–1999.* Jefferson, NC: McFarland & Company, Inc. Publishers, 2000, 9.
20. Al Kermisch. "From a Researcher's Notebook," *Baseball Research Journal* 28 (1999): 141–43, 142.
21. "Great Pitching: "Cy" Young's Wonderful Work Against the Quakers: Two Out in the Ninth When the Phillies Made Their First, Last and Only Hit," The *Cleveland Leader*, Friday, July 24, 1896, 3.
22. "Young's Record: It is One That Will Probably Stand for a Long Time: One Hit and a Shutout," *Cleveland Plain Dealer*, Friday, July 24, 1896, 3.
23. "Shut Out at Cleveland: Delahanty Secures the Only Hit Made Off "Cy" Young," *Philadelphia Record*, Friday Morning, July 24, 1896, 11.
24. "The Phillies Shut Out in the First Game at Cleveland," *Philadelphia Public Ledger*, Friday, July 24, 1896, page unknown.
25. "Boston May Give $10,000 for Young," *Baltimore Sun*, Friday Morning, August 27, 1897, 6.
26. "Baseball: News and Comment," *Sporting Life*, Volume 29, Number 3, April 10, 1897, 5.
27. "Base Ball Notes," *Providence Sunday Star*, Volume XXIX, Number 151, Sunday morning, May 4, 1884, 8.

CORRECTED BOXSCORE FOR CY YOUNG'S FIRST NO-HITTER

CLEVELAND SPIDERS
Manager: Patsy Tebeau

Batting, Fielding and Stolen Bases

Player	AB	R	H	BA	1B	2B	3B	HR	BB	SO	SH	SB	PO	A	E
Jesse Burkett, lf	4	0	1	0.250	1	0	0	0	0	0	0	0	2	0	0
Cupid Childs, 2b	3	2	1	0.333	0	1	0	0	1	0	0	1	0	4	0
Bobby Wallace, 3b	4	0	0	0.000	0	0	0	0	0	0	0	0	2	1	2
Jack O'Connor, 1b	4	1	2	0.500	2	0	0	0	0	0	0	0	13	0	0
Ed McKean, ss	4	1	0	0.000	0	0	0	0	0	0	0	0	3	3	1
Ollie Pickering, cf	3	1	1	0.333	1	0	0	0	1	0	0	1	2	0	0
Ira Belden, rf	3	1	2	0.667	2	0	0	0	1	1	0	0	1	0	0
Chief Zimmer, c	2	0	0	0.000	0	0	0	0	1	0	1	0	3	2	0
Cy Young, p	3	0	1	0.333	1	0	0	0	0	0	0	0	1	3	0
Totals	30	6	8	0.267	7	1	0	0	4	1	1	2	27	13	3

Pitching

Player	IP	H	SO	BB	HBP	WP	B	W	L	LOB	DP	BE
Cy Young, p	1	0	0	0	1	0	4	0	1	9	0	3
Totals	1	0	0	0	1	0	4	0	1	9	0	3

CINCINNATI REDS
Manager: Buck Ewing

Batting, Fielding and Stolen Bases

Player	AB	R	H	BA	1B	2B	3B	HR	BB	SO	SH	SB	PO	A	E
Bug Holliday, rf	4	0	0	0.000	0	0	0	0	0	0	0	0	1	0	0
Dummy Hoy, cf	4	0	0	0.000	0	0	0	0	0	1	0	0	2	0	0
Bid McPhee, 2b	3	0	0	0.000	0	0	0	0	0	1	0	0	1	6	0
Jake Beckley, 1b	3	0	0	0.000	0	0	0	0	0	0	0	0	15	0	0
Tommy Corcoran, ss	3	0	0	0.000	0	0	0	0	0	0	0	1	1	5	0
Charlie Irwin, 3b	3	0	0	0.000	0	0	0	0	0	1	0	0	1	3	0
Eddie Burke, lf	3	0	0	0.000	0	0	0	0	0	0	0	0	1	1	1
Pop Schriver, c	3	0	0	0.000	0	0	0	0	0	0	0	0	2	0	0
Billy Rhines, p	1	0	0	0.000	0	0	0	0	1	0	0	0	0	2	0
a) Claude Ritchey	1	0	0	0.000	0	0	0	0	0	0	0	0	0	0	0
Totals	28	0	0	0.000	0	0	0	0	1	3	0	1	24	17	1

a) batted for Rhines in ninth

Pitching

Player	IP	H	SO	BB	HBP	WP	B	W	L	LOB	DP	BE
Billy Rhines, p	4	0	1	0	0	1	2	0	3	8	8	1
Totals	4	0	1	0	0	1	2	0	3	8	8	1

Umpire-in-Chief: Kick Kelly at HP

Runs by Inning

	1	2	3	4	5	6	7	8	9	Totals
Cleveland Spiders	2	0	0	1	0	0	0	3	x	6
Cincinnati Reds	0	0	0	0	0	0	0	0	0	0

PLAY-BY-PLAY OF CY YOUNG'S FIRST NO-HITTER

Date: Saturday, September 18, 1897 vs Cincinnati Reds **Location:** League Park in Cleveland, OH
Game Time: 1:00 PM local **Attendance:** 2500 **Weather:** Fair with brisk northerly winds, about 70°F

FIRST INNING
Cincinnati Reds Batting
Holliday grounded out to short
Hoy popped out to first
McPhee grounded out to second
Cincinnati 0 runs, 0 hits, 0 LOB; Cleveland 0 errors
Cleveland Spiders Batting
Burkett out on an unknown play
Childs doubled to right
Wallace out, Childs to third
O'Connor singled, Childs scored
McKean popped to Burke in left but Burke muffed it and
     O'Connor scored
Pickering out on an unknown play
Cleveland 2 runs, 2 hits, 1 LOB; Cincinnati 1 error

SECOND INNING
Cincinnati Reds Batting
Beckley grounded out to Young
Corcoran out on an unknown play
Irwin out on an unknown play
Cincinnati 0 runs, 0 hits, 0 LOB; Cleveland 0 errors
Cleveland Spiders Batting
Belden walked
Zimmer walked
Young out on an unknown play
Burkett out on an unknown play
Childs out on an unknown play
Cleveland 0 runs, 0 hits, 2 LOB; Cincinnati 0 errors,
     Cincinnati 1 WP

THIRD INNING
Cincinnati Reds Batting
Burke out on an unknown play
Schriver out on an unknown play
Rhines flied out to center
Cincinnati 0 runs, 0 hits, 0 LOB; Cleveland 0 errors
Cleveland Spiders Batting
Wallace out on an unknown play
O'Connor out on an unknown play
McKean out on an unknown play
Cleveland 0 runs, 0 hits, 0 LOB; Cincinnati 0 errors

FOURTH INNING
Cincinnati Reds Batting
Holliday hit to Wallace at third who made a poor throw and
     Holliday was safe
Hoy flied out
Holliday was out trying to steal second
McPhee struck out
Cincinnati 0 runs, 0 hits, 0 LOB; Cleveland 1 error
Cleveland Spiders Batting
Pickering walked
Belden singled (beat out a bunt hit), Pickering went to second
Zimmer sacrificed, Belden to second and Pickering went to third
Young made an infield hit, Belden to third and Pickering was
     caught at home plate
Burkett singled scoring Belden and Young was caught at third
Cleveland 1 run, 3 hits, 1 LOB; Cincinnati 0 errors

FIFTH INNING
Cincinnati Reds Batting
Beckley flied out

Corcoran hit to McKean at short who made a poor throw
     and Corcoran was safe
Irwin struck out
Corcoran stole second and was out trying to steal third
Cincinnati 0 runs, 0 hits, 0 LOB; Cleveland 1 error
Cleveland Spiders Batting
Childs out on an unknown play
Wallace out on an unknown play
O'Connor out on an unknown play
Cleveland 0 runs, 0 hits, 0 LOB; Cincinnati 0 errors

SIXTH INNING
Cincinnati Reds Batting
Burke out on an unknown play
Schriver out on an unknown play
Rhines walked
Holliday hit to Wallace at third who fumbled and Holliday
     was safe at first, Rhines went to second
Hoy went out to O'Connor
Cincinnati 0 runs, 0 hits, 2 LOB; Cleveland 1 error
Cleveland Spiders Batting
McKean out on an unknown play
Pickering out on an unknown play
Belden struck out
Cleveland 0 runs, 0 hits, 0 LOB; Cincinnati 0 errors

SEVENTH INNING
Cincinnati Reds Batting
McPhee out on an unknown play
Beckley out on an unknown play
Corcoran out on an unknown play
Cincinnati 0 runs, 0 hits, 0 LOB; Cleveland 0 errors
Cleveland Spiders Batting
Zimmer out on an unknown play
Young out on an unknown play
Burkett out on an unknown play
Cleveland 0 runs, 0 hits, 0 LOB; Cincinnati 0 errors

EIGHTH INNING
Cincinnati Reds Batting
Irwin out on an unknown play
Burke out on an unknown play
Schriver out on an unknown play
Cincinnati 0 runs, 0 hits, 0 LOB; Cleveland 0 errors
Cleveland Spiders Batting
Childs walked and stole second
Wallace flied out
O'Connor singled, Childs went to third
McKean forced O'Connor, Childs scored
Pickering singled and stole second, McKean to third
Belden singled to short left scoring McKean and Pickering
Zimmer forced Belden
Cleveland 3 runs, 3 hits, 0 LOB; Cincinnati 0 errors

NINTH INNING
Cincinnati Reds Batting
Ritchey batted for Rhines and hit sharply to Young for an out
Holliday grounded out to Wallace
Hoy struck out
Cincinnati 0 runs, 0 hits, 0 LOB; Cleveland 0 errors
Cleveland Spiders Batting
Did not bat
Cleveland 0 runs, 0 hits, 0 LOB; Cincinnati 0 errors

Bacteria Beat the Phillies

The Deaths of Charlie Ferguson and Jimmy Fogarty

Jerrold Casway

Between the years 1888 and 1891, the National League Philadelphia Phillies lost two prominent ballplayers on what promised to be contending teams. In an age when the life expectancy for American men was 46 to 53, it was surprising to see athletically-fit young men in their mid-twenties die before their expectant lifespan.[1] This fate, however, was not unanticipated. The late nineteenth century was still lacking medicines for infectious diseases and questions persisted about how these illnesses were contracted and spread. Baseball players, in spite of their athletic conditioning, were just as susceptible as the general population to the ravages of disease. The perceived invulnerability of the healthy athlete was just a delusionary product of a ballplayer's notoriety.

Typhoid fever, diphtheria, and Consumption (tuberculosis) were the troubling diseases for men who travelled widely, worked in confined and crowded spaces, and practiced lifestyles that ran down their immune systems. Once a body lost its resistance to disease, the factors from exposure took their toll.

Both typhoid fever and tuberculosis were bacteria-borne. The typhoid bacteria grew in the intestines and blood stream and were induced by contaminated water, unpasteurized dairy products, raw eggs, and the unwashed skins of raw vegetables and fruit. In general, the disease was a product of improper sanitation. It led to high fevers, abdominal pains, headaches, and constipation. A person carrying the disease might not be affected by it, but could pass it on to more susceptible victims. In 1891, typhoid death ratios in Chicago were 174 per 100,000 people.[2] Tuberculosis was more threatening and widespread.

Tuberculosis was often called Consumption because the disease wasted a body through its pulmonary affliction: a person was, in essence, "consumed" by the bacteria. The Greeks called it the "wasting disease." Tuberculosis was also quite contagious: coughing, sneezing, spitting would expel infectious droplets, sometimes in a blood form. It was said that in the late nineteenth century, an afflicted person could infect 10 to 15 people a year.[3] Weight loss, fatigue, chest pains, and bloodied sputum were the most apparent symptoms. By the turn of the century, tuberculosis was the leading cause (25%) of death in the United States.[4] Vulnerability to the bacteria often was brought on by a weakened immune system that could be accelerated by excessive drinking and smoking. But the congregating of people was the decisive factor for the disease's transmission.

The incidence of tuberculosis among ballplayers never reached epidemic proportions. We only know of eight recorded deaths among late nineteenth-century ballplayers. Jimmy Fogarty, the Phillies' fleet-footed outfielder, was the most prominent victim. The same could be said for typhoid fever. Only the deaths of four ballplayers were attributed to this illness. Again, the Phillies had the most significant victim, their star pitcher and batsman Charlie Ferguson.[5] For the unfortunate Phillies, both players were considered critical pieces for a pennant-contending ball club.

Ferguson was born in rural Charlottesville, Virginia, during the Civil War on April 17, 1863. His father was a baker and an entrepreneurial businessman in a largely Irish community known as Random Row. How Charlie picked up an interest in baseball is not known, but the war had greatly popularized the game in the South, especially a border state like Virginia. Although there was speculation that he attended the University of Virginia, no record of his enrollment exists. It is probable that he played ball with a team that had some affiliation with the university in his hometown in 1882. His play attracted the attention of a Richmond merchant who owned a ball club in the Virginia capital. In 1883, Ferguson signed and pitched for that Richmond club. His performance at Richmond caught the attention of scouts for the new Philadelphia baseball franchise. Under the management of Al Reach, the club signed Charlie Ferguson in 1884 for $1500.

In his first season, the twenty-one-year-old Ferguson had a 21–25 record in 417 innings. His ERA was 3.54 for a team that finished 39–73. Before the start of the following year, Ferguson married the eighteen-year-old Mary Smith. The coming season also gave notice of his baseball potential. He was 26–20 with an ERA at 2.22. He even pitched the franchise's first no-hitter against the Providence Grays. But Ferguson also showed great promise with the bat and played 15 games in the outfield. He actually led the team in batting average, .306 in 235 at bats. Nothing he did in 1885 prepared the league for his next season's performance. Ferguson was 30–9 with a 1.98 ERA. His WHIP was .976, the second best in the National League. He finished the season with 11 straight wins.

However, at the end of August 1886, Ferguson and some of his teammates became sick during an extended heat wave on a western road trip because of "bad water in the west." Initially, Ferguson and George Wood were sent home to recover, but when Charlie returned to the team his illness re-emerged. Again he asked Harry Wright for permission to leave the ball club. These incidents may have foretold that something was wrong with the Phillies' ace pitcher. Although Ferguson was enjoying his best season, he had pitched 396 innings after a 405-inning campaign the previous year. He might have been 23 years old, but those were a lot innings for a pitcher who also played the outfield. Actually there were two main issues affecting the young Ferguson. First, Charlie complained of a weak arm and general fatigue when the team left Philadelphia on that last road trip. But Wright refused to give him permission to return to his Charlottesville home. Ferguson was torn by this decision because he did not want to take a "French leave" of the team.[6]

Ferguson asserted that he was too weak to perform up to his own standards. He said he had been overworked in the previous Detroit series and got very little offensive support from the team. Charlie confessed that he did not welcome bearing the brunt of the pitching load in Chicago the way he was feeling.[7] He said, "I have worked hard and faithfully and have given my manager very little trouble by always trying to please him." Ferguson told reporters that Wright did not appreciate the gravity of his condition. Unable to get Wright's support, Ferguson took a train out of Chicago and went home to Virginia. He claimed he was bedridden for ten days and had a doctor's certificate to validate his condition.[8] A few of his teammates doubted his illness and said it was a case of "home sickness" or "chicken heartedness."[9] This commentary made little sense. It was probably an expression of some players' frustration with Charlie's state of mind. He was worn out and was distressed about his salary and with a troubling situation at home. Another factor was that Ferguson was a hypochondriac, "a confirmed

crank on the subject of health." Apparently, he was frequently afflicted with imaginary ailments. He even carried a medicine chest on road trips. It was said that Ferguson "swallowed enough medicine to kill an ordinary healthy man." His teammates joked that he would pitch a good game whenever he was ailing.[10] But manager Wright believed Ferguson was imagining one of his illnesses and was upset by the departure of his star player and suspended him for the remainder of the season. He also fined him $200 and threatened to blacklist him for his actions.[11] When Ferguson returned to Philadelphia at the end of the year, he told John Rogers, the team's litigious treasurer, that "I will lick someone before I leave this city … [without my full] salary."[12]

Not spoken about during this controversy was the fact that Ferguson was worn down, possibly setting the stage for his eventual date with typhoid fever. Although newly married, the young Ferguson was still a fashionable man-about-town, who kept a high-profile lifestyle. Between the on-field demands on his physicality and his after-hours activities, Ferguson's resistance was put in jeopardy.

As Ferguson was wearing down, he again returned to the topic of compensation. Few in the league pitched or played more innings than Charlie, but he was dealing with a franchise that had the lowest salary scale in the league. It was judged that no Phillies player approached the league's $2000 maximum. Not to be overlooked was Charlie's grievance about last season's $200 fine. Having been paid $1800 for each of the last two years, Ferguson believed his performance had earned him a raise. He reacted by joining three teammates in early November 1886 in demanding enhanced contracts for the upcoming season.[13] To make extra money Ferguson and many of his teammates planned to play an extended exhibition tour in Cuba that winter. Ferguson, however, had second thoughts and for unspecified reasons stayed home in Virginia with his wife and their ailing baby.[14]

The Phillies, like other clubs, were feeling the pressure for higher salaries from the newly-formed players' Brotherhood. Ferguson and a number of his teammates were early and active members of this unionized organization. They responded by refusing to go south for spring training unless the team acceded to their salary demands. Ferguson held out for $3000. Eventually, he relented and said he would sign for $2800. Harry Wright, however, was only authorized to offer him $2500. Charlie refused this offer and remained in Philadelphia. *The Sporting News* reported that any ball club would gladly pay this "crack" pitcher $3000. But manager Wright believed that Ferguson would eventually come around before the team returned from the south. In the meantime, he coached baseball at Princeton College. He said he would return to Richmond after his coaching commitment was over.[15] Caught in a financial bind, Ferguson relented and signed for $2500, a $700 raise over his last contract.

He did not disappoint management. He was 22–10 with a 3.00 ERA, third best in the league even though he was put off by the new pitching rules affecting the pitching box and the placement of his pivot foot.[16] Ferguson also became the team's second baseman when he was not pitching. He batted .337 and led the team with 85 RBIs. More remarkably, unlike 1886, he finished the year in a flurry. The Phillies won 16 out of their last 18 games. Charlie either pitched or played the field in each of these contests. He was 7–0 as a pitcher with a 1.75 ERA and batted .361. Thanks to his efforts, the Phillies moved into second place behind the power-laden Detroit Wolverines. Ferguson's performance was so impressive that a number of teams offered to buy his contract. It was reported that one club proposed $10,000 for Charlie's services. President Al Reach rejected all offers for his star player.[17]

Unfortunately, Ferguson's season was marred by the tragic death in June of his infant daughter. As indicated above, Charlie threw himself into his ball playing. He appeared in 72 of 128 games (59%), had 264 at bats, and pitched 297 innings. Nevertheless, he went out to the West Coast after the season and played ball until his arm gave out. At this point a weary Ferguson returned east.[18] It was obvious that the rigors of the 1887 season had sapped his strength and brought on another bout of the exhaustion that had afflicted him at the end of 1886.

Ferguson was depleted and very much run-down. He had lost some of his 170 pounds. In this weakened condition he was exposed to contaminated liquids or was infected by a bacteria carrier. Initially, Ferguson appeared normal and again coached baseball at Princeton. After he belatedly signed his 1888 contract, he played second base in early April preseason exhibitions against the American Association Athletics. Although Ferguson's offense was lacking, he did play well in the field and was considered the team's regular second baseman.[19] By mid-April 1888 he began to exhibit signs of the illness. It began with a high fever that was first diagnosed as malaria. But when red spots appeared on his chest, the diagnosis changed to typhoid. He was now confined to bed in his Broad Street residence in north Philadelphia for about three weeks. It was hoped that this convalescence would quell the disease. President Reach responded by bringing in Dr. William Pepper, a renowned physician at the University of Pennsylvania Hospital. He joined two other doctors who were attending Ferguson. Using hypodermic injections, they stabilized Ferguson's blood pressure, but his high fever remained unbroken.

On Saturday, April 28, his illness took a turn for the worse. By noon he sank into unconsciousness and all hope began to fade.[20]

Early that evening teammates began to arrive. He awoke when they spoke to him. Ferguson asked about that afternoon's game against New York. They told him they had lost and he softly commented, "We are certainly having bad luck this year." Ferguson then asked Sid Farrar to come closer and said, "Sid, I am afraid I am going to die." Before Farrar could respond, Charlie again lost consciousness. The players went to get Ferguson's young wife, Mary, who was reluctant to enter the room. Soon after her coming to his side, the doctor pronounced him dead. She became hysterical and passed out. By the time he died, most of his teammates, with the exception of Al Reach, John Rogers, and Harry Wright, were at the house.[21]

The Sporting News joined other publications in mourning and lauding this extraordinary athlete. He had turned 25 only 12 days before his death. The paper said, "He was a gentleman of the highest degree and a great ballplayer. He had more friends than any player on the club."[22] Ferguson was what we call today a five-tool player. He did everything well. His teammates and friends organized a benefit game for Ferguson's widow. The exhibition raised $406. The Phillies also paid his medical and funeral expenses. He was buried in Maplewood cemetery in Charlottesville, Virginia.[23] Ferguson, like his father, was investment-conscious and his wife was left a number of Charlottesville properties.

The Phillies abruptly lost their star player to a bacterial infection. Many teams commemorated Charlie by wearing black armbands. But his ball club knew they could not replace a man whom the Boston press called "Ferguson Furioso."[24] No pitcher could fill that void in their rotation. They did find someone to take his place at second base, a youngster from Cleveland named Ed Delahanty.

Four years later the team suffered another loss, the death of their starting center fielder, Ferguson's teammate, Jimmy Fogarty. His death, too, resulted from a deadly bacterial infection that sapped the vitality of the franchise.

Fogarty was born on February 12, 1864, in San Francisco. His father was a railroad foreman who moved his family to Colorado before settling in California. Jimmy was the fourth of six children. Affable and companionable, Fogarty did what he pleased and enjoyed opportunities that came his way. Besides his spirited Irish personality, he was blessed with great speed and athletic coordination. Jimmy initially played baseball for two years in the California League with the local Haverly ballclub. He soon realized that money, notoriety, and competition for baseball were better on the east coast. This recognition drew him to the new franchise in Philadelphia. In 1883, Fogarty at the age of 19 was good enough to earn a place on an experimental reserve team. Playing third base, he convinced Al Reach to retain him at lower pay as a substitute player when the reserve system was scrapped. Fogarty was confident that he could win a starting position if an opportunity arose. In 1884, under the new Phillies manager, Harry Wright, he got his chance when outfielder John Manning was beaned by a pitched ball. Fogarty took advantage of this situation and became the Phillies' regular center fielder.[25] Within a few seasons he was acclaimed as a superior outfielder and a champion base stealer. Playing alongside Ed Andrews and George Wood, the outfield was a stable unit until Sam Thompson switched clubs and young Ed Delahanty was tried in left field. On occasion, Fogarty also played the infield and was used as a "change" pitcher when the staff was overworked.

In his first season, Fogarty played in 97 games and his batting average was only .212. The next year he raised his batting average to .232 in 111 games. In 1886 the 22-year-old Fogarty began to come into his own. He batted .293, playing in only 77 games because of an injured knee. But his physical condition did not keep Jimmy from non-ballfield distractions. He chafed over his annual salary of $1400. At the end of the year he joined Ferguson and others demanding a raise. Fogarty warned that the $1600 offered by the club, "won't get him for another season."[26] The youngster even threatened Harry Wright that he might not come east in 1887.[27] Despite this rhetoric, Fogarty was thinking entrepreneurial. He and the Phillies' groundskeeper opened a "cosy little saloon" near the Phillies new ball park at Broad and Lehigh.[28] His most controversial endeavor was an exhibition tour in Cuba. This commitment disappointed his friends in California, but Fogarty had money and adventure on his mind.[29]

The tour was organized by an enterprising insurance man, James P. Scott, and officials from the local Athletic Association club. The exhibition did not live up to its expectations. Expenses for two travelling teams were excessive. There was also competition from a famous touring Spanish bullfighter. Profits were made, but they were not satisfactory for ballplayers like young Fogarty. He claimed Scott had guaranteed him $200 above the sharing of gate receipts. Fogarty refused to play until he was paid or got a return boat ticket back to the States. Scott and his partners condemned Fogarty's contentious behavior. They complained that he had not paid his tailor debts and bar bills. They also castigated him for disruptions at their hotel. Fogarty was accused of bringing disreputable people into the residence where they conducted themselves with scandalous behavior.[30] Other players joined Fogarty in disputing the profit-sharing plan. The discontent that followed disrupted the exhibition tour. In spite of these problems, Fogarty returned to the States and reconciled with the Phillies after they gave him a $500 raise to $1900.

In 1887, the Phillies finished second and Fogarty had a .261 batting average in 126 games. He scored 113 runs, and led the league with 82 walks. He also stole 102 bases (as then defined) and had 39 outfield assists. During the season Fogarty stole 38 bases in 27 consecutive games. In one game he swiped six bases.[31] Nevertheless, he still managed to get himself in trouble. On the train ride south for spring training he harassed an elderly black passenger who threatened to defend himself with a concealed screwdriver.[32] A more serious problem was the drinking binges that Fogarty conducted when the Pittsburgh club came to the Quaker City. Detectives followed Fogarty and his companions. They reported that on consecutive nights the ballplayers were drunk and disruptive. Fogarty was fined twenty-five dollars over and above an earlier forfeiture of fifty dollars.[33] Accustomed to leading a demanding night life, Fogarty finished out the year without any further problems. However, he did overextend himself by organizing his teammates after the season on a western exhibition tour. They played games in Cincinnati, Chicago, Santa Fe, and Las Vegas, New Mexico, before arriving for a series of games in Los Angeles.[34] After the tour Fogarty remained in the west until March 1888.

Wherever Jimmy Fogarty appeared, he sported a profligate lifestyle. In California, Philadelphia, or any city on the National League circuit, the flamboyant Fogarty was surrounded by his many friends and supporters. He even belonged to the Union Republican Club in Philadelphia and was the confidant of many well-placed people. His nicknames of "Master Jeems" and "The Foge" testified to his temperament and public persona as a popular man about town. Jimmy earned his reputation by keeping early morning hours

OLD JUDGE CIGARETTES Goodwin & Co., New York.   OLD JUDGE CIGARETTES Goodwin & Co., New York.

Charlie Ferguson (left) and Jimmy Fogarty (right) each died of maladies that would be unlikely to be fatal today, Ferguson from typhoid fever and Fogarty from tuberculosis.

at all-night social clubs. This fraternizing did nothing to quell his serious drinking, heavy smoking, and avid gambling habits. Such vices certainly contributed to his often erratic actions. Affable and charming, Fogarty could also be mean-spirited and bigoted, especially when he was drinking. Many of these traits came to a debilitating head during the next year's baseball season.

The 1888 season was a difficult one for Fogarty. His batting average slipped to .236 and though he played in 121 games, he stole only 58 bases. Most contemporaries associated this decline with three problems. Baseball analysts said the advantage of 1887's four-strike rule allowed him to lead the league in walks. In 1888, his tactic of taking too many pitches caused him to be less effective at the plate. Then there was the developing relationship with veteran outfielder George Wood. These "gayest young men" were inseparable late-night "sunrise socialites." Both were constantly chided for their partying and their influence on teammates and visiting players.[35] Their on-field performances suffered as a result.

Perhaps the most distractive influence was the growing union movement in professional baseball. The players' Brotherhood, formed in 1885, attracted support from players who were upset with the prevailing reserve clause and static salaries. The Brotherhood was a ready-made cause for the restive Fogarty. Only 24 years of age, Fogarty was weaned on clubhouse union talk of many of the Phillies' older and more militant players.

Nine of the club's 13 players supported the union's positions. When Art Irwin's politics forced him to step down as team captain, Fogarty moved to ingratiate himself to manager Harry Wright. However, Wright should have known better then to consider the volatile Fogarty. He reminded Jimmy that he needed to be smart and use his brains. Fogarty, the wiseacre, responded, "You can't throw your brains to first base and put a man out."[36]

Within a few weeks, he resigned his captaincy.[37] In spite of these distractions, Fogarty recovered his focus in 1889. He played in 128 games, had a .259 batting average and led the league in stolen bases (99), putouts (302), and assists (42). He also fielded at an impressive .961 clip, committing only 14 errors. But Fogarty's real test came at the end of the 1889 season when he accompanied Albert Spalding's overseas baseball tour.

On the tour Fogarty was exposed to the Brotherhood's leaders, such as John M. Ward, Fred Pfeffer, Ned Hanlon, Jimmy Ryan, and of course George Wood. On the long sea voyages Fogarty was further indoctrinated to the union's policies. When the touring players learned that the club owners had reneged on the salary cap promises and the reserve clause concessions, the commitment for a strike-driven players' league was cast.

Soon after Fogarty arrived stateside, he declared, "We've got to get more money out of the game .... We attract the fans, but the owners pocket the money."[38] One owner replied, "would to heaven we could be such slaves and draw salaries from $3,000 to $5,000 for seven months work—no, play."[39] Fogarty and his mates said they were subjected to a kind of "gilded bondage."[40] Club magnates labeled the players as "hot-headed anarchists" and "seditious malcontents."[41]

The players responded with a league of their own. The union league was made up of jointly-run franchises, operated by capitalist backers and ball playing employees. Each player signed a one-year contract with a two-year option to renew. Reserve and salary classification contracts were prohibited, gate receipts were shared, and home clubs got concession profits. Under these guidelines Fogarty signed with the Philadelphia union club in which he invested $2000 of his own money.

Sometime after the 1889 season, Fogarty returned to the west coast where he and Mike Kelly worked to unionize minor league ballplayers. On February 6, 1890, Fogarty returned to the Quaker City to an enthusiastic welcome. He was named captain of the players' team and worked incessantly to get a site for the new local Brotherhood ballfield. All this travelling and stress began to take its toll on Fogarty. As the 1890 season approached, he fell ill. At first doctors thought he might have typhoid, but in reality he had contracted tuberculosis. Initially, George Wood was installed as Fogarty's "head nurse." The "Foge" recovered from the first attack, but he had not fully shaken off the bacterial infection. Once the season started, however, the weakened Fogarty was determined to lead his club to a profitable year.

By mid-May, the club was playing less than .500 ball, Fogarty's batting average was around .230, and the club's attendance reflected the team's disappointing play. At this point the ball club's major stockholders began to question Fogarty's leadership. Reminiscent of the Cuban fiasco of 1886, Fogarty fell out with the team's directors, primarily the club's president, Henry Love. An ongoing feud festered between the two men. George Wood tried to placate Fogarty, but the matter had gotten out of hand. Fogarty eventually resigned the captaincy and refused to play as long as Love stayed in office. Jimmy complained about a sore foot, an injured knee, and a bad cold. The crisis was resolved when new investors replaced Love and his supporters. But Fogarty for the remainder of the season was an inconsistent player. His stamina was drained and he was disillusioned with the whole union experiment.

Hereafter I am out for the "stuff" and will play ball for money in every sense of the word. I am done with honor and all such nonsense in connection with baseball. I stuck with the Brotherhood but the Brotherhood had not stood by me.[42]

The Philadelphia Quakers of the Brotherhood finished the season in fifth place. Fogarty was 7–9 as a manager/captain. He played in only 91 games, his batting average a lowly .239, and stole 36 bases. At the season's end the union league and its ball clubs were no more. Investors made do with their losses and players looked to mend their relationships with their former teams. But the once graceful darling of center field had pushed his body beyond its capacity. His knees were not in good condition, his hands had been burnt by a curtain fire in his bedroom, and his respiratory system was again exhibiting symptoms of tuberculosis.[43] This condition was not surprising given his lifestyle and the strains of the past year. Fogarty's consumptive bacteria were dormant and were waiting for the athlete's body to weaken.

Jimmy Fogarty believed rest and the recuperative climate of California would allow him to recover his health and strength. Meanwhile, the Phillies debated Jimmy's status. President Reach and manager Wright were willing to forgive the likeable and repentant ballplayer. Colonel Rogers, the sour-tempered club treasurer, with reluctance agreed to take Fogarty back.[44] Jimmy accepted his reprieve and arrived in Philadelphia in early February 1891. He appeared to be in good health and spirits. Feeling like his old self, Fogarty celebrated. He hung out with his old cronies and made the rounds of his favorite night stops. But the cold weather and his long hours produced a bad cold that triggered his pulmonary problems.

His condition accelerated and within a few days he was admitted to St. Joseph's Hospital under the care of the Sisters of Charity. After his discharge it was only a matter of time before he had a serious relapse. For the next few months the ailing Fogarty went from home to home of different friends. No one was more attentive than his close companion, George Wood. But Fogarty was a stricken man. Both his father and brother had suffered the same affliction. By the end, "The Foge" was emaciated and weighed about ninety pounds. He was now regularly attended to by a local priest. Fogarty's constant companion was a bible that he kept on his lap.[45]

On May 20, Jimmy Fogarty took his last labored breath. He was only 27. His body was embalmed and conveyed in a wreath-covered coffin by train to San Francisco where he was buried. Philly players wore black arm bands and the Union Club flew their flag at half-mast. Meanwhile, Billy Hamilton, who was purchased during the strike season, took over center field and the base paths for the player known to all as "Master Jeems."

Within a four-year span the Phillies lost two of their most popular and promising stars to dreaded bacteria-driven illnesses. Their deaths were a shock to other ballplayers, who lived their lives as if they were immune to such infections. Unfortunately, the habits of their celebratory lifestyles and their public exposures made them susceptible to whatever was circulating in their environment. Standing buckets of drinking water, congested dressing quarters, eating on the run, and hours spent on soot-ridden trains created a petri-dish setting for disease.

In this era ballplayers were responsible for their medical care. As a result, they often put off treatment believing they would recuperate in time. The problem was that pulled muscles responded to rest but that was not the case with infectious bacterial diseases. Stricken victims had little hope of recovery. Neither the victim's youth nor an athlete's conditioning could ward off the onslaught of a ravaging illness. Death by way of a bacterial infection was as assured as a pitched ball crossing home plate. For the Phillies the passing of these two young charismatic players shadowed the ball club into the new century. With these deaths, the ball club also lost something of its character and vigor from which it slowly recovered. The teams that followed never lacked dominant players—Delahanty, Thompson, Lajoie, Flick, and Hamilton each made the Hall of Fame—but these players lacked the appeal and charisma of Ferguson and Fogarty. And though both players had their issues with management, their sudden deaths from unseen bacteria took something from the life of the ball club and perhaps the city they represented. ■

Notes

1. The 46 age figure takes infant mortality into consideration. Fifty-three years was a more agreeable number for the late nineteenth century. "Were there old people in 1900?" This life expectancy topic came from an Internet source dated February 24, 2014: Thadeusktsim.wordpress.com
2. "1900 Flow of Chicago River Reversed," *Chicago Timeline*, March 7, 2007, Chicago Public Library.
3. T.B. Fact Sheet (Google) from World Health Organization, November 2010 and July 2011.
4. C. Davis, "Tuberculosis Facts," December 8, 2014, Google.
5. Christy Mathewson died from tuberculosis after his lungs were weakened during a gas training accident in France.
6. A "French leave" is a leave without permission or saying goodbye.
7. *The Sporting News*, September 27, 1886; September 20, 1886.
8. Ibid., September 9, 1886; September 13, 1886.
9. *Sporting Life*, July 14, 1886; September 22, 1886. It may have been that his pregnant young bride was yearning for his return.
10. Ibid., May 9, 1888.
11. *The Sporting News*, October 25, 1886; September 13, 1886.
12. Ibid., October 25, 1886.
13. *Sporting Life*, November 17, 1886.
14. Ibid., November 3, 1886.
15. *The Sporting News*, March 26, 1887.
16. *Sporting Life*, June 15, 1887.
17. Paul Hoffman, SABR BioProject.
18. *The Sporting News*, December 17, 1887; The Sporting Life, November 2, 1887; November 9, 1887; November 23, 1887.
19. Ibid., March 28, 1888; April 4, 1888; April 18, 1888.
20. *Philadelphia Inquirer*, April 30, 1888.
21. Public Ledger, April 30, 1888; *The Sporting News*, May 9, 1888.
22. Ibid., May 5, 1888.
23. *Sporting Life*, May 16, 1888; March 28, 1896.
24. Ibid., September 29, 1888.
25. J. Casway, "Jimmy Fogarty and the Brotherhood Movement," *Nineteenth-Century Notes*, Spring 2014, 1–2; Public Ledger, May 21, 1891; *Sporting Life*, May 23, 1891; "Jimmy Fogarty File," Baseball Hall of Fame, undated clipping.
26. *Sporting Life*, November 17, 1886.
27. Ibid., December 14, 1886.
28. Ibid., October 6, 1886.
29. Ibid., November 10, 1886.
30. Ibid., November 3, 1886; November 12, 1886; November 24, 1886; December 1, 1886; December 8, 1886; December 29, 1886; *The Sporting News*, January 22, 1887.
31. *Sporting Life*, August 31, 1887.
32. Ibid., March 23, 1887.
33. Ibid., July 13, 1887.
34. Ibid., November 23, 1887.
35. *The Sporting News*, July 28, 1888; The Sporting Life, August 1, 1888.
36. *The Sporting News*, May 22, 1889.
37. *Sporting Life*, July 10, 1889.
38. F. Lieb & S. Baumgartner, *The Philadelphia Phillies*, New York: Putnam, 1953, 32.
39. *Sporting Life*, April 3, 1889.
40. *Philadelphia Inquirer*, March 8, 1889.
41. Ibid., November 16, 1889; *Spalding Guide*, 1890, 11–26.
42. *Philadelphia Inquirer*, June 16, 1890. For details of Fogarty's Brotherhood experience see J. Casway, "Jimmy Fogarty and the Brotherhood Movement," *Nineteenth-Century Notes*, Spring 2014, 3–4.
43. *Philadelphia Inquirer*, August 24, 1890; September 7, 1890.
44. Ibid., December 26, 1890.
45. *Public Ledger*, May 21, 1891.

The Chadwick Awards

IN NOVEMBER 2009, SABR established the Henry Chadwick Award, intended to honor the game's great researchers—historians, statisticians, analysts, and archivists—for their invaluable contributions to making baseball the game that links America's present with its past. In addition to honoring individuals for the length and breadth of their contribution to the study of baseball and their deepening of our enjoyment of the game, the Chadwick Award educates SABR members and the greater baseball community about sometimes little-known but vastly important research contributions, thus encouraging the next generation of researchers.

The roster of the previous 35 Chadwick honorees includes researchers from the past and present: Some are our colleagues, others our predecessors. All have contributed greatly to the field. This year we add five names to the ranks, and present their biographies, written by SABR members, here.

John Dewan by Sean Forman

JOHN DEWAN has spent his career bringing sports statistics to baseball fans and analysts starving for information. Growing up on the South Side of Chicago, Dewan developed his interest in baseball and statistics while listening to White Sox games on the radio with his father and playing Strat-O-Matic with friends on his front steps. Dewan grew up playing various Chicagoland bat-and-ball games—baseball on concrete diamonds, 16-inch slow pitch, "Fast Pitching" and "Kick Baseball"—and attending White Sox games at Comiskey Park. "We never missed a bat-day double-header, Dewan says. "It was the main source of my baseball equipment growing up." Dewan remains a Sox fan and says Paul Konerko's Game Two grand slam in the 2005 World Series is the greatest single sporting moment he's experienced.

Dewan attended Loyola University, where he majored in Mathematics and Computer Science…and also met his future wife, Sue. He settled into a career as an actuary and continued to enjoy baseball, but not really considering it more than a hobby. But then a co-worker gave Dewan a *Bill James Baseball Abstract* in the early 1980s, and everything changed. "Bill James was doing baseball analytics with baseball statistics in the same way that I was doing insurance analytics with insurance statistics," Dewan recalled. "That was the turning point of my career. I knew that I could have much more fun working with baseball numbers than I could working with insurance numbers." A few years later, when Bill James announced the creation of Project Scoresheet, Dewan called directory assistance in Lawrence, Kansas, to get James's number; within a month, he was writing data-collection software, and within a year he was the Executive Director of Project Scoresheet.

Soon after, Dewan met Dick Cramer, a fellow programming sabermetrician. Cramer, a 2015 Chadwick Honoree, had co-founded STATS, Inc., which was the first company that provided advanced, play-by-play-based data to Major League Baseball teams. Dewan and Cramer re-launched STATS with Dewan as CEO, and STATS LLC rode the beginning of the personal computing and Internet age to become the leading producer of real-time and advanced statistics for American sports (and perhaps worldwide). STATS data powered new, exotic box-score presentations and provided detailed pitch-by-pitch accounts of every event on the field, which created new ways to study in-game strategy or other nuances of the game.

Dewan and his fellow owners sold STATS to Fox Sports in 2000 and, following a brief stint with Fox and the expiration of his non-compete agreement, Dewan co-founded Baseball Info Solutions, for which he now serves as CEO. BIS has pioneered the collection of defensive data and provides data to both MLB franchises and media outlets.

Dewan has always been interested in measuring player fielding, dating back to his time playing Strat-O-Matic as a child. "At STATS, we had better data. We had zones that we recorded for where each batted ball was hit. We developed Zone Ratings, and…published these analytics in the annual *Baseball Scoreboard*." For Dewan, fielding is a never-quite-solved problem with more and more aspects worthy of study. "One of the keys [to measuring fielding] is tracking more and more data elements that enable you to look at all these [aspects of fielding]. We are constantly adding more elements to track at BIS."

John's wife Sue was an early employee at STATS. "Her work as the head of the IT department for STATS in the early days of the company led to all the later success that our technology enabled us to accomplish," Dewan says. The two of them now live on the North Side of Chicago. They share a love of Olympic Sports, having attended five Olympiads together, and continue to root for the White Sox. In January 2000, they founded the Dewan Foundation to support mission work in Central America and Africa, and have taken more than fifteen mission trips themselves.

Larry Lester by Rob Neyer

LARRY LESTER comes by his life-long interest in Negro Leagues baseball as naturally as anyone, maybe ever: He was born in 1949 and raised in Kansas City, Missouri, and numbered among his childhood friends Robert Paige, elder son of legendary Satchel.

In 1965, Lester was 16 years old when Satchel Paige made his last appearance in the major leagues, a three-inning stint with the Kansas City Athletics. The A's played in Municipal Stadium, just five blocks away from Lester's home. And of course Lester made sure to be there. He was one of the wise and lucky few; Paige was hired as a promotional stunt, but somehow fewer than 10,000 paying customers showed up.

For ol' Satch, his three shutout innings were one last brilliant fight against Father Time. But young Larry was in a fight against time of his own, as he wrote some decades later:

… and Cinderella's clock was ticking for me, too. I had left my two younger sisters, Cookie and Brenda, at home by themselves. They had promised not to tattle on me, but only if I could get back before daddy. As I ran through the front door I could hear my father come in through the back. We met half way into the house. Of course, I was loaded down with a game program, ball cap, and other diamond goodies. I smelt like hotdogs, burnt popcorn and cracker jacks. I was flat busted. Boy, was I in a heap of trouble!

My father went baritone and demanded, "Did you leave your sisters at home by themselves?" I froze like a batter looking at a third strike. For a moment I thought, "Should I even bother to answer?" I was speechless and just waited for the guillotine to drop!

Suddenly, a voice emerged from the bedroom. I looked up and it was my grandmother from Fort Smith, Arkansas. Grandma Geraldine Williams had come to help celebrate my mother's 36th birthday. Knowing her grandson's love for the game, she put her hands on her hips and she proudly lied and said, 'George, I've been with the girls all evening.'"

Twenty-five years after that memorable night at Municipal Stadium, Lester co-founded Kansas City's Negro Leagues Baseball Museum, where he served as Research Director and Treasurer from 1991 through 1995. According to Lester's website, "The Museum's current static exhibition and informational kiosks were developed from Lester's personal collection of historic photographs, accompanied with his captions written from archival news clippings."

In 1995, Lester left the NLBM and founded NoirTech Research, Inc., "combining his expertise in research and technology to strategically track the African American experience in sports and entertainment."

From 2001 through 2004, Lester co-chaired the National Baseball Hall of Fame and Museum's ground-breaking Negro Leagues Researchers & Authors Group (NLRAG), which unearthed huge amounts of new data about Negro Leagues baseball for the "Out of the Shadows" research project. In 2006, Lester served on the Hall of Fame's Special Negro Leagues Committee, which—relying largely on information compiled by NLRAG—elected 17 new members with ties to black baseball as players, managers, and executives.

The longtime chairman or co-chairman of SABR's Negro Leagues Committee, Lester organizes the annual Jerry Malloy Conference. He's also written or co-written many of the seminal works about the Negro Leagues, including books about the East-West All-Star Game; Rube Foster; black baseball in Detroit, Kansas City, Chicago, and Pittsburgh; and black baseball's first World Series. Simply put, it's difficult to imagine the state of Negro Leagues research today without Larry Lester.

Today, Lester lives in Raytown, Missouri, just outside Kansas City, with his wife Valcinia. The Lesters have three grown daughters: Tiffany, Marisa, and Erica Joi. Among his current projects, Lester is working on a comprehensive Negro Leagues encyclopedia, filled with the information he has spent much of his life discovering.

Norman L. Macht by John Thorn

Octogenarian **NORMAN L. MACHT** has lived a baseball life that all of us may envy. It began in a minor league broadcast booth alongside Ernie Harwell, and extended to front-office stops in Lanett, Alabama; Eau Claire, Wisconsin; and Knoxville, Tennessee. It continued through the writing of more than thirty baseball books, many of them for young people, on up to a magisterial three-volume biography of Connie Mack, with whom Macht may now be said to share the title of The Grand Old Man of Baseball. Indeed his meticulously researched multivolume biography may occupy in baseball literature a position of parallel standing with those by Carl Sandburg (Lincoln), Douglas Southall Freeman (Washington), Dumas Malone (Jefferson), and Robert Caro (Johnson).

Along the way Macht served 12 years as an officer and director of SABR between 1992 and 2005, wrote articles for its publications, took a hand in founding two research committees, and was chairman of the national convention committee1997–2009 It is an honor now for SABR to recognize his lifetime achievement in baseball research by presenting him with the Henry Chadwick Award.

Norman Macht saw his first major league game at the Polo Grounds in 1935, when he was six years old. His baseball aspirations took a turn after a Dodgers tryout camp in Cambridge, Maryland. Relying on a "great changeup, but nothing to changeup from," he lasted two-thirds of an inning and was told to come back later, when he could throw harder, something they said they couldn't teach. Reorienting his energies toward the front office, he apprenticed with the Atlanta Crackers, while keeping the official stats for three minor leagues for the Howe News Bureau. He also worked as a statistician for broadcaster Ernie Harwell, who would become a lifelong friend. In 1951 he was the 21-year-old business manager of an independent team, the Valley Rebels of the Class D Georgia–Alabama League.

Returning from four years' service in the Air Force during and after the Korean War, he was the business manager of the Eau Claire Braves for two years, then the Knoxville Smokies for one year. But, with the advent of television among other factors, the minor leagues were shrinking. He became a stockbroker. But how to stay linked with baseball? Freelance writing and authorship seemed the ticket. Macht made contact with

Dick Bartell, a boyhood hero of his formative New York Giants years, and the two collaborated on *Rowdy Richard: A Firsthand Account of the National League Baseball Wars of the 1930s and the Men Who Fought Them*, published in 1987. He went on to work on a couple of books with Brooklyn pitching star Rex Barney, and wrote many young-adult biographies in the Chelsea House series, "Baseball Legends," including volumes on Ty Cobb, Satchel Paige, Babe Ruth, and Lou Gehrig. He has also written several books on topics of less abiding interest than baseball, such as Money and Banking (2001).

In a splendid reminiscence of his early years in the game ("Memories of a Minor-League Traveler," published in the 2010 *National Pastime*), Macht wrote of a chance encounter in 1948:

> As I described in the preface to my Connie Mack biography, Atlanta was a regular stop for major-league clubs barnstorming north from spring training. The Athletics were in town for two games.
>
> Connie Mack was sitting on a park bench in left field while his team took batting practice. I decided I'd like to meet him. He was 85. I was 18. I walked out and introduced myself and shook hands—I remember bony but not gnarled fingers—and sat down. I asked him something about some team that was in the news—it might have been a clubhouse fight or something of that nature. He answered politely, patiently, assuring me that whatever it was wouldn't affect the team's performance on the field. I asked him about this and that—an 18-year-old's questions, devoid of any great insight or import. After a few minutes I thanked him for the opportunity to talk with him and took my leave. I had no idea that I would be writing his biography sixty years later.

When he first conceived of the Mack biography in the mid-1980s, he knew it would be only the second in the field—following a smallish Putnam biography penned by Fred Lieb. He thought it would be a single-volume work of some 300 pages. And there was Connie Mack's ghosted autobiography, *My 66 Years in Baseball*, published in 1950. After nearly three decades of largely pre-Internet research, Macht jokingly called his work, completed this past year with a third volume, *My 66 Years in Researching Connie Mack*.

Its actual title, of course, is *Connie Mack and the Early Years of Baseball* (2007); *Connie Mack: The*

Turbulent and Triumphant Years, 1915–1931 (2012); and *The Grand Old Man of Baseball: Connie Mack in His Final Years, 1932–1956* (2015). All three volumes, running to more than 2000 pages, are published by the University of Nebraska Press.

Macht and his wife Sherie now reside in Escondido, California. Future baseball researchers may view archival materials (much of it available via online request) from his Mack biography at Southern Methodist University's DeGolyer Library in Dallas, Texas.

Tom Ruane by Mark Armour

TOM RUANE has spent nearly his entire life in the idyllic town of Poughkeepsie, New York, in the Hudson River Valley. Like many of us, he developed his love of baseball from playing it as a child and stuck with it even as his skills left him, as they inevitably do. Aside from a brief childhood fling with the Twins, his rooting loyalty has shamelessly bounced between the Mets and Yankees depending largely on the two teams' places in the standings at a given time.

Tom received a BA in English (Creative Writing) from SUNY New Paltz in 1976, but smartly hedged his bets with a BS in Computer Science from Union College in 1980. He was granted employment as a computer programmer for IBM in 1980 and, defying the volatility in the industry, has remained there ever since. He continued writing—his short stories appeared in magazines and journals throughout the 1980s, and he even shopped around a novel—but he eventually gave up this dream in favor of starting his family. He married Eileen Travis in 1988, and the couple has raised two (very tall) boys: Joe and Pat, both frequent SABR convention attendees.

As someone who loved baseball and understood what computers could do, Tom almost inevitably began creating his own baseball (and football) simulations, which improved his programming skills while also furthering his own understanding of how baseball teams score and prevent runs. Once he discovered the *Bill James Baseball Abstracts* and *The Hidden Game of Baseball*, he became interested in doing his own research, and of course he had the necessary skills to do so.

Tom joined SABR in 1991, and a few years later began extensive research into how teams were constructed throughout the twentieth century. That project resulted in several articles in *The Big Bad Baseball Annual*, and more importantly became the genesis of an online transactional database that Tom and others have regularly expanded and corrected. It is now being maintained and improved at Baseball-Reference.com.

By the late 1990s Tom had become a very active member of SABR's online listserv. If you asked a research question on SABR-L in those years, Tom often was the one who answered it, and his answers were usually small pieces of research, detailed and organized enough that the original question and several potential follow-up questions had been answered. Often Tom would not wait for questions to be asked, but would simply post answers to his own questions: What team had the most home runs hit by players in their final season? The simple answer was the 1968 New York Yankees, but Tom was never satisfied with the simple answer, so readers of SABR-L got lots of tables and methodology. In 1998 Tom attended his first SABR convention, and has been a valuable part of the SABR scene ever since.

Sometime in 1997 Tom began volunteering for Retrosheet, including the laborious and necessary proofing of event files. His participation continued to grow until it became his primary research outlet, and he became a Retrosheet board member in 2004. Tom's primary focus has been the expansion of Retrosheet's website from primarily a repository for play-by-play data files and the specialized software that could be used to manipulate it to a place for baseball fans to go to find textual play-by-play for tens of thousands (soon hundreds of thousands) of games. A few years later Tom helped start and manage Retrosheet's Box Score Project, an effort to create online box scores which, as of 2016, is complete back to 1913. Tom also conducts his own studies using Retrosheet data, and publishes them all on their website.

Tom has done all of this with selfless dedication, kindness, and good humor. He has been one of the leading lights of the baseball research community for twenty years and, fortunately, shows every indication that he will remain so for some time to come. ■

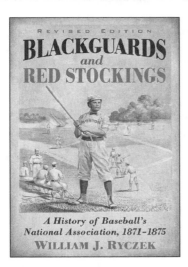
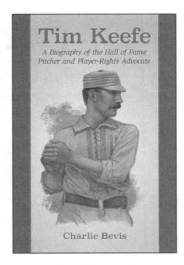

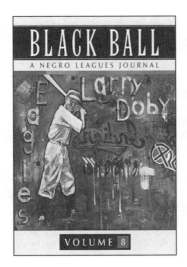
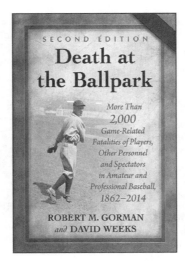
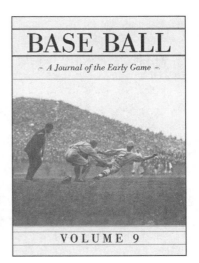

Contributors

BRUCE S. ALLARDICE is a Professor of History at South Suburban College, near Chicago, and has authored numerous articles on the Black Sox, along with biographies of the Black Sox gamblers for the SABR BioProject. His article on "The Spread of Baseball in the South Prior to 1870" received SABR's McFarland Award in 2013.

MARK ARMOUR is the founder and director of SABR's Baseball Biography Project.

DR. JERROLD CASWAY is the Dean and Professor Emeritus at Howard Community College in Columbia, Maryland. He has written many articles on nineteenth-century baseball and was a featured keynote speaker at the Baseball Hall of Fame. He has written a biography on Ed Delahanty in the *Emerald Age of Baseball* (2004) and McFarland will publish his book, *The Culture and Ethnicity of Nineteenth-Century Baseball*, this coming year.

SEAN FORMAN is a longtime SABR member and the creator of Baseball-Reference.com.

RYAN GANTNER has a Ph.D. in Mathematics from the University of Minnesota and teaches mathematics at St. John Fisher College in Rochester, New York. Like most projects of his, this one developed as an offshoot of a student research project. He is new to SABR but hopes to guide students in this direction in the future.

ROGER A. GODIN has been a SABR Member since 1977. He is the author of *The 1922 St. Louis Browns: Best of the American League's Worst* and various *BRJ* articles. His principal research and writing is in the American aspect of hockey, about which he has written two books and a number of monographs. He serves as the NHL Minnesota Wilds' team curator and resides in St. Paul.

RICHARD HERSHBERGER writes on early baseball history. He has published in various SABR publications, and in *Base Ball: A Journal of the Early Game*. He is a paralegal in Maryland.

JEFFREY N. HOWARD is an Associate Professor of psychology at Northern State University in Aberdeen, South Dakota. Dr. Howard received his PhD in Human Factors Psychology from Wichita State University. His research interests include music-cognition, decision-making, and cross-sensory modality investigations. He also holds master's degrees in clinical and experimental psychology, as well as a bachelor's degree in radio-television journalism.

Because fate frowned upon him, **WADE KAPSZUKIEWICZ** is a lifelong fan of the Cleveland Indians. While watching Jose Mesa blow the save in Game Seven of the 1997 World Series, he began thinking about Golden Pitches—and whether fans of any other teams had their hearts similarly broken by them.

STEPHEN R. KEENEY is a lifelong Reds fan and a new SABR member. He graduated from Miami University in 2010 with degrees in History and International Studies, and from Northern Kentucky University's Chase College of Law in 2013. After passing the bar exam he moved from Cincinnati to Dayton, where he works as a union staff representative and lives with his wife, Christine.

NORM KING lives in Ottawa, Ontario, and has been a SABR member since 2010. He has contributed to a number of SABR books, including *Thar's Joy in Braveland: The 1957 Milwaukee Braves, Winning on the North Side. The 1929 Chicago Cubs*, and *A Pennant for the Twins Cities: The 1965 Minnesota Twins*. He

thought he was crazy to miss his beloved Expos after all these years until he met people from Brooklyn.

JAPHETH KNOPP received a B.S. degree in Religious Studies and M.A. in American History from Missouri State University and is currently enrolled in the History Ph.D. program at the University of Missouri. He lives with his wife, Rebecca Wilkinson, and their son Ryphath. He can be contacted at Japheth.knopp@gmail.com

BRIAN MARSHALL is an Electrical Engineering Technologist living in Barrie, Ontario, Canada and a long time researcher in various fields including entomology, power electronic engineering, NFL, Canadian Football and recently MLB. Brian has written many articles, winning awards for two of them. He has two baseball books on the way on the 1927 New York Yankees and the 1897 Baltimore Orioles. Brian is a long time member of the PFRA. While growing up, Brian played many sports. He aspired to be a professional football player but when that didn't materialize he focused on Rugby Union and played off and on for 17 seasons.

ROB NEYER began his career as a baseball writer/analyst working for Bill James, later at STATS Inc. and then for many years at ESPN.com. His books include *The Neyer/James Guide to Pitchers* and *Rob Neyer's Big Book of Baseball Blunders*.

RUSSELL ORMISTON is an assistant professor of economics at Allegheny College in Meadville, Pennsylvania. He studies sports economics, labor economics and human resource management and can be contacted at rormisto@allegheny.edu.

PETE PALMER is the co-author with John Thorn of *The Hidden Game of Baseball* and co-editor with Gary Gillette of the *Barnes and Noble ESPN Baseball Encyclopedia* (five editions). Pete worked as a consultant to Sports Information Center, the official statisticians for the American League 1976–87. Pete introduced on-base average as an official statistic for the American League in 1979 and invented on-base plus slugging (OPS), now universally used as a good measure of batting strength. He won the SABR Bob Davids award in 1989 and was selected as a charter member of the Henry Chadwick Award. Pete also edited (with Thorn) seven editions of *Total Baseball*. He previously edited four editions of the *Barnes Official Encyclopedia of Baseball* (1974–79). A member of SABR since 1973, Pete is also the editor of *Who's Who in Baseball*.

JACOB POMRENKE is SABR's Director of Editorial Content, chair of the Black Sox Scandal Research Committee, and editor of *Scandal on the South Side: The 1919 Chicago White Sox* (2015). He lives in Scottsdale, Arizona, with his wife, Tracy Greer, and their cats, Nixey Callahan and Bones Ely.

A SABR member since 1979, **JOHN THORN** is the Official Historian of Major League Baseball.

DON ZMINDA has worked for STATS LLC since 1990—first as Director of Publications and now as the company's Director of Research for sports broadcasts. He has co-authored or edited many baseball books, including the annual *STATS Baseball Scoreboard* (1990–2001) and the SABR BioProject publication *Go-Go to Glory: The 1959 Chicago White Sox*. A Chicago native, Don is a graduate of Northwestern University (BS Journalism, 1970) and lives in Los Angeles with his wife Sharon.